FOOTPRINTS OF VICTORY OVER RACISM – VOLUME 1
RAYS OF VICTORY WORKBOOK SERIES

FOOTPRINTS OF VICTORY OVER RACISM – VOLUME 1

RAYS OF VICTORY **WORKBOOK** SERIES

his Book Belongs to:

_____
(Your Beautiful Name)

Jesus Christ in you is greater than the unclean spirit of racism. Let His Footprints lead you to daily victory over racism.

FOOTPRINTS OF VICTORY OVER RACISM – VOLUME 1

RAYS OF VICTORY <u>WORKBOOK</u> SERIES

FOOTPRINTS OF VICTORY OVER RACISM:

In the Secret Place With God
(Volume 1)

40 DAYS OF READINGS FROM THE

RAYS OF VICTORY SERIES:

"<u>NAILING RACISM TO THE</u>

<u>*CROSS*</u>*"*

∞∞∞∞∞∞∞∞ ♦ ♦ ♦ ♦ ♦ ∞∞∞∞∞∞∞∞

Illuminating daily guideposts for God's rays of victory over racism

∞∞∞∞∞∞∞∞ ♦ ♦ ♦ ♦ ♦ ∞∞∞∞∞∞∞∞

Be free forever from 'Pharaoh's' bitter yoke and move beyond racism

Dr. Jacyee Aniagolu-Johnson

FOOTPRINTS OF VICTORY OVER RACISM – VOLUME 1

"Footprints of Victory Over Racism: In the Secret Place with God – Volume 1," Copyright 2002-2013, Jacinta Aniagolu (Jacyee Aniagolu-Johnson). Printing Rights by Marble Tower Publishing, LLC. All rights reserved. Unauthorized duplication is prohibited by law and the eighth commandment.

Inspirational excerpts from "Rays of Victory: Nailing Racism to the Cross" Copyright 2002-2013, Jacinta Aniagolu (Jacyee Aniagolu-Johnson) All rights reserved.

No part of this book may be reproduced, stored in a retrieval system, or transmitted by any means, electronic, mechanical, photocopying, recording, or otherwise, without written permission from the author and publisher, except by a reviewer who may quote brief passages in a review.

Churches and other non-commercial interests such as non-profit organizations may reproduce portions of this book without written permission of Marble Tower Publishing, provided that the text does not exceed 500 words and the text is not material quoted from another publisher or author. When reproducing text from this book please include the following credit line: "Footprints of Victory Over Racism: In the Secret Place with God – Volume 1" by Jacyee Aniagolu-Johnson, published by Marble Tower Publishing, LLC. Used by permission.

FOOTPRINTS OF VICTORY OVER RACISM – VOLUME 1

Edited by Chad Steenerson (www.christianeditor.net)
Also Edited by Uché Aniagolu (Ebony WoodHouse Productions)
Cover design by Marble Tower Publishing, LLC, Copyright 2012-2013

Editing Style:
Please note that the editing style presented in this book by the second editor, Uché Aniagolu, is meant to emphasize reverence of God, His Son Jesus Christ and His Holy Spirit. For example, verbs that describe actions of God may be capitalized. This editing style may differ from what you are accustomed to, but we chose it for the reason noted above.

First Paperback Edition
ISBN 978-0-9789669-5-9

Printed in the United States of America by Marble Tower Publishing, LLC

FOOTPRINTS OF VICTORY OVER RACISM – VOLUME 1

Publisher's Cataloging-In-Publication Data
(Prepared by The Donohue Group, Inc.)

Aniagolu-Johnson, Jacyee.
 Footprints of victory over racism : in the secret place with God / Jacyee Aniagolu-Johnson. -- 1st pbk. ed.

2 v. ; cm. -- (Rays of victory series. Workbook series)

"Illuminating daily guideposts for God's rays of victory over racism."
 "Inspirational excerpts from 'Rays of Victory: Nailing Racism to the Cross'"--T.p. verso of both volumes.
 ISBN-13: 978-0-9789669-5-9 (pbk.: v. 1)
 ISBN-10: 0-9789669-5-3 (pbk.: v. 1)
 ISBN-13: 978-0-9789669-6-6 (pbk. : v. 2)
 ISBN-10: 0-9789669-6-1 (pbk. : v. 2)

 1. Racism--Religious aspects--Christianity. 2. Spiritual warfare. 3. Christian life. I. Aniagolu-Johnson, Jacyee. Nailing racism to the cross. II. Title.

BV4599.5.R33 A54 2011
248.4

FOOTPRINTS OF VICTORY OVER RACISM – VOLUME 1

Some Scripture taken from the HOLY BIBLE, KING JAMES VERSION, Cambridge, 1769. (Public Domain).

Some Scripture taken from the HOLY BIBLE, NEW LIVING TRANSLATION (NLT) Copyright 1996 by Tyndale Charitable Trust. Used by Permission of Tyndale House Publishers.

Some Scripture taken from the HOLY BIBLE, NEW INTERNATIONAL VERSION ® (NIV). Copyright NIV 1973, 1978, 1986 by International Bible Society. Used by permission of Zondervan. All rights reserved.

Some Scripture taken from the HOLY BIBLE, NEW KING JAMES VERSION ® (NKJV). Copyright 1979, 1980, 1982, 1999 by Thomas Nelson, Inc. Used by Permission of Thomas Nelson, Inc. All rights reserved.

Some Scripture taken from the HOLY BIBLE, GOOD NEWS BIBLE (GNB) published by The United Bible Societies. Copyright American Bible Society, 1966, 1971, 1976, 1992.

Dedication

This book is dedicated to our Heavenly Father, God Almighty—the God of righteousness, justice, equity and all goodness enveloped in One—our only one and true Living God, who offered us all the gift of eternal salvation through His Son, our Lord and Savior Jesus Christ.

To my dear father, Justice Anthony Aniagolu and my mother Lady (Mrs.) Maria Aniagolu whom I love dearly and who first taught me about God, His profound love, mercy, faithfulness and grace, and His holy justice against any form of evil, wickedness, oppression and injustice.

FOOTPRINTS OF VICTORY OVER RACISM – VOLUME 1

To the memories of Olaudah Equiano (Gustavus Vassa), Saint Katharine Drexel, Malcolm X (Malcolm Little) and his wife Betty X (Betty Shabazz), Reverend Dr. Martin Luther King Jr. and his wife Coretta Scott King, Medgar Wiley Evers, Walter Max Ulyate Sisulu, Steve Biko, James Chaney, Andrew Goodman, Michael Schwerner and Chief Gani Fawehinmi. Also, special dedication to President Nelson Rolihlahla Madiba Mandela, Winnie Madikizela-Mandela, and to all other civil rights leaders, who have boldly stood against injustice, oppression and repression, bad governance and other forms of wickedness in their community, district, borough, county, state or country, that positively impacted the world as a whole.

To all those who dedicate(d) their lives against all odds to the fight against racism or ethnic prejudice, injustice and oppression, and to many others who lived and died for justice and equality; and those who continue to fight for justice in every nation of the world.

Finally, to all those, regardless of race, ethnicity or nationality, who need God's awesome power, His rays of victory, to deal with and overcome racial prejudice or discrimination—may your individual victory through God's beams of justice come speedily as you abide in His

Holy Word and presence through our Lord and Savior Jesus Christ.

Acknowledgement

My foremost gratitude is to God my Heavenly Father for His free gift of salvation through His Son, my Lord and Savior Jesus Christ, and His Holy Spirit Who dwells within me. It is He Who inspires and empowers me daily to overcome any and all challenges, including my experiences with racial prejudice and discrimination.

To my dear father, Justice Anthony Aniagolu and my mother Lady Maria Aniagolu whom I love dearly for being wonderful parents and for all they did for me and my siblings.

My special gratitude goes to my husband, Lamonte, who remains my earthly rock of Gibraltar, and through whom God continues to teach me His expression of true and unconditional love that has no bounds. I love you very much.

My special gratitude also goes to my sister, Maryanne, a lovely woman of God—thank you for continuing to help me to better understand how to hear the true voice of God and how to spend endless quality time in God's holy presence through prayer, thanksgiving and worship. I love you very much.

To my sister Uché, I thank God for the sweet fragrance of Jesus Christ in you. You are an embodiment of servanthood—selfless sacrificial giving, and it is the greatness of God in you through Christ that empowers you to humble yourself to serve others; I have no doubt that God will magnify His glory in your life through Jesus Christ. I love you very much.

To my sister Chi-Chi who's giving spirit surpasses anyone that I know—May Luke 6:38 remain like a wellspring within you and may God continue to bless you and enrich your life beyond your wildest imagination through Jesus Christ! I love you very much.

To my brother Kizito whose deep and genuine love for God helps me to stay focused on Matthew 6:33; may the power of God's Holy Word continue to promote you from faith to faith and from glory to glory, in the awesome Name of our Lord and Savior Jesus Christ. I love you very much.

To the rest of my family, Tony, Emeka, Chuka, Lolly and Nwachu, I remain forever grateful to God for your lives, individual families and accomplishments. It is my prayer that John 3:16 will be and remain alive in your hearts. I love you very much.

Special thanks to Reverend (Prophet) Michael Galleta at the Genesis Upper Room Church, San Jose, California. Reverend Michael first prayed for the success of the Rays of Victory Series manuscript and has for many years covered my family with powerful prayers of faith. God has spoken to me through him in many profound ways—and may God continue to bless you, your wife Minister Yvonne Galleta and children, and your entire congregation.

To David and Fortune West and the Ocean of Mercy Prayer Ministry in Cork, Ireland, I would like to thank God for your spiritual covering of the Rays of Victory project through your prayers and encouragement with the Holy Word of God. As you continue to spread the good news of the Gospel of Jesus Christ, may you continue to be seen as manifested light of Jesus Christ onto nations, and may God continue to diffuse the fragrance of Christ through you to win souls.

To my sisters in the Lord Jesus Christ, Chinwe Igwegbe-Lane, Nonye Igwegbe and Cathy Agada, thank you for all your prayers and support and powerful prophetic words that sustained me during the final "birthing" stage of the RAV book series. May our Heavenly Father continue to take you from faith to Faith and from glory to Glory, in the awesome Name of our Lord and Savior Jesus Christ!

My heartfelt thanks to Minister Sarah Allred at the Genesis Upper Room Church, whom God used her prayer ministry to touch me in a profound manner. Thank you, Sister Sarah, for allowing God to use you to help me refresh my walk with Him. May He continue to bless you!

I would like to thank Bishop (Dr.) Don Meares, and Elders Kevin Mathews and Peyton Gray at the Evangel Cathedral, Upper Marlboro, Maryland, who have been a blessing to me through their teaching and preaching. I thank you for helping me to continue to better understand God's Holy Word and to grow spiritually. I would also like to especially thank Elders Kevin Mathews and Peyton Gray, who prayed for the success of the "Rays of Victory Series—thank you very much for continuing to allow God to use you in the most tremendous ways.

To the rest of my friends and prayer partners who prayed with and for me for the success of this book and the entire Rays of Victory Series—may God continue to bless you immensely in the awesome Name of our Lord and Savior Jesus Christ!

Finally, to the Body of Jesus Christ (all Believers in Him and all of God's genuine priests and ministers around the world), regardless of denomination, race, ethnicity or nationality, may God's favor and blessings always overflow in your lives as you continue to spread the good news of the Gospel of our Lord and Savior Jesus Christ, and further His powerful ministry that is firmly rooted in true and pure Love, which is God Himself.

Stereotypes, Prejudice, Discrimination

"The terms stereotype, prejudice, discrimination, and racism are often used interchangeably in everyday conversation. But when discussing these terms from a sociological perspective, it is important to define them: *stereotypes* are oversimplified ideas about groups of people, *prejudice* refers to thoughts and feelings about those groups, while *discrimination* refers to actions toward them; and *racism* is a type of prejudice that involves set beliefs about a specific racial group. Stereotypes can be based on race, ethnicity…almost any characteristic. They may be positive (usually about one's own group…but are often negative (usually toward other groups, such as when members of a dominant racial group suggest that a subordinate racial group is stupid or lazy). In either case, the stereotype is a generalization that doesn't take individual differences into account…Where do stereotypes come from? In fact new stereotypes are rarely created; rather, they are recycled from subordinate groups that have assimilated into society and are reused to describe newly subordinate groups."

(Stereotypes, Prejudice, Discrimination. http://cnx.org/content/m42860/latest/content_info #cnx_attribution_header)

Power of the Prayer of Jabez

Like God did for Jabez, may He use the pain you have experienced from your racist offenders, the rejection you experienced from those who mocked you, the wicked words of racists who said that you were insignificant and not good enough because of your race, ethnicity, nationality, or any other reason, to bless and anoint you, enlarge your territory, keep you from evil, and make you a blessing to many, and not an instrument of pain to anyone, in the awesome Name of Jesus Christ, Amen.

Jacyee Aniagolu-Johnson, PhD

"Now Jabez was more honorable than his brothers, and his mother called his name Jabez, saying, "Because I bore him in pain." And Jabez called on the God of Israel saying, "Oh, that You would bless me indeed, and enlarge my territory, that Your hand would be with me, and that You would keep me from evil, that I may not cause pain!" So God granted him what he requested."

1 Chronicles 4:9-10

FOOTPRINTS OF VICTORY OVER RACISM – VOLUME 1

RAYS OF VICTORY **WORKBOOK** SERIES

What the Bible Says About Oppression

"He who oppresses the poor reproaches his Maker, but he who honors Him has mercy on the needy.
Proverbs 14:31"

"Learn to do good; seek justice, rebuke the oppressor; defend the fatherless, plead for the widow."
Isaiah 1:17

"If you see the oppression of the poor, and the violent perversion of justice and righteousness in a province, do not marvel at the matter; for high official watches over high official, and higher officials are over them."
Ecclesiastes 5:8

"Ransom me from the oppression of evil people; then I can obey your commandments."

Psalms 119:134

"LORD, you know the hopes of the helpless. Surely you will hear their cries and comfort them."

Psalms 10:17

"At that time I will put you on trial. I am eager to witness against all sorcerers and adulterers and liars. I will speak against those who cheat employees of their wages, who oppress widows and orphans, or who deprive the foreigners living among you of justice, for these people do not fear me", says the LORD of Heaven's Armies.

Malachi 3:5

"For this is what the Sovereign LORD says: Enough, you princes of Israel! Stop your violence and oppression and do what is just and right. Quit robbing and cheating my people out of their land. Stop expelling them from their homes, says the Sovereign LORD."

Ezekiel 45:9

Contents

Dedication 8
Acknowledgement... 11
Contents 20
What is Racism?... 23
Definitions of Racism 24
The Reason for this Book 27
How to Use this Book... 28
Preface 31
Introduction... 38
A Prayer of Salvation 50
Prayer after Profession of Salvation.......................... 52
Partnership Prayer... 55
CHAPTER 1 - The Disease Called Racism 57
CHAPTER 2 – Shut Out the Spirit of Racism 66
CHAPTER 3 – The Blood of Jesus Christ Delivers ... 76
CHAPTER 4 – Spiritual Decay and Racism 85
CHAPTER 5 – God's Touch for True Repentance...... 95
CHAPTER 6 – Dealing With Racism......................... 101
CHAPTER 7 – Focus Your Faith Against Racism 112
CHAPTER 8 – The Power of Our Faith Against Racism. 127
CHAPTER 9 – The Power of Faith Fuels Forgiveness 138
CHAPTER 10 – God's Kingdom Power in Us 144
CHAPTER 11 – God's Kingdom Power Against Racism 152

CHAPTER 12 – God's Illuminating Rays of True Spiritual Knowledge 161
CHAPTER 13 – Power of God's Grace Over Racism 172
CHAPTER 14 – Resist the Spirit of Racism 180
CHAPTER 15 – Remain Steadfast Against the Spirit of Racism 186
CHAPTER 16 – Jesus Christ in You is Greater than the Spirit of Racism 192
CHAPTER 17 – Feeling Under-represented, Outnumbered and Overpowered? 197
CHAPTER 18 – Discouraged by Experiences With Racism? 208
CHAPTER 19 – Forgiveness–A Form of Spiritual Cleansing 213
CHAPTER 20 – Dismantling Negative Effects of Racism 220
CHAPTER 21 – Are You Sick and Tired of Racism? 226
CHAPTER 22 – False Beliefs Perpetuate Racism 234
CHAPTER 23 – Are You Bound By Seeds of Hostility? .. 244
CHAPTER 24 – The Spirit of Racism and Self-Deceit 254
CHAPTER 25 – Are You Passing On the Tradition of Racism? 259
CHAPTER 26 – The Spirit of Racism Infects Children ... 267
CHAPTER 27 – A Spiritual Mind – A Guarded Gate Against Racism 277
CHAPTER 28 – True Spiritual Relationship – A Pivotal Force Against Racism 284
CHAPTER 29 – Are You Plagued By the Grasshopper Complex 297
CHAPTER 30 – Dealing With Racism in the Workplace . 306
CHAPTER 31 – No Room for Negative Effects of Racism 323
CHAPTER 32 – Carnal or Unrighteous Anger Against Racism 329
CHAPTER 33 –Unrighteous Anger is a Self-defeating Emotion 344

CHAPTER 34 – Righteous Anger Against Racism........... 354
CHAPTER 35 – Turning Unrighteous Anger into Righteous Anger 364
CHAPTER 36 – The Power Over Racism: Philippians 4:8-9 372
CHAPTER 37 – God Sees and Understands Your Pain and Anger 381
CHAPTER 38 – Racism Causes Self-Hatred Through Mind Distortion 394
CHAPTER 39 – Self-Hatred Fosters Self-Incarceration... 402
CHAPTER 40 – Solidifying God's Word Within You...... 408

What is Racism?

"A situation in which one race maintains supremacy over another race through a set of attitudes, behaviors, social structures and ideologies. It involves four essential and interconnected elements:

Power: *the capacity to make and enforce decisions is disproportionately or unfairly distributed.*

Resources: *unequal access to such resources as money, education, information, etc.*

Standards: *standards for appropriate behavior are ethnocentric, reflecting and privileging the norms and values of the dominant race/society.*

Problem: *involves defining "reality" by naming "the problem" incorrectly, and thus misplacing it."*

-- *Women's Theological Center, Boston, MA, 1994*

Definitions of Racism

"Any distinction, exclusion, restriction, or preference based on race, color, descent, or national or ethnic origin which has the purpose or effect of nullifying or impairing the recognition, enjoyment, or exercise, on equal footing, of human rights and fundamental freedoms in the political, economic, social, cultural, or any other field of public life."

-- The ICERD (International Convention on the Elimination of All Forms of Racial Discrimination)

∞∞∞∞∞∞∞∞∞∞∞ ♦ ♦ ♦ ♦ ♦ ∞∞∞∞∞∞∞∞∞∞∞

"Racism has not disappeared... we confront forms of racism that are covert or more complex..."

-- The International Council on Human Rights Policy

∞∞∞∞∞∞∞∞∞∞∞ ♦ ♦ ♦ ♦ ♦ ∞∞∞∞∞∞∞∞∞∞∞

"Racism is a system of inequality based on race."

-- Tim Wise

Reading Racism Right to Left: Reflections on a Powerful Word and Its Applications

(http://www.timwise.org/2010/07/reading-racism-right-to-left-reflections-on-a-powerful-word-and-its-applications/)

∞∞∞∞∞∞∞∞∞ ♦ ♦ ♦ ♦ ♦ ∞∞∞∞∞∞∞∞∞

"Racism involves physical, psychological, spiritual, and social control, exploitation and subjection of one race by another race...This means that racial discrimination and injustice are established, perpetuated and promoted throughout every institution of society - economics, education, entertainment, family, labor, law, politics, religion, science and war..."

-- Phavia Kujichagulia

(Recognizing and Resolving Racism: A Resource and Guide for Humane Beings)

∞∞∞∞∞∞∞∞∞ ♦ ♦ ♦ ♦ ♦ ∞∞∞∞∞∞∞∞∞

"Racism - Racial prejudice and discrimination that are supported by institutional power and authority. The critical element that differentiates racism from prejudice and discrimination is the use of institutional power and authority to support prejudices and enforce discriminatory behaviors in systematic ways with far-reaching outcomes and effects..."

-- Enid Lee, Deborah Menkart and Margo Okazawa-Rey (eds.) (Beyond Heroes and Holidays: A Practical Guide to K-12 Anti-Racist, Multicultural Education and Staff Development.)

The Reason for this Book

For every person, every child of God to know, understand and use the awesome power of God's Holy Word and His power within him or her through Jesus Christ to slay the goliath racism that they may encounter anywhere.

"You, dear children, are from God and have overcome them, because the one who is in you is greater than the one who is in the world."
(1 John 4:4, NIV)

∞∞∞∞∞∞∞∞∞ ♦ ♦ ♦ ♦ ♦ ∞∞∞∞∞∞∞∞∞

To receive the spirit of racism is to reject God's Holy Word.
To practice racism is to disobey God's Holy Word.
To reject the spirit of racism is to uphold God's Holy Word.

How to Use this Book

This book, "Footprints of Victory Over Racism – In the Secret Place with God, Volume 1," contains selected readings from the "Nailing Racism to the Cross Series," and is designed to help you in your daily meditation as you deal spiritually with the negative elements of racism. I suggest that you decide on a 40-day prayer and meditation, using this book as well as "One-on-One With God for Victory Over Racism," as your guide to powerful Scripture in God's Holy Book, the Bible. Let God's Holy Word guide and empower you to prayerfully defeat any influence of the foul spirit of racism in your life.

FOOTPRINTS OF VICTORY OVER RACISM – VOLUME 1

Read and meditate on God's Holy Word, the Holy Bible, and spend quiet time in prayer and worship. Supplement your Bible reading with daily reading of this book. I recommend that you read one chapter a day. At the end of each chapter are simple yet thought-provoking questions that are based on God's Holy Word. Try to answer all questions and also jot down your own thoughts and reflections and any revelations that you may receive from God while you pray. By revelations, I mean either realizations that you may have or prophetic enlightening or disclosure that God may deposit in your heart as you meditate on His Holy Word and on these devotionals. You may also choose to use the "Footprints Note Book 1: For Victory Over Racism," to write down your answers to chapter quizzes in this book.

You may also invite one or two friends or family, or your Bible study group if you belong to one, to join you in your daily meditation and prayer over the 40-day period. You may meet once a week with your devotional partner or group to share your individual testimony and how God is empowering you daily with the "Footprints" of Jesus Christ for victory over every form of racism that you may encounter.

FOOTPRINTS OF VICTORY OVER RACISM – VOLUME 1

This book is for every person, and especially Christian believers in our Lord and Savior Jesus Christ, through Whom God has given us authority over every form of evil, including racism (Colossians 2:9-10; Luke 10:18-19). Be assured that when Christ leaves His Footprints for you to walk in to follow Him (Psalms 77:18-20), He will lead you to sure victory over racism.

Preface

Some say that the Bible does not address racism. I say that not only does the Bible deal with racism—it unearths the vile spirit behind it. The Bible, God's Holy Word, tells us that all human beings regardless of race, ethnicity or nationality, are created in the excellent Image of God (Genesis 1:26-27)! After God created every person, He called him or her "simply gorgeous." No one is superior or inferior to anyone, and no one is better than anyone (Galatians 6:3). God punished Miriam's racial prejudice and backbiting (Numbers 12:10). Also, He dealt with Apostle Peter's racial prejudice (Acts 10:1-29). So, we may label individuals or a group of people negatively because we lack authentic spiritual knowledge, but God does not acknowledge any such label that is contrary to His Holy Word. You may be born and raised in a "ghetto," but you are not from there; no one is from there; God did not create any "ghetto," we humans did!

Racism is a plague of human society that has been around for centuries. It has become well-rooted in our cultures and may not end anytime soon. Jesus Christ met a Samaritan woman in Sychar, the city of Samaria, near the plot of land that Joseph inherited from his father Jacob who dug a well there. She came to draw water from the well and Jesus asked her for some water (John 4:4-7). Her response was: "Then saith the woman of Samaria unto him, 'How is it that thou, being a Jew, askest drink of me, which am a woman of Samaria? for the Jews have no dealings with the Samaritans.'" (John 4:9) She recognized Jesus to be a Jew and was focused on their tradition that separated Jews from the Samaritans.

Undoubtedly, Jesus knew everything about her and was more concerned about her salvation and showed no interest in her race or ethnicity. Had Jesus focused on the fact that she was Samaritan, which was irrelevant to Him, He would have walked away and she would have missed her miracle of meeting the Messiah, receiving her salvation, and her subsequent evangelism ministry in the city (John 4:10-26). How many miracles and blessings have we missed because we were focused on someone's race, ethnicity or nationality, not realizing that God sent them our way?

In the Book of Numbers Chapter 12, we read about how Miriam and Aaron began to speak spitefully against Moses, motivated by race and ethnic prejudice and underlining jealousy: "And Miriam and Aaron spake against Moses because of the Ethiopian woman whom he had married: for he had married an Ethiopian woman. And they said, Hath the LORD indeed spoken only by Moses? hath he not spoken also by us? And the LORD heard it." (Numbers 12:1-2) God was displeased with Miriam and Aaron and struck Miriam with leprosy, perhaps because she was the chief instigator and God saw that her motive was malicious. It took Aaron to plead with Moses on Miriam's behalf and Moses to plead with God on both their behalf for Miriam to be healed (Numbers 12: 3-16). You see, anyone can be racist, regardless of race, ethnicity or nationality. Therefore, we need to guard our heart and mind from the vile spirit of racism.

For individuals who have over time allowed the unclean spirit of racism to invade their soul, my hope is that this book will bring God's conviction to your heart, rather than condemnation. When God convicts you, He reveals to you, through His Holy Word and Holy Spirit, all hidden areas of your heart where racial prejudice resides, and shows you the necessary repentance that He requires. He offers you the opportunity to genuinely repent and change (Psalms 51:2, 2 Chronicles 7:14, 1 John 1:9) and gain a renewed mind in Jesus Christ (Romans 12:2; Ephesians 4:23-24).

The meditation excerpts in this book are readings from the Series, "Nailing Racism to the Cross." This is a 40-day daily meditation and workbook that is designed to help you gain personal victory over racism. For those of you who face injustice and oppression of racism, it is my prayer that as you journey through "Footprints of Victory over Racism, Volume-1" with me, you will understand the demonic origins of the foul spirit of racism and the source of its negative spiritual hold on you. I pray that you will become convinced that it is necessary for you to apply God's Holy Word, the Sword of the Spirit, against racism so you can permanently break down its stronghold on you. You have to believe that through Jesus Christ you have overcome racism!

The anointing of God's Holy Spirit in you breaks the yoke of the burden of racism on your soul (Isaiah 10:27). A renewed mind in Jesus Christ empowers you to ward off the potential destructive effects of racism on your psyche and in your life (Romans 12:2; Ephesians 4:23-24). Your understanding of the conquering power of God's Word within you (Romans 8:37) helps you to resist racists and deal strategically and victoriously with racism.

This book will show you a Christ-rooted approach on how to prevent buildup of the negative mental stronghold of racism and its potential lingering effects. Also, you will recognize potential damaging and lingering effects of racism, and learn how to eliminate them; you will learn how to remain fully aware of who you are in the spirit and in the natural; you will understand the essence of your spirit, which has the power of our Lord and Savior Jesus Christ, who lives in you, and the Holy Spirit of God, who also dwells within you through Him (1 Corinthians 2:12; 1 John 2:27); and you will learn how to constantly "guard" your heart and mind, and your sense of self: worthiness, regard, respect, esteem, confidence, competence, efficacy and efficiency, even when surrounded by the foul elements of racism.

Most importantly, you will learn how to free your mind forever from the daily assaults of racism. Racism and those who perpetrate it against you are enemies of God. Let God battle those who oppress you—let Him oppose those who oppose you—let Him be an Enemy to your enemies and an Adversary to your adversaries (Exodus 23:22). Allow God to make you His battleaxe against the foul spirit of racism operating in its human hosts (Jeremiah 51:20)—let God destroy the vile spirit of Haman on your behalf (Esther 7:6, 9:25).

Scripture Meditation

Let God battle those who oppress you—let God oppose those who oppose you—let Him be an Enemy to your enemies and an Adversary to your adversaries (Exodus 23:22)—and let Him gain victory for you—the battle is not yours but the Lords'.
- 1 Samuel 17:45-47

"But if thou shalt indeed obey his voice, and do all that I speak; then I will be an enemy unto thine enemies, and an adversary unto thine adversaries."
- Exodus 23:22

FOOTPRINTS OF VICTORY OVER RACISM – VOLUME 1

"Having canceled the charge of our legal indebtedness, which stood against us and condemned us; he has taken it away, nailing it to the cross. And having disarmed the powers and authorities, he made a public spectacle of them, triumphing over them by the cross."
- Colossians 2:14-15

"Despite racism that exists around you, you are endowed with great gifts, talents and abilities for success.
Jesus Christ nailed racism to the Cross."

- Jacyee Aniagolu-Johnson

Introduction

Every human being is created in the excellent Image of God, regardless of nationality, race, or ethnicity. In the eyes of God, all human beings are equal in humanity and dignity, and no person, race, ethnicity or nationality, is superior or inferior to another. God is multiracial, that is, all races encompassed in One (Him). We are all one race in Him. We, the human race, are all reflected in His excellent Image. Unfortunately, regardless of our nationality, race, or ethnicity, sometimes we do allow negative spiritual influences to operate within us. In many cases, such evil spiritual influences are received, nurtured, established, and institutionalized, and then spread through a tradition

> *Every human being is created in the excellent Image of God.*

of lies. They deposit and grow inside of us racial prejudices and discriminatory feelings and thoughts that become words, attitudes and actions against other people, and keep us bound by their stronghold. A stronghold is "a place of survival or refuge: one of the last strongholds of an age-old tradition"[1] [such as racism]. It is a "strongly fortified defensive structure."[2] A racist mindset is like a strongly fortified structure built by the vile spirit of racism that orchestrates racism and influences the hearts and minds of its human hosts to perpetrate and perpetuate prejudicial and discriminatory acts.

We can become trapped within a negative stronghold of racism, which defiles our hearts and locks up our minds with prejudices against individuals of other races, ethnicities or nationalities. Such a stronghold can keep our minds in ignorance, barring the undeniable truth from penetrating our hearts (2 Corinthians 4:3-4) that racism is contrary to God's will for our lives and for all humanity (Galatians 3:26-29). God has not authorized

God has not authorized the odious spirit of racism, or any other thing, to defile your heart.

the odious spirit of racism, or any other thing, to defile your heart (Proverbs 4:23; 1 Corinthians 6:19-20).

    The purpose of our existence is beyond our race, which is merely our racial genetic makeup that manifests as a specific color of eyes, texture, color and shade of skin, and shape of facial features or the physical form of a person's body. We have been created for God's glory (Isaiah 43:7); chosen to worship Him (1 Peter 2:9); called to worship Him (Romans 12:1; Psalms 95:6); and instructed to worship Him (Revelation 14:6-7). So, we exist to glorify and worship God our Maker, and to know, believe, understand and successfully live through His excellent plan and purpose (Jeremiah 29:11) for our lives to the splendor of His awesome Name. Our individual race is not our identity—our true identity is our redeemed and renewed spirit in Jesus Christ (Galatians 2:20; Colossians 2:9-10; Romans 8:1-2, 31-39). Our spirit is our "inner man" and is expressed within and through our soul and physical body, to define who and what we are.

> *Our individual race is not our identity—our true identity is our redeemed and renewed spirit in Jesus Christ.*

What are the human spirit, soul and body (1 Thessalonians 5:23; Hebrews 4:12) and what is the relationship, for us Christian believers, between these entities within a person? Every human possesses a spirit, which is the part of us that gives us the ability to have an intimate relationship with God through Jesus Christ (John 4:24). The human spirit is the spiritual aspect of man and it is through our spirit that God births life in us (Genesis 2:7), and into our soul. Our spirit connects us to God through Jesus Christ Who is our and the only Mediator: "For there is one God and one Mediator between God and men, the Man Christ Jesus…" (1Timothy 2:5). Our spirit communicates with God; and our spirit also communicates with the world through the expression of our soul in our physical body.

Regardless of race, ethnicity or nationality, we have all been created for God's glory.

Our soul is fueled by our "inner person," our spirit, and is expressed through our body in the physical environment. Our soul is the "bridge" between our spirit and our body; it is the earthly aspect of a human—it is the seat or locus of heart, mind, emotions, thoughts, will, motivation, resolve, willpower, understanding and personality.

OUTERMOST

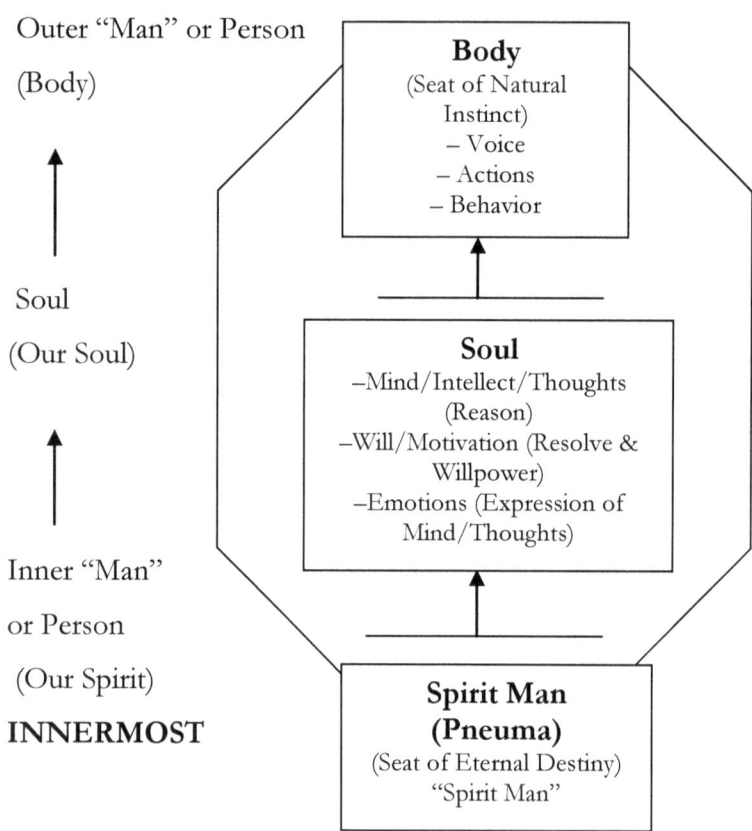

Outer "Man" or Person (Body)

↑

Soul (Our Soul)

↑

Inner "Man" or Person (Our Spirit)

INNERMOST

As Christians, we should worship God in spirit and truth (John 4:23-24). It is through our spirit that we are to stay in close communion with God through prayer, praise and worship, and draw nearer to Him. We are to always give praises to God, offer genuine thanksgiving to Him and worship Him, so that our souls—our hearts, minds, emotions, thoughts, will and resolve remain ruled by His spiritual preeminence rather than material or earthly issues such as racism. We are to abide in God's Holy Word, hear and obey Him.

What we need is for our inner person, our "spirit man," to dwell on God's Word so that our souls will be strengthened (Ephesians 3:16) and live in accordance with His Holy Word (Joshua 1:8; Romans 7:22). Then, our soul becomes guided more by things of God and less by things of the world. We either allow God and His Holy Word to direct our spirit, soul and body, or we give into the external world around us. My sister, Maryanne, explained it quite simply when she once said to me: "if you don't know who you are in Jesus Christ, then the things of the world will interest you." Yes, indeed—the world will rule you if you don't know who you are in Christ and you will not take your rightful victorious position in Him.

Evil, like racism, attempts to dominate our lives, by controlling our hearts and minds; but our renewed

> *"If you don't know who you are in Jesus Christ, then the things of the world will interest you."*

inner spirit man in Jesus Christ is empowered and equipped by the Holy Word and the Holy Spirit through Him, to overcome all evil. It is our relationship with God through our new identity and nature in Christ, our inner spirit man in Him, guided by the Holy Spirit, which makes it possible for our soul to live in accordance with God's Word. If we ignore the Triune God and His Holy Word, we are sure to be ruled by our external world (Romans 7:14, 12:2, 8:5-6, 11:23-25, 24-25; John 3:5-8,15:1-8; 1 Corinthians 2:9-14; Ephesians 4:23-24).

Racism, though fueled by negative spiritual elements and evil principalities, manifests itself against our soul and body through our fellow humans as external forces in our physical environment. For us as individuals to overcome the foul spirit of racism in our lives, we must believe, understand God's Holy Word, and live and abide daily in His Word, and also be guided in our daily actions by the Word and Holy Spirit. First, we come to understand that we are all made in God's excellent Image; and created equal in humanity and dignity (Genesis 1:26-27). This means that all human beings are one race in

Through Jesus Christ, our inner spirit man is empowered and equipped by the Holy Word and the Holy Spirit.

God, regardless of their earthly nationality, race, or ethnicity (Romans 12:5).

Second, by faith, once you (a Christian believer) have undergone spiritual rebirth through Jesus Christ, you become a new person in Him—that is, to be born again; and you will receive the promised gift of God's Holy Spirit (John 3:3, 6-7, 16; Galatians 2:20; Romans 12:2; John 15:26-27). When you become *truly* born again in Christ, you are justified (acceptable)—made holy and righteous and blameless (cleansed, made spotless or unblemished) to God through Christ (1 Corinthians 1:1-3, 6-11; John 17:19; Acts 20:32; Acts 26:18; Romans 15:16).

> *The Holy Spirit will lead you to all truth (John 16:13).*

Third, by faith, you receive the power of God's Holy Spirit (John 7:38; Acts 1:8) through Who you receive the revelation of Holy Word which becomes tangible to you. You will begin to understand God's Holy Word and receive its revelation power. The Holy Spirit will lead you to all truth (John 16:13) and teach you how to live like Christ on a daily basis (Philippians 2:5), if you follow Him and listen to Him. You will also begin to have a deeper understanding of God. You will come to know that He, the Triune God, the only One, true Living God of all humanity, is all power that is above all things in Heaven and on Earth, seen or unseen, and is larger than racism. He is the Great I AM—the Alpha and Omega

Our God is above all things, inclusive of racism, and its evil and foul intrigues.

(Revelation 1:8) Who has all power and might above all things (1 Chronicles 29:12; 2 Chronicles 20:6). Our God is above all things, inclusive of racism, and its evil and foul intrigues. His Only Son, Jesus Christ, whom He made the sacrificial Lamb offering for our eternal salvation, has, on our behalf, defeated all works of the devil, including racism (John 13:3).

As you read and meditate daily on God's Holy Scripture as your daily guidepost, it is my prayer that through God's directed true spiritual knowledge from His Holy Spirit, Who dwells within you; you will gain a new sense of spiritual-awakening for resisting racism and gaining individual victory over it. By the redeeming and conquering Blood of our Lord and Savior Jesus Christ and the power of God's Holy Word, His divine knowledge will equip you to understand and identify the vile spirit of racism and its human hosts and targets.

Through prayer and remaining steadfast in Jesus Christ Who is God's Living Word, He equips you with His army of warring angels to triumph over racism. As you face the daily challenges that racism sets before you, I pray that you will surrender and yield your spirit and soul (heart, mind, thoughts, emotions, will, resolve, attitudes and personality) to the Triune God and His Word, and receive and accept His conviction for a renewed and empowered mind through His Son, Who is our Lord and Savior Jesus Christ.

Through Jesus Christ, God has already given you the power to trample the evil spirit of racism.

The daily illuminating guideposts in this book are for your individual fortification with God's Holy Word, to empower you with His rays of victory over any form of racism—then, as you gain a Christlike mind by the power of God's Holy Word (Romans 12:2; Ephesians 4:23-24), you will become like an impenetrable shield against racism and its destructive elements (Psalms 91:4; 2 Samuel 22:29-37; Ephesians 6:10-18; Psalms 84:11; Romans 8:37). Through Jesus Christ, God has already given you the power to trample the evil spirit of racism (Luke 10:19).

I pray that as you believe and receive God's Holy Word, and accept Jesus Christ as your Lord and Savior, the power of His Holy Spirit would become activated within you—and through Christ you would become more than a conqueror of racism (Romans 8:37) and every other challenge that you may encounter in your life (Mark 11:24).

Chapter Quiz

1. Which race is created in the excellent Image of God?

   _____

2. Which race does God's Holy Word say is the superior race?

   _____

3. Which race does God's Holy Word say is the inferior race?

   _____

4. Racism is a kind of spiritual stronghold. Why?

   _____

5. True or false: Our race, ethnicity, skin shade or color is so important that it is the purpose for our creation and existence. Explain your answer.

---

6. What has God equipped us with to fight and defeat the evil spirit of racism and racism?

∞∞∞∞∞∞∞∞ ♦ ♦ ♦ ♦ ♦ ∞∞∞∞∞∞∞∞

Reflections:

_____

_____

_____

_____

Chapter References:
1. <u>http://www.thefreedictionary.com/stronghold</u>
2. *wordnetweb.princeton.edu*

∞∞∞∞∞∞∞∞ ♦ ♦ ♦ ♦ ♦ ∞∞∞∞∞∞∞∞

Now, let us say a prayer of salvation
(See next page)

∞∞∞∞∞∞∞∞ ♦ ♦ ♦ ♦ ♦ ∞∞∞∞∞∞∞∞

A Prayer of Salvation

On this day, _____, I, _____ confess with my mouth that the Lord Jesus Christ is my personal Savior; I believe that He shed His Blood for me on the Cross of Calvary and that God raised Him from the dead for my eternal salvation. I repent of my sins and ask God to forgive my sins through the mighty Blood of Jesus Christ.

On this day, _____ by my faith, I, _____ believe that I am now saved by the precious Blood of Jesus Christ. I believe in the Triune God: God the Father, God's Son, Jesus Christ and God the Holy Spirit. I believe that in the Name of our Lord and Savior Jesus Christ, I will receive God's powerful and holy anointing by the baptism of His Holy Spirit that will release from my heart the flowing rivers of Living Water, in Jesus' Name, Amen. Thank you Father Lord God, for on this day, _____, in the Name of Jesus Christ, I, _____ am Born Again

Scripture Meditation:

"For God so loved the world that He gave His Only Begotten Son, that whoever believes in Him should not perish but have everlasting life." – John 3:16

"But what does it say? 'The word is near you, in your mouth and in your heart' (that is, the word of faith which we preach): that if you confess with your mouth the Lord Jesus and believe in your heart that God has raised Him from the dead, you will be saved. For with the heart one believes unto righteousness, and with the mouth confession is made unto salvation." – Romans 10:8-9

"He who believes in Me, as the Scripture has said, out of his heart will flow rivers of Living Water." – John 7:38

"That which is born of the flesh is flesh, and that which is born of The Spirit is spirit. Do not marvel that I said to you, 'You must be born again.'" – John 3:6-7

Prayer after Profession of Salvation

Dear glorious Heavenly Father, thank You that I am born again by the precious Blood of Jesus Christ. I accept my renewed spirit in Him.

Dear gracious Father, I thank You for making me aware that I have spiritual and mental shackles from my experiences with racism. Thank You for revealing to me all areas where I am shackled. Thank You for giving me total release and freedom from the intrigues of the foul spirit of racism. I reject the evil tradition of racism and all that it stands for. I forgive anyone who has hurt or offended me in any manner, including my racist offenders.

Dear precious Father, by my faith in Your Holy Word, I believe that You have answered my prayers in the precious Name of Jesus Christ. In the Name of Jesus Christ and by Your enabling grace, Lord God, I know that I can and that I have gained victory over any form of racial oppression and injustice.

Thank You, awesome Father, for Your marvelous rays of victory over racism on my behalf, and for Your limitless and boundless power within me through Jesus Christ, Amen.

Scripture Meditation:

"And whatever you ask in My Name, I will do, that the Father may be glorified in the Son. If you ask anything in My Name, I will do it." – John 14:13-14

"Pray without ceasing; in everything give thanks; for this is the Will of God in Jesus Christ for you." – 1 Thessalonians 5:17-18

"And whenever you stand praying, if you have anything against anyone, forgive him that your Father in Heaven may also forgive you your trespasses." – Mark 11:25

"Until now you have asked nothing in My Name. Ask and you will receive, that your joy may be full." – John 16:24

FOOTPRINTS OF VICTORY OVER RACISM – VOLUME 1

"Don't copy the behavior and customs of this world, but let God transform you into a new person by changing the way you think. Then you will learn to know God's Will for you, which is good and pleasing and perfect." – Romans 12:2

Partnership Prayer

I commit to spending quality time in prayer, worship and thanksgiving, and meditating on God's Holy Word, to receive His powerful and winning strategies for my daily victory over racism. This I shall do only by the grace of God, in the Name of our Lord and Savior Jesus Christ and through daily guidance by the Holy Spirit. I stand in agreement with my prayer partner(s) _____ believing that through the redeeming precious Blood of Jesus Christ, God has taken away the burden of racism, its reproach and yoke of destruction from all areas of my life. I stand in agreement with my prayer partner(s) _____ believing that the precious Blood of Jesus Christ has permanently destroyed and removed the power of the burden of the foul spirit of racism in my life, in Jesus' Name, Amen.

_____
Your Name

_____
Prayer Partner's Name

_____
Dr. Jacyee Aniagolu-Johnson
(Author remains in agreement with you)

"Again I say to you that if two of you agree on earth concerning anything that they ask, it will be done for them by My Father in heaven." – Matthew 18:19

"It shall come to pass in that day that his burden will be taken away from your shoulder, and his yoke from your neck, and the yoke will be destroyed because of the anointing oil." – Isaiah 10:27

CHAPTER 1 - The Disease Called Racism

Many people consider racism to be simply a bad cultural habit or a product of an ignorant tradition that has been passed on from one generation to another. However, racism is much more than that. It is a disease, a spiritual infirmity, with a vile spiritual origin that has been received and sustained by a tradition of spiritual and carnal lies in many societies. God did not authorize racism and will never approve of it or any other form of demonic influence. Racism is expressed as prejudices and discrimination; bigotry that is

Racism is a disease with a spiritual origin.

driven by one's racial makeup, ethnicity, nationality or other distinction. As Christian believers, we know that a spiritual ailment needs to be dealt with first by spiritual means so that change is made possible in the physical environment.

In Mark 9:16-27 Jesus Christ clearly demonstrated that a disease which is of a spiritual origin can only be cured using a spiritual approach when He delivered a young man from demonic possession (Matthew 4:24, 8:16, 8:28; 17:17-19). Racism manifests itself in the form of a spirit of demonic possession and whoever is being inhabited or influenced by this foul spirit can only be delivered from it by God's power through Jesus Christ.

God did not authorize racism and will never approve of it or any other form of demonic influence.

You cannot be delivered from the foul spirit of racism if you are racist and in denial of it. You must first acknowledge and confess that you are racist, repent in the Name of Jesus Christ, to be delivered from the stranglehold of that foul spirit.

The disease of racism in those who practice, perpetrate and perpetuate it can also become a disease of destruction of the souls of those who are its targets.

When I talk about the human soul, I also refer to our heart, mind, emotion, thought, will, motivation, resolve and willpower. Racism can take a toll on our minds whether we want to admit it or not. It can distort our thinking, attitudes, behavior and personality, and disconnect us from the truth, especially the truth about our value to ourselves, our loved ones, those in our circle of influence, our own society and to the world as a whole (John 4:9-10; Acts 10:14-15, 28-29).

Racism will try to make stagnant and unfruitful in you the hope, charity and love that you have and are capable of showing or sharing with others (John 4:9).

Your negative experiences with racism can distort your thinking.

Experiences with racism have convinced many that they are underachievers, even those of us who are born again believers (spiritually reborn in Jesus Christ); by this, I mean children of the Most High God who have received Jesus Christ into their hearts as their Lord and Savior. As a result, many of us limit ourselves through our own negative mindset, thoughts, emotions, actions, lack of motivation, will and resolve. Are you one of those individuals? Have you allowed your experiences with racism to limit your mind, dreams and aspirations?

Many have been deceived to believe racist lies about who they or others are, and they have forgotten that every man and woman (including them) is created in the Image of a perfect, excellent and Holy God. They never knew or no longer believe that God, our Father in Heaven, has not authorized and never will approve of any form of oppression or injustice, including racism (Isaiah 54:15,17; Jeremiah 1:19). They have become oblivious to the truth that God has never permitted the perpetrators of racism to try to muddle up the hearts and minds of those who have been targets of racism.

> *The attacks of racism on your soul are usually silent and destructive over time, if you don't resist, reject, rebuke and renounce them with God's Holy Word.*

Bear in mind that the spirit of racial prejudice, racism, bigotry, intolerance, narrow-mindedness—against others, can germinate within anyone of us as beliefs and become a stronghold which manifests as a mindset. In no time, the vile spirit of racism can quietly become deeply rooted within the soil of our hearts and minds, and spring forth as racist thoughts, words, emotions and actions that fuel our attitudes, behavior and personality; that is, if we allow ourselves to be willing human vessels for the loathsome spirit of racism. For those who use their human power to perpetrate and perpetuate racism, the negative spirit behind racism perverts willing human souls, making them its earthly vessels who believe, spread, celebrate and institutionalize its lie—that they are superior to or better than those they taunt or oppress by their racist words and actions.

For those who are targets of the foul spirit of racism, the effects of racism can disorganize your mind and thought process, and your belief in who and what you are. Racism can muddle your perception of yourself, that is, who you are in your mind. It can scramble and defile your heart and mind, and pervert your entire soul. Racism can give you a wounded and defeated soul, a victim mentality, leaving your mind in a state of permanent mental defeat and confusion about your true self, and your purpose and worth. As a result, you may wish for the rest of your life that you were a person of a

Racism can give a defeated soul if you allow it.

different race, rather than celebrate who God created you to be.

Racism's attack on your soul is usually silent and destructive as it eats into your heart, mind, emotions, will, resolve, thoughts, attitudes, actions, attitudes, personality and behavior, and finally, your physical body succumbs to ill health brought on by racism-inflicted stress. Regardless of who you are, your socio-economic status or specific and unique situation in life—whatever this may be, if you are a target of racism, over time your daily experiences with racism have the potential to unsettle your soul and ravage your heart, mind, emotions, will, resolve, and thoughts. Also, it can negatively impact your attitudes, actions, reactions, personality and behavior, as well as derail you from your God-driven purpose. However, this can only happen if you don't tap into the awesome power of God's Holy Word by the revelation knowledge of His Holy Spirit through our Lord and Savior Jesus Christ.

Jesus Christ has nailed racism to the Holy Cross on your behalf.

Christ is the Victor and Conqueror (Romans 8:35-37; Psalms 144:1-2) over all evil, including challenges like racism. Jesus Christ made you more than a conqueror over all evil, including racism (Romans 8:37). If you do not receive the awesome power of God's Holy Spirit through Jesus Christ, then racism can have its way in and with you—especially your mind or psyche, and your emotions, thoughts and thought process, willpower, resolve, and perceptions—as well as your daily actions, reactions and behavior. If you allow it, the foul spirit of racism can and will consume your entire being (1 Peter 5:8-9).

Thank God there is good news for you! If you feel rejected because of racism, you shouldn't, because Jesus Christ has nailed racism to the Holy Cross on your behalf (Colossians 2:14-15); He has given you God's divine victory over racism (1 John 5:4-5). He has overcome the world on your behalf, and racism that exists in it (John 16:33). When Jesus Christ, the "Stone" the builders rejected became the "Cornerstone" (Matthew 21:42), you too became the cornerstone over racism.

Jesus Christ, the "Stone" the builders rejected became the "Cornerstone" (Matthew 21:42).

Now, roll up your sleeves and begin to dig into God's Holy Word to receive His awesome power over the obnoxious spirit of racism. Call unto God and let

Him show you great and mighty things that you did not know (Jeremiah 33:3) about gaining spiritual and material victory daily over racism and the foul spirit behind it.

Chapter Quiz

1. From a Biblical perspective, what kind of infirmity or disease is racism?

---

2. Explain ways through which racism could take root within your soul.

---

3. Explain ways through which racism could attack your heart, mind and thoughts.

---

4. What is the foul spirit of racism? Does it attack your spirit, your soul or both? Explain your answer.

∞∞∞∞∞∞∞ ♦ ♦ ♦ ♦ ♦ ∞∞∞∞∞∞∞

Reflections:

_____

_____

_____

_____

∞∞∞∞∞∞∞ ♦ ♦ ♦ ♦ ♦ ∞∞∞∞∞∞∞

CHAPTER 2 – Shut Out the Spirit of Racism

We all have to face the truth at some point and admit that whenever we are harboring prejudiced or racist feelings, we have actually opened the "door" of our heart to the foul spirit of racism, and whether knowingly or by ignorance, we become a recruit of and recruiter for this despicable spirit, and therefore an agent for fostering racial prejudice and discrimination in our family, community, county, district, borough, province, state, country and the world.

Racism can give you a defeated and crippled mind.

Here's a word of caution: Never open up your soul to the vile spirit of racism—the evil spirit of Haman (Esther 7)!

The vile spirit of racism can attack anyone's heart, regardless of race, ethnicity or nationality, and socioeconomic status. Your material wealth can only shield you from the vile spirit of racism to an extent. In reality, only the Triune God can give you full protection from the evil spirit of racism. You can be wealthy, loaded with material things, and still have a heart and mind that is scrambled and confused by the despicable spirit of racism. There are many wealthy and highly successful individuals who are plagued spiritually by the odious spirit of racism. As a result, they have acquired either superiority or inferiority complexes about their race, ethnicity or even nationality.

Racism is contrary to God's Holy God and a direct attack on Him.

Daily, they wish either to be of the "preferred race or ethnicity" and think they are inferior, or they believe they are in fact of the "preferred race and feel superior to others and think they are better than other people of other races or ethnicity.

If you give the foul spirit of racism access to your soul, its negative effects on your heart and mind can mask or limit God's awesome power within you and present you with a counterfeit and corrupted copy of your true self. The vile spirit of racism can

God Himself is multi-racial and as such is fully reflected in every race.

pollute your heart, mind, thoughts, emotions, motivation, will, resolve, dreams and aspirations. It can devour your entire soul, if you allow it (1 Peter 5:8-9). A racist's mind is like foul smelling refuse land filled with rotten, toxic debris without the fragrance of Jesus Christ. Racism can put you in a spiritually diseased state with a defeated and crippled mind making you to lose positive spiritual focus. Anyone that loses focus on Jesus Christ and the Holy Spirit also loses focus on God's Holy Word and on God Himself in Whose perfect Image you are created.

God Himself is multi-racial and as such is fully reflected in every race. He created all of humanity and each of us reflects His beautiful and excellent Image. Your specific race, ethnicity and image are a reflection of God's own Image (Genesis 1:26-27). As a born again Christian, your authentic spiritual identity and nature is in Jesus Christ Who has reconciled your spirit to God (2

Corinthians 5:18). So never let anyone fool you into believing the lie that their race is superior or inferior to yours—this is a lie of the devil, the enemy of your soul, and there is no truth in him, as Jesus Christ has declared (John 8:44).

If racism is defeating you, it should not because God is on your side (Romans 8:31). Consider racism and the evil spirit behind it a serpent and scorpion spirit (Luke 10:17-19)—a fierce lion seeking to devour your soul (1 Peter 5:8-9). So, resist this foul and demonic spirit by standing firm in your faith—for through Jesus Christ, God has given you the power to trample upon fierce lion, scorpion and serpent spirits (like racism) under your feet and over all the power of the enemy and no harm will come upon you (Psalms 91:13; Luke 10:19).

Consider racism and the evil spirit behind it a serpent and scorpion spirit.

Racism may sometimes unnerve or rattle you, but it lacks true spiritual power and authority to permanently defeat you (2 Corinthians 4: 8-9), because you are more than a conqueror through Jesus Christ (Romans 8:37). I encourage you today to go to your holy place of worship—God's secret place with you (Psalms 91:1-3) and ask Him to show you great and mighty strategies (Jeremiah 33:3), to help you gain daily victory over racism.

Racism may sometimes unnerve or rattle you, but it lacks true spiritual power and authority to permanently defeat you (2 Corinthians 4: 8-9).

If you would *abide* in Jesus Christ—He will *abide* in you and He [God] will *abide* in you through Christ. If God's Word *abides* in you, He will give you your heart's desire through Christ (John 15:1-8). God will give you all other things that you seek if you seek Him first and His righteousness (Matthew 6:33). If you are obedient to God's Word, He will bless and promote you (Deuteronomy 28:1-14). He will make you the head over racism and not the tail under it (Deuteronomy 28:13).

Now is the moment for every one of us to resign from being a recruit of the vile spirit of racism, if we have been, because this obnoxious spirit is from the kingdom of darkness. We have the choice through Jesus Christ to be delivered from the darkness of racism into God's Kingdom of Light (Colossians 1:13). No matter who you are—a pastor or bishop, catholic or non-catholic priest, bishop or cardinal, monk, nun, senior pastor, evangelist, church worker, elder, deacon, apostle, prophet, lawyer, doctor, other health care professional or worker, engineer, scientist, teacher, homemaker, policeman, politician, computer expert, news anchor, journalist, comedian, small business owner, government worker—whatever your profession may be—I urgently suggest that we all accept this free offer through Jesus Christ—to be delivered from the darkness of the evil spirit of racism into God's Kingdom of Righteousness where light, virtue, truth, honesty, rectitude, decency, morality, uprightness, equity, justice and holiness rule. Don't believe the lies of the devil anymore. The truth is that the foul spirit of racism is contrary to God's Holy Word and is a direct attack on God Himself, Who created all of humanity (1 Corinthians 8:12). The belief in the superiority or inferiority of one race over another or one individual over another is a falsehood, for it is in God's excellent Image that we are all made; every race is within Him as one race—the human race.

> *Don't believe the lies of the devil anymore. Believe the truth of God's Holy Word—racism is contrary to God and against His Holy Word.*

If I am speaking to you, please hear me out today. You do not need to continue on the fruitless paths of disobedience to God's Word that the evil spirit of racism has led you on. Wherever you are now, you can choose at this very moment to begin the process of expelling the unholy spirit of racism from within you. This foul spirit of racial hostility and hatred must not have either temporary or permanent residence in you.

Wherever you are Jesus Christ is right there with you now—receive Him in your heart—this time not just by mere words—but in truth. Yes, He is waiting for you to offer a prayer of repentance (2 Chronicles 7:14) to change your prejudiced and racist ways.

> *The belief in the superiority or inferiority of one race over another or one individual over another is a falsehood.*

Don't delay another minute, because the despicable spirit of racism does not deserve any more residence within you, me or anyone else, for we are God's holy temple that should never be defiled by any unclean spirit—not by the foul spirit of racism, and certainly, not by any other unclean spirit (1 Corinthians 3:16-17).

Self-check: Are you infected by the foul spirit of racism, either as its perpetrator or its target? If you are, don't delay anymore, for Jesus Christ is knocking at the door to your heart (Revelation 3:20; John 10:7,9). So, open the door now and receive God's redeeming power by the precious Blood of our Lord and Savior Jesus Christ, Who can and will cleanse you of the vile spirit of racism and its negative effects—but this can only happen if you *truly* let Him into your heart and life. From this moment, by the awesome power of God's Holy Spirit through Christ, you will cease to be racist, if you were one; or you will cease to perceive yourself to be a victim of racism.

I urge you to repent of any racist thoughts or actions, and from this moment *truly and honestly* receive Jesus Christ in your heart as your Lord and Savior and start to meditate on God's Holy Word. Humbly, ask for His divine revelation by His Holy Spirit, Who will dwell within you when you receive and confess Jesus as your Savior, Lord and Master, and Redeemer of all humanity. Through Him, God will start the good work of pruning and purifying you (Malachi 3:2-4)—and He will expel the wicked spirit of racial prejudice and discrimination—the vile spirit of racial hostility, dislike and hatred from within you forever, nullifying any and all of its actions and effects on you.

Are you infected by the foul spirit of racism?

Chapter Quiz

1. Do you have any prejudice(s) against another race or ethnic group? If you do, identify and list your prejudices.

   _____

2. If you have developed racial or ethnic prejudices, how might this have happened?

   _____

3. How could God's Holy Word help you get rid of those racial or ethnic prejudices?

   _____

4. What steps should you take to shut out the foul spirit of racism?

   _____

5. What does John 8:44 tell you about the devil who is the "father of all lies," and how he presents racist lies to you and uses the foul spirit of racism against you and others?

   _____

∞∞∞∞∞∞∞ ♦ ♦ ♦ ♦ ♦ ∞∞∞∞∞∞∞

Reflections:

_____

_____

_____

_____

∞∞∞∞∞∞∞ ♦ ♦ ♦ ♦ ♦ ∞∞∞∞∞∞∞

CHAPTER 3 – The Blood of Jesus Christ Delivers

One might ask how it is possible for an individual to defeat racism, an age-old tradition that has become an intricate, interwoven part of society. The answer is simple: our individual victory over racism is only possible because of the awesome power of God's grace that lies with and within us through Jesus Christ (1 John 4:4), Who is our Conqueror and Victory over the world (1 John 5:4-5; 1 Corinthians 15:57). God's grace to us—Jesus Christ is already within you and me, and we can tap into it when we are tired, weak and exhausted, to draw our daily strength and

Choose to dismantle and destroy racism by truth of God's Holy Word.

victory (2 Corinthians 12:9). This strength and victory cannot be drawn from any other source, as the world may want to believe; rather, it is drawn from a divine release from God's powerful Word through Jesus Christ. It is drawn from the empowering of God's Holy Spirit Who dwells within us who are believers in Christ. Through prayer, worship, praise, meditating on God's Holy Word, and daily communion with God through Christ—and divine guidance through His Holy Spirit Who dwells within us, this spiritual release and revelation is activated by our own faith and belief in God, His Holy Word, which is God Himself—and acceptance of His Son Jesus Christ, our Savior and Redeemer, our Lord and Master.

Jesus Christ is our Conqueror and Victory over racism—and over the world.

If God allowed His only Son to die for us (John 3:16), what then is it that He cannot do for you and me? He has given you the power to speak life or death, to create or destroy (Proverbs 18:21)—so use that power to frustrate, suffocate, defeat and destroy the wicked plans of the foul spirit of racism against your life—choose to dismantle and destroy racism and build upon only the truth of who and what God says you are. God has not given you a timid spirit that you should allow yourself to be controlled by fear of racism or any other form of evil or negative situation or challenge; rather, He has given you a spirit of power, love and soundness of mind—yes, He has given you strength of will power, self-discipline and self control (2 Timothy 1:7) which you can use victoriously against racism.

As a born again believer, you have to believe the absolute truth that the power of God is unquenchable within you through Jesus Christ. If you believe God and His Holy Word, He will demonstrate His power and glory to you through Christ, against the evil spirit of racism (Romans 9:17; Ephesians 1:18-23; John 11:40). This is the victory that Christ gained for you and I by His crucifixion and resurrection (1 John 5:4-5; John 11:25); for He conquered evil on our behalf on the Holy Cross of Calvary—and by His precious Blood, we have the same victory. Allow God in the Name of Jesus Christ to help you stand in Christ's victory so that you can conquer every form of evil

> *Let God oppose those who oppose you—let God be an enemy to them.*

coming against your life, including devious and destructive influence of racism in your life (1 John 5:4).

Until you start experiencing in your daily life the victory that Jesus Christ has obtained for you, you cannot really say that you are living the power of God's Word, and applying the power of the anointing of His Holy Spirit within you. If your life is still being led into defeat by daily challenges, including racism, then you have yet to get on the path of triumph with Jesus Christ, and God's fragrance through Him has not fully permeated your life (2 Corinthians 2:14). However, you can activate God's power within you by receiving Jesus as your Lord and Savior, repenting of your sins, and meditating on His Holy Word and living by it—and spending intimate quality time of prayer, worship and thanksgiving in His holy presence (2 Chronicles 7:14; Psalms 91:1-3). If you allow God's Word to abide in you (John 15:7), then the radiance of God's awesome grace will through Jesus Christ, give you strength and transform you into more than a conqueror of racism or any other challenge that you may encounter (Romans 8:37). Then, as you believe

> *You have been spiritually stamped and validated by the precious Blood of Jesus Christ.*

God's Word by your own faith, you will begin to see the manifestation of God's awesome power and glory (John 11:40)—although racists may gather around and against you, they will not prevail against you (Jeremiah 1:19; Isaiah 54:15, 17).

Racism, whether subtle or overt, is a form of spiritual perversion and oppression that manifests itself in our physical world, and God hates oppression or violence against anyone, regardless of race, ethnicity or nationality (Jeremiah 22:3; Isaiah 61:8; Ezekiel 45:9; Psalms 11:5). He fights for the oppressed and unjustly treated (Exodus 3:7-10, 23:9,22,23; Deuteronomy 26:6-9; Psalms 9, 10:4, 12:14, 35, 37, 121, 127, 140:12; Isaiah 25:4). When you are confronted with racism, go to God in prayer, plead your case before God (Psalms 7:1-2; 35) and then through forgiveness release your racist offenders to Him (Mark 11:22-25).

Racism can never change God's love for you.

Be obedient to God's Holy Word and let Him battle those who oppress you—let God oppose those who oppose you—let Him be an Enemy to your enemies, and an Adversary to your adversaries (Exodus 23:22; Psalms 18:1-3; Psalms 35:1-3)—let Him gain victory for you—the battle is not yours but the Lords' (1 Samuel 17:45-47). As you continue to stand on God's holy ground of integrity (Ephesians 4:1), God will act on your behalf and your enemies will surely become God's enemies—and who can stand before God's power? Who can oppose His might and win? (Romans 8:31; Job 9:4)

From now on, let your spiritual and mental motto be: "Through Jesus Christ, I am above racism and its evils." Let these words become deeply rooted in your heart and mind. Know that God loves you so much (Romans 8:35-39) and that through Jesus Christ, He has redeemed you and made you His righteous child and heir, and co-heir with Christ in His glorious Kingdom (Romans 8:16-17). This means that your negative experiences with racism or other challenges can never change God's love for you (Romans 8:38), nor can such experiences ever overtake you when you are fully clothed in God's spiritual armor (Ephesians 6:13) that is sustained by daily prayer of faith in Jesus Christ. So if God loves you no matter what, then He has set the most solid and immovable foundation for your life and existence—your salvation and victory

> *God has given you a spirit of power, love and a sound mind (2 Timothy 1:7).*

through Jesus Christ. For this reason, you can overcome racism because the power of God the Father Who is in you through Jesus Christ, is greater than any evil, seen or unseen (1 John 4:4), including racism.

If you abide in God's Word daily (John 15:1-8), it will empower you daily with the truth about who you really are in Jesus Christ—and you will be fruitful despite the influences of racism around you. God's holy truth, if you will receive and apply it daily in your life, will forever set and make you free from the pangs of racism (John 8:31-32). You have been spiritually stamped and validated by the precious Blood of Jesus Christ, Who is your victory over the world (1 John 5:4-5, 16:33), and racism lacks the authority or power to change this holy truth.

Jesus Christ is your victory over the world (1 John 5:4-5, 16:33)

∞∞∞∞∞ ♦ ♦ ♦ ♦ ♦ ∞∞∞∞∞∞∞∞
Chapter Quiz

1. As a Christian and a child of the Most High God, explain one spiritual approach (based on the

Bible) that you can apply to gain daily victory over racism.

_____

2. How can you shake off the spirit of fear of racism?

_____

3. How can you shut the door to your heart to the foul spirit of racism?

_____

4. Racism is a form of spiritual perversion and oppression. Explain why and how.

_____

5. What Holy Scripture declares you to be more than a conqueror through Jesus Christ? How can you apply that Scripture to truly become more than a conqueror of racism?

_____

∞∞∞∞∞∞∞∞ ♦ ♦ ♦ ♦ ∞∞∞∞∞∞∞∞

Reflections:

_____

_____

_____

FOOTPRINTS OF VICTORY OVER RACISM – VOLUME 1

∞∞∞∞∞∞ ♦ ♦ ♦ ♦ ∞∞∞∞∞∞

Chapter 4 – Spiritual Decay and Racism

If you do not *read, receive, know and apply* God's Holy Word, if you do not meditate on it daily and exercise your believing faith in His Word through Jesus Christ, you run the risk of slipping into a state of spiritual decay or complacency (Revelation 3:14-17). This opens the door to your soul for the enemy (the devil) to mount attacks on any and all areas of your life.

Racism can create doubts within you about who you are.

Spiritual decay also creates access for the foul spirit of racism to launch a formidable attack against your soul and penetrate your heart, mind and thoughts, negatively impact your emotions, motivation, will and resolve, and influence or direct your attitude, actions, personality and behavior, in a manner that is contrary to God's Holy Word, plan and purpose for your life.

If you are in a state of spiritual decay, the effects of racism can create doubts within you about who you are, what you are and the height of success that you are capable of achieving. It can misinform you about your true spiritual content and try to fill you with lies about who you are (John 8:44; 2 Corinthians 2:11). For example, when the foul spirit of racism demeans you through one of its human subjects, you may begin to believe that who and what you are is inferior, unacceptable, unworthy and of little or no significance to the world. When this happens, you may begin to function based on a defiled 'photocopy' of your true self. This is not your true self, but the fabricated self that the odious spirit of racism and its custom-made lies that it designs for you, to destroy your perception of your true spiritual image, identity and nature—all in your mind.

We are created in God's excellent Image.

Anyone who functions based on a photocopy of their God-designed original blueprint, rather than the original itself, could easily be defiled and deceived by lies and made to believe anything about him or herself. Such a person could begin to see him or herself as a "victim" of racism that attempts to devalue their worth already predetermined by God to be worthy through the precious Blood of Jesus Christ.

By your mere creation and existence through conception and birth, God already expressed His approval of your life. Before your conception, He knew you and designed your creation (Jeremiah 1:5)—He loved you and He created you in His excellent Image. By offering His only Son Jesus Christ for your salvation (John 3:16), He expressed His boundless and eternal love for you (Romans 8:35-39). Then, by being spiritually born again through Jesus Christ (John 3:3), you have become justified through Christ and the process of your sanctification has begun (Revelation 12:10).

God's Holy Word will renew your mind.

By doing this, God once again expressed His love for you, by offering you eternal salvation through the redeeming power of the precious Blood of His only Son Jesus Christ. God placed His Stamp of Validation and Ownership on you—His Holy Spirit Whose awesome power raised Christ from the dead (2 Corinthians 1:20-22; Ephesians 1:15-23; 2 Timothy 1:13-14). He, Christ, is the resurrection—through which the guaranteed deposit of the anointing power of His Holy Spirit dwells within you. Spiritual decay will blind you to this truth, that is, God's fundamental truth about Jesus Christ in you and the real you in Him (2 Corinthians 4:3-6).

So, if you are one of many people whom racism has defeated spiritually and mentally and who lacks a sense of purpose, focus or direction, that is a sign of a spiritual crisis and decay within you. Don't let this lie continue to fester within you—end it now by crying out "Abba Father" to God in prayer for help and begin to read, know and meditate on His Holy Word (Romans 8:15; Galatians 4:6). Let God's Holy Word abide within you, renew your mind (Romans 12:2) and refresh you with a new breath of God (Genesis 2:7). Let it create a new birth in you and a new kind of consuming fire (Hebrews 12:28-29). Let the Fire of the Holy Spirit through Jesus Christ, cause a reawakening of your spirit and bring new life within your soul, and sharpen discernment of your renewed mind (Genesis 2:7; John 3:6; Galatians 2:20; 2 Corinthians 5:17; John 7:38; Romans 10:9-10, 12:2).

God created and validated you through Jesus Christ.

Once you go to God in prayer, with humility and honesty, and through the guidance of His Holy Spirit already in you, He will begin to reveal spiritual things to you in the most subtle and yet awesome ways (Jeremiah 33:3). He will give you clarity of mind to understand His excellent purpose that He designed especially for your life. God will open your spiritual eyes (2 Corinthians 3:16-18), begin to renew your mind with His Holy Word (Romans 12:2; Ephesians 4:23-24), and give you new spiritual sight and knowledge to begin to appreciate His wonderful future for your life (Jeremiah 29:11). However, for this journey with God to begin, you must first receive Jesus Christ in your heart and receive the power of the Holy Spirit (Romans 10:9-10; Acts 1:8). Then, you must begin to abide in God's Holy Word for the amazing process of revelation of His Word by His Holy Spirit to begin to take place in you.

Let God's Holy Word abide within you, renew your mind and refresh you with a new breath of God.

God can only open your spiritual eyes for you to begin to see your true worth and life's purpose when you invite and receive Jesus Christ into your heart, and then, receive the power of God's Holy Spirit within you. Through prayer (thanksgiving, praise and worship), with meditation on His Holy Word, and without doubt in your heart or mind, you will live in daily obedience to His Holy Word. Then, as you draw nearer to God, He, too, will draw nearer to you (James 4:8). Your trusting relationship with God will cause your desires to begin to align with God's desires for you and His purpose for your life; and then, God shall grant you your heart's desires in accordance with His will for your life, as He has promised in His Word (Psalms 37:4; Psalms 20:4; Matthew 6:33).

God may choose to use obvious or subtle miracles, a friend, a co-worker, your pastor, a family member, anyone else or circumstances to reveal more of Himself to you, and also, He will reveal Himself directly to you in any manner that He chooses (Deuteronomy 4:29). One thing is certain: When you ask Him to reveal to you the only true reality about who you are, He certainly will do so once you begin to acknowledge Who He is (Matthew 16:13-19; Matthew 91:14-15), as He has promised in His Holy Word. God will take away your spiritual blindness, transforming you into a mirror image of His glory in Jesus Christ (2 Corinthians 3:18; 1 John 3:2; 1 John 3:-2-3). Then, you will see your Christlike image only through God's Eyes in accordance with His Word, and not as a racist's or as anyone else's negative presentation of yourself to you.

God's Holy Word fortifies you against racism.

The validation of God's perfect Image, His love for all humanity, regardless of race, ethnicity or nationality, was manifested in Flesh as His Son Jesus Christ, Who died for our salvation (John 3:16)—and in you whom He loved and created and validated through Christ Whom you have accepted as your Lord and Savior. Thus, through Christ, God's Stamp of Validation is already in and on you and me, and this is a crucial, life-giving, preserving and restoring foundation—His Stamp of Ownership in and on you and is sealed by His deposit of His Holy Spirit in you.

If you accept, understand and grow in and with the knowledge of God's Word, He will fortify you against any potential destructive effects of racism or any other adversity or negative circumstance (Psalms 91). God will become your shield and buckler (Psalms 91:4)—your daily protection against any false mindset orchestrated by any form of evil, including the obnoxious spirit of racism. His Holy Word promises us in Psalms 91:14-15 (NKJV): "Because he has set his love upon Me, therefore I will deliver him; I will set him on high, because he has known My name. He shall call upon Me, and I will answer him; I will be with him in trouble; I will deliver him and honor

God has His Stamp of Ownership in and on you.

him." Your genuine love for the Triune God guarantees you victory through Jesus Christ Whom you have accepted as your Lord and Savior. God's Word, Which is inseparable from God Himself, will transform your mind into a victorious, fortified "battlefield" (Philippians 4:4-9; Psalms 119:9-16; Psalms 91:1-4) against the intrigues and wiles of the enemy of your soul, the devil. Remember that it is also the devil who originates, orchestrates and directs the despicable spirit of racism.

God's Holy Word will empower you to pull down and demolish any argument or posturing that racism sets up against the knowledge of God, and you will take captive every foul thought of racism and make it obedient to Jesus Christ (2 Corinthians 10:3-6). God's Word will serve as your "Bridge" over your troubled waters—over your experiences with racism, and will give you daily individual victory over the deceitful schemes of racists.

God's Word will serve as your "Bridge" over your troubled waters.

Yes, in the awesome Name of Jesus Christ, God will bring down every "counsel of Ahithophel" being set up against your life (2 Samuel 15:31, 17:1-23).

Chapter Quiz

1. How can you build and fortify your faith against racism?

   _____

2. Explain how spiritual complacency or decay can open up your soul to defeat through the evil spirit of racism.

   _____

3. Why must you never see yourself as a victim of racism or of the foul spirit of racism?

   _____

4. If God has validated you through Jesus Christ, can racism declare you to be unworthy or inferior? Explain your answer.

   _____

5. Why must you always see yourself as a victor over racism and of the loathsome spirit of racism?

   _____

Reflections:

_____
_____
_____

∞∞∞∞∞∞∞ ♦ ♦ ♦ ♦ ♦ ∞∞∞∞∞∞∞

Chapter 5 – God's Touch for True Repentance

If you have a racist mindset, thoughts, motives or attitudes, I urge you to open up your spirit and soul for God's conviction (not condemnation) to touch you with His love. Through His Holy Spirit within you, He will reveal to you all hidden areas of your heart where racial and ethnic prejudice resides and the necessary repentance and changes required (2 Chronicles 7:14; John 16:8; Acts 10:27-29). For those who practice racism, any form of racism is more than just a bad cultural attitude that one needs to unlearn—it is a form of evil spiritual possession—it is a form of injustice and oppression, and as such, an offense against humanity and

> *Racism is a demonic influence and a sin against God.*

an assault against God, Who is the Creator of all humanity (1 Corinthians 8:12). Racism is also a manifestation of demonic influence. It is disobedience of God's Holy Word. Therefore, it is a sin against God Himself. Just like any other sin, true repentance and turning away from such actions is required (2 Chronicles 7:14).

The Greek meaning of the word translated "repentance" is "metanoia" which means "change" (meta) and "mind" (noia)—to have a change of mind. Therefore, turning away from sin (such as racism) is repentance; it is an act of will and a decision to turn toward God (2 Chronicles 7:14; Acts 3:19). Repentance through Jesus Christ makes it possible for us to witness the manifestation of the glory of God's Word and His anointing presence within us. It requires us to accept a change in the right direction, away from our negative and wrong paths. To repent from our old and racist ways, we need to allow God's Word to truly penetrate our hearts and minds, and purge our wrong ways of thinking.

God's Holy Word trains your heart, mind and thoughts.

The Word of God will begin to train our thoughts, mind and heart as it takes root within us. His Holy Spirit Who dwells within us will become our Best

Friend, Teacher, Counselor, Guide, Educator, Comforter, and Mind- and Eye-opener, and will reveal to us only God's holy truth about the equality of all people regardless of race, ethnicity, nationality or any other discriminating factor that humans have received and accepted from the devil, the father of all lies (John 8:44). God's Holy Spirit in us leads us to all truth, God's Holy Word— and nothing less (John 16:13). God's Word offers us the only truth that there is and convicts our hearts, if we truly receive it. Then, we shall come to know God's truth, which will make us free (John 8:32). God's Holy Word will make us free, if and only when we *truly* believe and receive it in our hearts as the truth, and apply it in our lives. Then, it cancels the lies of the devil in our hearts and minds.

The rich diversity of the human race is a blessing to humanity.

God's Holy Word inspires true repentance in us, and this has great rewards. Through the precious Blood of Jesus Christ, we are liberated from all of our sins and the lies of the devil, whether subtle or overt—and we are delivered from our own destructive and harmful actions against ourselves and others. The liberating Word of God, if we *truly* receive it in ours heart, will release us from bondage to any wicked traditions, including racism (Colossians 2:8; Matthew 15:3; Mark 7:13).

Genuine and honest repentance through Jesus Christ offers us a fresh new beginning that allows us to start building a new and wholesome relationship with God. We begin to develop love and respect for the racial and ethnic diversity that exists in the human race. God's Word teaches us how to positively build upon the rich diversity of the human race, rather than use race as a divisive or destructive weapon against any individual or group. Then, we come to understand that with God's Word we build up lives, but with racism and its lies we tear down lives.

With God's Word we build up lives, with racism we tear down lives.

To those who have been targets of racism, God wants all of humanity to be saved through Jesus Christ (John 3:16). Therefore, we must all pray for the repentance of our prejudiced and racist attackers (Matthew 5:44), even as we use the power of God's Word, by spiritual warfare, against the foul spirit of racism operating in them, to tear down the stranglehold of their racist activities.

Allow God's Holy Spirit within you to reveal to you each day true spiritual knowledge and wisdom that paralyzes racism and its negative effects. Forgiveness is one way to silence the foul spirit of racism that operates through your racist offenders. Let your daily meditation on God's Holy Word and the guiding revelation of His Holy Spirit within you become a quiet and empowering daily spiritual refresher and rebuilder of your mental ammunition. With this, you will begin to cultivate the right spiritual mindset, and developmental endurance for resisting racism and gaining daily victory over every experience with racism. Then you will develop a spiritual, racism-proof armor that shields you from the fiery darts of the odious spirit of racism—and you are able to deal victoriously with racism in your physical environment.

Develop a spiritual, racism-proof armor that shields you from the fiery darts of the odious spirit of racism.

∞∞∞∞∞∞∞∞ ♦ ♦ ♦ ♦ ∞∞∞∞∞∞∞∞

Chapter Quiz

1. Can and will God forgive your sins if you repent? Why? How?

   _____

2. Can and will God forgive prejudiced and racist people if they repent? Why? How?

   _____

3. Can the Holy Spirit help you recognize the sin of prejudice and racism in you, if you let Him? Why? How?

_____

4. True or false: Does God expect you to forgive and pray for prejudiced or racist people to change their ways? Explain your answer.

_____

5. How can you develop a spiritual, racism-proof armor to shield you from the fiery darts of the odious spirit of racism?

_____

∞∞∞∞∞∞∞∞ ♦ ♦ ♦ ♦ ♦ ∞∞∞∞∞∞∞∞

Reflections:

_____
_____
_____
_____

∞∞∞∞∞∞∞∞ ♦ ♦ ♦ ♦ ♦ ∞∞∞∞∞∞∞∞

CHAPTER 6 – Dealing With Racism

Racism is a form of spiritual and psychological terrorism because it attacks your soul and aims to pollute your heart and mind, and distorts your perception of yourself and others. It is also a manifestation of negative, unseen spiritual influences (Ephesians 6:12-13) in our physical, visible environment. God has not authorized and does not authorize racist practices, because His Word has said a resounding NO to any kind of injustice or oppression (Exodus 2:23-35, 3:7-10; Psalms 103:6)—and racism is not an exception. If anyone directs racial prejudice or discriminatory actions against you, they are

> *Racism is a form of spiritual and psychological; terrorism.*

not actually attacking you, but God, Who is your Creator (1 Corinthians 8:12). Therefore, the racist offender or oppressor is waging a war against God Himself (Acts 26:14-15), and no one can win any battle against God. Simply put, as a born again believer you have God's victory through Jesus Christ. God's power and might fights for His people and delivers justice (Exodus 3:16-17) to and for those who love and acknowledge Him (Psalms 91:14-15); who trust and obey His Word (Romans 10:11; Psalms 119:100; Proverbs 3:5-6)—and who praise and worship Him and abide in His Word (Psalms 18, 37, 91). So, the battle against racism is not yours but the Lord's (1 Samuel 17:47); and He, *Jesus Christ has overcome racism on your behalf.* Christ, has already won the battle for you (John 16:33). You are a child of God and He takes on your battles, if you submit to His Holy Word and let Him be your shield and buckler through the protective covering of the precious Blood of Jesus Christ (Psalms 91:1-4; James 4:7).

When you submit to God's Word and resist the devil, who comes against you in the form of racism, he will flee from you (James 4:7-8). Knowing this now, when you experience any form of racism, injustice, persecution or oppression, stand firm on God's Word in the Name of Jesus Christ; act in accordance with His Word—refrain from vengeance or insult even when the opportunity presents itself, and then watch God gloriously manifest victory on your behalf. God will direct your steps and actions—a sure path to His divine victory over racism. The foul spirit of racism is an accuser of God's children, but the power of Jesus Christ within you has already overthrown this unclean spirit on your behalf (John 16:33; Revelation 12:9-10; 2 Corinthians 2:11; Revelation 20:10). Jesus Christ has canceled the charges of racism against you by nailing them to the Holy Cross (Colossians 2:14-15).

Racism is designed to degrade your view of your self-worth as a person, because it attacks the inner core of who you are—it is designed to devour, distort or destroy in your mind God's blueprint of the real you (1 Peter 5:8; John 10:10a). It is designed to deceive you about the truth of what God has said about you (Psalms 40, 41, 42, 45), and to present you with subtle and blatant lies (John 8:44), and untruth about your worth and the purpose of your creation. It presents you daily with only negative images about you and other people of your race or ethnicity; so racism is out to destroy your psyche and life, if you allow it (John

Racism cannot and will not destroy you!

10:10a), but you cannot allow it to do so, for Jesus Christ has already overcome every evil on your behalf, including racism (1 John 5:4-5; Colossians 2:14-15; John 16:33). Christ has given you life more abundantly and the vile spirit of racism and its human recruits do not have the power or authority to change this truth (John 10:10b).

Perhaps at work you may be skipped over for promotion, paid less than a less-qualified co-worker because of your race, ethnicity or nationality, left out of discussions on important work-related issues, given fewer challenges and less-significant tasks, not acknowledged for your work and contributions and so on. Nonetheless,

Walk in the position of Christ's power and authority in you for divine victory in your life.

these attacks should remain on the outside of you, if you truly knew whose you were, and if you believed that God had (and still has) wonderful things ahead for you (Jeremiah 29:11).

For you to be able to endure trials like racist schemes and plots against you and not allow such evil to dig into your inner core, you must wear God's full armor through Jesus Christ (Ephesians 6:10-18) and believe that racism is merely a test of your faith and is one of the many afflictions that you as a child of God will face (Psalms 34:19; Acts 14:22, 1 Peter 1:6-7; James 1:3). God has delivered you from all such afflictions through Christ (Isaiah 61:1-3). You must believe that racism is not a dominant force that has any real authority or power to defeat or destroy you when the power of God's Word dwells powerfully within you (2 Corinthians 4: 8-18). You must believe and affirm that racism cannot and will not destroy you (2 Corinthians 4:8-9). Know and believe without any shadow of doubt that because God is on your side, nobody and nothing, including racism and the evil spirit behind it and its human recruits, can be against you (Romans 8:31).

God's Holy Word is the Sword of the Spirit against racism.

As you face daily challenges like racism and other adversities of life, you have to consciously and subconsciously believe in the supreme power of God's Word against and above all evil. Apply God's Holy Word in your life when you deal with the many cleverly presented racist situations in our present-day world. Plead your case before God in prayer and watch Him rise up in your defense (Psalms 34, 35, 68:1). God has promised to be a shield of protection (Psalms 91) for those who have submitted their lives to the precious Blood of His only Son, Jesus Christ. It is therefore our responsibility to read, know, believe and receive God's Word, and to apply it to our lives for us to receive the blessings and promises of God's Word (Joshua 1:8; Deuteronomy 28:1-14). It is up to us to walk in the position of Christ's power and authority in us for divine victory in our lives. This is what brings to our lives victory and triumph. Therefore, the Sword of the Spirit, that is, God's Word, is the most powerful weapon that has ever existed which can dispel, scatter and destroy spiritual and carnal enemies of God, that is, any form of evil, including racism (Ephesians 6:17; Psalms 68:1-3). Through Christ, you have His authority and power over evil (Ephesians 1:20-23; Luke 10:18-19; Philippians 2:9-11; Hebrews 1:3-4); and as a believer in Jesus Christ, maximize the use of His authority and power in you, because under His precious Blood you are fully covered and secured to gain your individual victory over racism.

Racism is designed to degrade your self-worth as a person.

God's Holy Word is a spiritual weapon, the Sword of the Spirit that you and I must fight with, and not solely with physical weapons. God's Word is the divine power that demolishes all strongholds. God's Word manifests His awesome power that weakens, dismantles and destroys evil spiritual or physical weapons. We must learn to apply God's Word to demolish arguments, influences, points of view, advice and opinions, as well as every posturing that racism sets up against the knowledge of God.

We must take captive, that is, imprison, incarcerate, lock up, confine and cage every racist thought or action to make it obedient to Jesus Christ (2 Corinthians 10:4-5). The Word of God will only work for you when you read, listen, hear, believe and retain it in your heart and mind (John 11:40, 15:1-8), and live and act in daily obedience to it (Joshua 1:7-9). Hearing, believing and knowing God's word is what activates your inherent faith, that is, God's gift of the measure of faith within you (Romans 12:3; Romans 10:17).

Your obedience pleases God (1 Samuel 15:22). Your faith pleases God (Hebrews 11:6). Your faith will move the "mountain" of racism out of your way (Matthew 21:21-22; Mark 11:22-24). Believe that nothing is too hard for God to do (Jeremiah 32:27).

The power of your faith is greater than the foul spirit of racism.

Genuine faith brings God's holy power and might over any circumstance or situation on your behalf. This then brings God's promises and miracles into your daily life. Once your inherent measure of faith is activated, and as it grows and matures by applying God's Word, it can be fine-focused against any form of racism, whether hidden or blatant, or any other challenge that you may be experiencing. Such activated faith will rightly claim your legal spiritual position in Jesus Christ, Who has on your behalf overcome all adversities, including racism. Christ has overcome the world on your behalf (John 16:33), and so have you through Him (1 John 5:4). Only by activating your faith in Christ and standing in His victory for you, can you too become more than a conqueror over racism and other trials that you may encounter in your life (Romans 8:37). Through faithful belief in the power of God's divine Word and sustained focus and hard work, God will surely give you spiritual, mental and material victory over challenges like racism and other forms of life's tests, trials and tribulations. The power of your own faith against the obnoxious spirit of racism is greater than its intrigues and vile product—racism.

> *You, child of God, are the light of the word that shines brilliantly over the darkness of racism.*

Know that through Jesus Christ, you already have overwhelming victory over the darkness of the odious spirit of racism, a defeated foe by God's Kingdom of Light (John 1:5; 1 John 1:5). God has given Jesus Christ, Who lives in you, all authority over any evil that attacks you (Matthew 28:18). So if you understand the power of the authority that God gave Christ (Ephesians 1:15-23), then you will put your faith in Him because you know without a doubt in your heart that you, too, have His power and authority over any and all evil, including the spirit of racism. Once you grasp the power of Christ's anointing in you, your faith moves to a higher level and you are able to call out your victory from the unseen to the visible realm (Romans 4:17). You, child of God, are the light of the world (Matthew 5:14) that shines brilliantly over any darkness, for where God is, there can never be any form of darkness (1 John 1:5; Isaiah 9:2). Through Jesus Christ, God's holy Light in you will dazzle and confuse racism around you. God's Light in you through Christ suffocates and obliterates the evil darkness of racism.

Your faith will move the "mountain" of racism out of your way!

∞∞∞∞∞∞∞∞ ♦ ♦ ♦ ♦ ∞∞∞∞∞∞∞∞

Chapter Quiz

1. Why is racism a form of spiritual and psychological terrorism?

2. Can racism degrade your true self-worth in Jesus

Christ, or your view in your mind of your true self-worth? Explain.

___

3. How can you guard your heart, mind, emotions, thoughts, will, resolve, dreams and aspirations against the evil spirit of racism?

___

4. What spiritual weapons are most effective against the foul spirit of racism and its effects?

___

5. True or false: Carnal, and not spiritual weapons of warfare, are most effective against the vile spirit of racism. Explain your answer.

___

6. True or false: If you are able to subdue the vile spirit of racism through spiritual warfare, then you are able to defeat racism that exists in your physical environment. Explain your answer.

___

7. Who has already gained victory for you over racism?

___

∞∞∞∞∞∞∞∞ ♦ ♦ ♦ ♦ ♦ ∞∞∞∞∞∞∞∞

Reflections:

___
___

∞∞∞∞∞∞∞∞ ♦ ♦ ♦ ♦ ∞∞∞∞∞∞∞∞

Chapter 7 – Focus Your Faith Against Racism

"Faith is being sure of what we hope for and certain of what we do not see" (Hebrews 11:1 NIV). The NKJV says, "Now faith is the substance of things hoped for, the evidence of things not seen" (Hebrews 11:1).

God's Holy Word powers our built-in faith.

Faith is a spiritual force and substance. When you have faith, this spiritual substance in you gives you a quiet and certain confidence, assurance and inner knowledge that what you are hoping and praying for through Jesus Christ is already done and established, even before you see any material evidence that it has happened. Faith brings the substance of what you hope for first into spiritual evidence, then into physical manifestation. So, we must live by faith (Romans 1:17) and must walk by faith and not by sight (2 Corinthians 5:7). To have faith is to believe in something, to fully trust, to be confident that what you believe in is indeed true and will without doubt eventually become a tangible reality. Faith is also accepting God's will even when it seems to contradict what you hoped and believed for, because God's thoughts are not our thoughts and His ways are not ours either (Isaiah 55:9). Our authentic faith yields to God's holy will because He has the complete view of all things and we don't.

Your faith in God fuels you to trust Him and His Word.

To have faith in God is to believe Him and His Word, and to be fully convinced of the truthfulness, faithfulness and reliability of God Himself, His Word and everything else that pertains to Him (Joshua 21:45; Isaiah 55:11; Matthew 24:35; Hebrews 13:5). The foundation of your faith in God is having trust and confidence in God through Jesus Christ, your Savior, Lord and Master, Justifier, Sanctifier, Cleanser, Healer, Deliverer and all goodness encompassed in One. Such faith leads you to entrust your entire being to Him (Psalms 118:8; Proverbs 3:5-6).

God's Word tells us that each of us has received a measure of faith (Romans 12:3). So how can we grow and bolster our faith, and always retain and maintain it? How can we get our faith to work in our lives in such a manner that its power would dominate, grow and smother the negative effects of the rugged terrain of challenges and obstacles placed before us by evil such as racism? (Matthew 17:20-21; Mark 11:22-24) How can we transform our mustard-seed faith into a daily, victorious harvest and triumph over racism? How do we grow the inherent measure of faith within us? (Romans 10:17; Luke 17:6; Matthew 17:20)

Believe in God's faithfulness and rely solely on Him.

Since God has given each of us a measure of faith to start with; and for our faith to spring into spiritual action, we must initiate and activate its growth by first accepting the redeeming power of Jesus Christ, Who shed His Blood on Mount Calvary for the salvation of all humanity. Then, we receive the promised Holy Spirit of God, Who births a new spiritual life in us and activates God's Holy Word within us, as we begin to meditate and dwell on it. We must believe the absolute truth of God's Word that never fails, for our God does not relent on His promises through Jesus Christ (1 Samuel 15:29; Numbers 23:19). God's Holy Word builds our faith

(Romans 10:17). We must read, meditate and believe God's Holy Word and let it soak our heart and mind and abide in us—this positions us to ask God for anything and receive it through Jesus Christ and according to God's will for our life. God's blessings and promises for us are for us to live a victorious life—in accordance with God's holy will for our lives (John 15:7; Jeremiah 29:11). As we are led by God's Holy Spirit, we must live our lives in daily communion with God through:

Focus your faith against racism.

- **Constant prayer (praise, thanksgiving):** 1Thessalonians 5:17; Matthew 14:23; Mark 1:35-37; Mark 6:46; Mark 14:35, 39; Luke 5:15-16; Luke 3:21-22; Luke 9:18; Colossians 4:2; 1 Chronicles 16:9; Psalms 144:9; Psalms 145:10.
- **Relentless and perpetual worship:** 1 Chronicles 16:29; Psalms 34:3; John 4:23-24; 1 Corinthians 14:25; Psalms 29:2; Psalms 95:6; Hebrews 12:28; Hebrews 1:6; Revelations 4:10-11; Psalms 45:11; Psalms 99:5; Psalms 132:7; Psalms 5:7; Philippians 3:3; Psalms 14:2.
- **Spiritual fasting:** Luke 2:36-37; Luke 4:1-2; Daniel 10:2-3, Esther 4:3; Isaiah 58:5-8; Joel 2:12-

13; Exodus 34:28; Acts 9:9-12; Acts 13:2; Psalms 35:13; 1 Samuel 7:3-14; Ezra 8:21-23; Psalms 35:13.

We must meditate day and night on God's Word (Joshua 1:7-9). He, God, never leaves nor forsakes us (Hebrews 13:5) and nothing can ever separate us from His divine love (Romans 8:35-39). We must believe in the absolute truth of God's Word, which gives us new spiritual life, refreshes and renews our hearts and minds. We must then also live our daily lives in accordance with His Holy Word. Daily, we must release our offenders through daily forgiveness; this includes those who hurt or harm us; those who rub us the wrong way or distress us; those who abuse or insult us by their racist practices (Mark 11:25). We have no other option than to forgive our racist offenders, if we want God to forgive our own sins Jesus Christ (Ephesians 4:32; Colossians 3:13; Matthew 6:14; Mark 11:25).

Meditate day and night on God's Word.

Examine yourself. What is the level of your faith in God? Can your faith withstand the fiery darts of racism, or will it wither under the pressure of racist oppression, being ostracized, repressed, oppressed, outnumbered or physically overpowered in your environment? (Ephesians 6:11-17; 1 Peter 5:9) God will allow your faith in Him to be tested in order for you to show that it is pure and strong; the fiery darts of racism could be one of such tests. Just as fire tests and purifies gold, your faith will be tested by many trials, including your experiences with racism (James 1:3; 1 Peter 1:7), but God has also promised to create a way of escape when He determines that you are being tested beyond what you can take (Psalms 34:19; 1 Corinthians 10:13). Knowing this, you should not fall for the devil's tricks with an ungodly response when you are tempted by the foul spirit of racism that seeks to devour your soul (1 Peter 5:8-9).

Fire your faith against racism.

Like fuel that powers the engine of a car, the Word of God powers our built-in measure of faith, our faith fortifies our spirit, and that in turn drives our soul and body. In response to our faith and faith-fueled prayers, through Jesus Christ, God fires-up His invisible army against our challenges and obstacles and demolishes them before our very own eyes (2 Kings 6:8-17; Psalms 97:2-3; Exodus 9:23; Daniel 10:12-13). This is what our activated faith can and will do against any kind of racism that we may experience. Activated faith is a spiritual weapon of mass demolition. Through your activated faith, the Word of God will grow and multiply within you, giving rise to a continuous cycle and steady stream of sustained and amplified spiritual ammunition. Through this process, your daily life becomes a package of miracles that is sure to guarantee a victorious life in Jesus Christ—despite racism around you.

Be assured that because of your love and commitment to God, He will use the foul intrigues of racism as stepping-stones of victory for your life (Romans 8:28; Psalms 91:14-16; Isaiah 26:3-4). Racism may remain a huge phenomenon around you, but one that lacks the power to permanently stifle, limit or stop you in any way. By your activated faith in His Word, power, might and glory, God will release you from the oppression of racism (Exodus 3:7-10). He will hear your cry for His mercy and justice, and deliver you from the clutches of your racist offenders (Exodus 3:7-10; Psalms 7:1-2; Psalms 18:1-3, 13-19, 37-42, 46-49).

Faith works from within and not from without.

Focusing your faith against racism is only possible by hearing and meditating on God's Word (Romans 10:17), and most importantly, by believing His Word and acting on it (John 11:40; John 7:38). This also means spending quality time in worship of God in spirit and in truth

(John 4:24), and prayer to Him through Jesus Christ—and inviting the presence of His Holy Spirit to reveal the deeper meanings of His Living Word to you, to saturate your heart and mind in it (Jeremiah 33:3; John 14:26; 1 Corinthians 2:12-13).

As you travel through societies' rugged and often times racist terrain, your individual journey of life with Jesus Christ and the Holy-Spirit gives us a winner mentality and empowers your mind against challenges and obstacles like racism. For many of us, the difficulty of traveling the normally tough roads of life is often worsened by our daily experiences with racism, but our belief and unwavering faith in God becomes our main spiritual armor to deal with it and become victorious. Our faith in God fine-focuses our hearts and minds on His Holy Word, His powerful guiding spiritual light (Psalms 119:105), that takes us from the ugly paths of oppression and injustice of racism to God's holy freedom and justice.

With God's holy light racism cannot darken your path.

It's up to each of us to nurture and grow the measure of the free gift of faith that is within us. Faith works from within and not from without us, so that our inward person is in complete control of our outward person. Therefore, when the devil, who is the enemy of your soul, lies to you and tells you that racism is a huge monster that you cannot stand up to and gain victory over, by faith reject the lie—and declare, in the Name of Jesus Christ: "I am equipped with God's spiritual sling and stone and my unwavering and sustained faith, and I am propelled by the power of God's Holy Word, His awesome Holy Spirit fire power, against the so-called giant of racism" (1 Samuel 17:45-47; Hebrews 12:29). Such faith will become the foundation of your belief system, and by the authority God gave to you through Jesus Christ (Luke 4:6, 36; Matthew 28:18), whatever you bind on Earth is bound in Heaven and whatever you loose on Earth is loosed in Heaven (Matthew 16:19).

God has equipped you with the power of His Word to resist and defeat racism.

Therefore, by your faith in God's Holy Word through Jesus Christ, I urge you to exercise the authority of Christ and bind the foul spirit of racism and its evils, and loose your heart and mind from its 'Pharaoh's clutches' forever. All things are possible for those who believe God—yes, believe that all things are possible for you from God through Jesus Christ! (Luke 1:37)

Jesus Christ is God's grace to us. Christ is more than sufficient for each of us to gain individual victory over racism. Therefore, exercise your faith in Christ to position yourself to become a recipient of His victory for you. Many people have never exercised their own spiritual faith and authority given to them through Jesus Christ (1 John 5:4); some fail to sustain it and others do not truly believe in its possibility or power. Lack of faith is a sin (Romans 14:22-23), and displeasing to God Himself (Hebrews 11:6).

For the power of God to work on your behalf, you must hear it, receive it, embrace it, believe it, and activate the measure of faith He has given to you (Romans 12:3). Most people have been raised to believe the world's system that echoes daily in their ears that racism is a prevailing force against their lives. Few have shut their ears to this lie while opening their ears to hearing the truth that God is the only dominant and prevailing force in their lives and that racism is no match for the power of God which dwells in us (Ephesians 1:15-23). God made you in His excellent Image and has given you dominion on Earth (Genesis 1:26-27) and it is up to you to exercise that spiritual authority and dominion through Jesus Christ.

To gain victory, you have to believe the absolute truth of God's Word.

Our goal must be to focus our faith against racism

and surrender our daily experiences with racism to God. Our belief and unwavering faith in Jesus Christ must therefore become our major guiding spiritual light that focuses our mind daily on God, Who is the great Light, the powerful Source of that guiding light (Habakkuk 3:4).

Your love for God keeps you focused on His Word!

God will give you clarity of mind and purpose and excellence in your daily work and walk with Him—all of which would elevate your spirit and soul above the evil intrigues of racism and set you on the right course for your well-being. If you trust and believe God, He will make you the head above racism and not the tail beneath it (Deuteronomy 28:13). Through Jesus Christ, when the light of God shines in and on you daily (Psalms 119:105), racism and its evils will not be able to darken His brilliant paths of triumph for you. Through Christ, God has made you more than a conqueror over racism (Romans 8:37)—more than an overcomer of it.

Daily, you must take on the responsibility of remaining focused on God's spiritual guiding Light, His Holy Word, as the lamp that shines light on your path (Psalms 119:105). This light can only illuminate your path as you study and meditate on His Word. You must give reverence to God's awesome holiness within your heart, mind and daily living, through thanksgiving, prayer and worship. This takes your focus away from the negative events happening around you, because many times the extent of the negativity of such events is enough to sway your faith away from the awesome power of God. When your love for God keeps you focused on His Holy Word and you walk in His holy ways, He will reveal Himself to you in a manner that will serve as your "Holy Bridge," your triumph and your testimony over the daily problems you encounter. In Jeremiah 33:3, God promises us: "Call unto me, and I will answer thee, and show thee great and mighty things, which thou knowest not."

The obnoxious spirit of racism is like foul-smelling refuse that needs to be disposed of for the stench to be dispelled—use God's Holy Word to exterminate the foul, smelly racism that tries to attack your soul. The power of God through Jesus Christ disposes the refuse of racism and dispels its stench. When your faith is focused on God, your mind is filled with the true reality about His awesome power. If you focus your faith on God's Holy Word, power and might, your faith will target your anger, fears, worries, pain and anxieties about racism and God will demolish the raised fences, bars and huddles set

> *God is your "Holy Bridge," your triumph and your testimony over the daily problems you encounter.*

before you by those who use racism against you. God will level the mountains of racism and bring down its carnal "giants." God will slay the goliaths of racism that stand in your way. When you allow your faith to be dwarfed by your fear of adversities such as racism, you give the vile spirit of racism and its recruits (your racist offenders), access to your soul. Fear will begin to take root, placing its stranglehold of spiritual weakness and discouragement within you.

Fear will exclude faith and invite unbelief into your mind and heart and you will begin to attribute real power to your racist offenders when real power resides only with and in God. So learn to focus and target your faith against your fear of racism, its evils or illusionary powers, for God has not given you a spirit of fear, but of power, love and a sound mind (2 Timothy 1:7). He has given you clear-mindedness, a sharp sense, and self-discipline.

Fear will exclude faith and invite unbelief into your mind and heart.

Jesus Christ has elevated your spirit above the wicked schemes and plots of your racist offenders and His light and glory will be with you at all times. He has equipped your soul with the power of His Holy Word to resist the devil and his evil schemes that include racist attacks against your job, career, family, education and your life in general (James 4:7-10). By your faith in God through Jesus Christ, your racist attackers will always remain at the losing end of their own evil plots. If you trust God to handle your experiences with racism, He will make your racist attackers your "foot stool." (Psalms 110:1)

Chapter Quiz

1. What is faith? Reference at least one Holy Scripture that deals with faith and explain how you can apply it to your life against racism.

   _____

2. How can you focus your faith against racism and the evil spirit of racism?

   _____

3. By faith, who has elevated your spirit above racism and the foul spirit of racism?

   _____

4. What negative force can dwarf your faith against racism or the foul spirit of racism and can bring you defeat?

   _____

5. How can you apply Mark 11:23 to slay the "giants" of racism that come against your life?

   _____

6. How can you elevate your spirit and soul against racism?

∞∞∞∞∞∞∞∞ ♦ ♦ ♦ ♦ ♦ ∞∞∞∞∞∞∞∞

Reflections:

_____
_____
_____
_____

∞∞∞∞∞∞∞∞ ♦ ♦ ♦ ♦ ♦ ∞∞∞∞∞∞∞∞

Chapter 8 – The Power of Our Faith Against Racism

Our faith, salvation and hope in Jesus Christ is the solid foundation of our relationship with God. It is our firm and unwavering conviction in the limitless, boundless and awesome love and power of God in us through Jesus Christ. Undoubting faith means believing without any uncertainty that with God through Christ, all things are possible in and for your life (Luke 1:37; Matthew 19:26).

Trust God for Who He is—God.

Is it really possible for our faith not to waver? After all Apostle Peter, whom Jesus Christ revealed Himself to as the "Rock," had faith that wavered sometimes (Matthew 14:27-31; Mark 14:66-71). Even the father of faith, Abraham, seemed to have run "out of patience" when he agreed to his wife Sarah's back-up plan to conceive a child with her maid servant Haggai, as she (Sarah) was trying to help God's ultimate plan for an heir from his loins (Genesis 16). Remember that Abraham, the father of faith, was also human like you and I. It was out of fear for his life that he told the half truth about Sarah being only his sister and not his wife (Gen 12:12-20, 20:1-18). Did Abraham trust God to protect his life when he concealed that Sarah was his wife? Yes, most likely, but his human nature, his flesh was afraid; and it was fear that motivated the half truth that he told.

> *The vile spirit of racism has no authority over your life unless you give it access.*

As believers, what must we do to prevent our faith from fluctuating or faltering for a prolonged period? I believe that abiding daily in God's Word, along with prayer, thanksgiving and worship fortifies our faith daily. Also, professing God's Word and constantly bringing to our remembrance compelling testimonies of our faith, offer reminders of the power of God's Word, and our individual and collective faith in His Living Word—simply put, trusting God for Who He is—God.

So, when your faith wavers, it would only be for a transient moment.

You must acknowledge and believe that God has the power to make the impossible become possible (Luke 1:37) anywhere and everywhere, and thus He can make the impossible become possible in your own life (Matthew 19:26). God remains the same from yesterday, today and forever, through eternity (Hebrews 13:8). The same power of God that freed the ancient Israelites from the yoke of Pharaoh (Exodus 3:7-8), took Elijah up to Heaven in a chariot of flames (2 Kings 2:11). Through Jesus Christ God cured and still cures diseases and sicknesses, made and still makes the blind to see, raised and still raises the dead back to life (Books of Matthew, Mark, Luke and John, Acts, etc). It is the same power of God—the power of His Holy Spirit that resurrected Jesus Christ (Luke 24:2-9), and Christ Himself Who is the resurrection and the life (John 11:25), can and will bring victory in your own situation. Through Christ, the power of God's Holy Spirit subdues the evil intrigues and wicked schemes and manipulations of the vile spirit of racism.

God has the Power to make the impossible become possible.

Racism is endemic and deeply rooted in the

hearts of many individuals, including many persons who are in powerful positions of authority over us, both in the church and secular world. So, we sometimes feel powerless and helpless because we think that it is impossible for us to conquer racism and its intended negative impact upon our daily life.

Untiring faith consumes adversities.

We feel like grasshoppers, and therefore, we tend to acquire a grasshopper mentality (Numbers 13:33). This type of mentality manifests from thinking small, and feeling inferior or inadequate, or believing that you are of a lower, substandard, or second rate level.

While you are thinking you are powerless over racism and the foul spirit of racism, imagine God looking at you from His heavenly realm and saying to you in Ezekiel 37:1-14, "Prophesy to these dry bones to listen to the Word of the Lord." (Ezekiel 37:4); My child, you have my power within you to bring new and refreshed life to the dry bones—to make "dead" yet good dreams and aspirations in your life come alive again. Just try Me and see that your situation is not too hard for Me to handle —see that My Hand is not too short (Isaiah 59:1) to demolish racism on your behalf. Try Me and see that nothing is impossible for Me to accomplish in your life (Luke 1:37).

Stop being afraid of racism and racists! Stop professing that racism is a "giant" over your life! Stop seeing yourself as powerless "dry bones" without life that cannot stand against the evil spirit of racism (Ezekiel 37:1-14). Stop declaring racism as the authority in your life and begin declaring the Triune God—God the Father—God the Son—and God the Holy Spirit, as the only Authority in your life. Stop declaring that you are a victim of racism; rather declare that you are a victor over racism. Start to prophesy and declare to yourself "...Dry bones, listen to what the LORD is saying to you, "I, the LORD God, will put breath in you, and once again you will live. I will wrap you with muscles and skin and breathe life into you. Then you will know that I am the LORD." (Ezekiel 37:4-6)

No mountain is too high for God to bring down.

Declare only the power of the One and only true Living God in your life. Declare God's Holy Word as the only real power and authority that dominates your life! Racism has no real power or authority over your life. It is you who have the power and authority of Jesus Christ in you over the foul spirit of racism (Book of Esther). It is also you who have the power and authority to surrender your mind and heart and entire soul to the evil schemes of the foul spirit of racism! (Numbers 13:33)

The vile spirit of racism tests our faith (Romans 5:1-4; James 1:2-3). Having unwavering faith is having the belief that through Jesus Christ during every second, minute, hour, day, week, month and year, the Holy Spirit of God dwells abundantly in your life and God's Living Word remains like a blazing fire of hope within and around you (Romans 5:3-5)—and therefore, a consuming fire against the foul spirit of racism and its unfruitful product racism that comes against your life (Hebrews 12:29). The power of unwavering faith = power of hope = power of patience = power of endurance = manifestation of God's glorious power in our lives = radiance of God's power in our lives = prayer answered! And yet, undoubting faith is not a spiritual formula. It is simply the intangible spiritual substance (Hebrews 11:1) that guarantees manifestation of God's promises into tangible results based on His Word that never lies or fails, and His awesome purpose for our lives (Joshua 21:45; Isaiah 55:11; Mark 13:31; Jeremiah 29:11). As born again believers, unwavering faith makes God's Word become "Flesh" and tangible in our lives; and it brings victory to our doorstep. God's promise to us,

No form of racism is too intricate for God to untangle, expose or destroy.

which we gain by sustained, undoubting faith in Him and His Holy Word, is that through Jesus Christ our faith turns into spiritual boldness and triumph that materializes into spiritual and material victory and success (Mark 11:23; 1 John 5:4).

God has given every living human an intrinsic measure of faith (Romans 12:3) and the ability to develop and gain more faith to the point of unwavering faith and even supernatural faith. But God has also given us free will, and thus the option to either gain and develop more faith or let it remain dormant or forever "lost" in dormancy. So, we have the choice to actively work to develop our faith by stepping out boldly into positive action based on God's Living Word and promises (James 2:20). We have the choice to implement our faith by a forward and positive move, and a continuous, active and conscious will to gain and build up our confidence in the Triune God, His Holy Word and the limitless and boundless power of His glory.

Unwavering faith turns into a fireball that explodes into an unquenchable fire.

To continuously grow your faith, you need to study the Word of God daily, and understand it for practical daily living through revelation and guidance by God's Holy Spirit. When you face problems and difficulties like racism, you need to dwell in God's Holy Word, meditate on it, absorb and soak it into your heart and your entire soul being, and then stand on the Spiritual Rock, Jesus Christ. There are no better options, so don't let the devil deceive you into believing otherwise.

Acquiring mature and untiring faith is a voluntary action or act of will toward having complete and unquestioned confidence, assurance, sureness, reliance, trust, certainty and belief in the existence and power of God in our lives through Jesus Christ. God cannot be seen with our natural eyes, so many doubt His existence, and because faith cannot be seen, many fail to recognize the need to acknowledge, grow and mature it to experience God's limitless power in their lives by their own faith. Yet, as intangible and unseen faith might be, through Jesus Christ it has the conquering power of God that is greater than any army of human soldiers, weapons of mass destruction or any other form of carnal power. Through Jesus Christ, our unwavering faith is a matchstick within our spirit and soul—it activates His holy fire power in us. With the power of His Holy Word, and our fervent prayers, worship, thanksgiving and fasting, such faith turns into a

Acquiring mature and untiring faith is a voluntary action.

fireball that explodes into an unquenchable fire. Untiring faith consumes adversities, giving rise to hope, patience and ultimately daily miracles in our lives.

Determined faith is therefore a comfortable, wonderful and permanent state of trust in God, Who is the First and the Last, the Beginning and the End, the Alpha and the Omega, and a God Who remains ever faithful and unchangeable (Malachi 3:6)—our God, the only Triune God, Whose power guarantees us triumph over the adversities that we face.

Well-grounded faith is also having full belief and understanding that no rugged terrain or mountains, including racism in our individual journey of life, is too big for God to diminish or remove. No such mountain is too high for God to bring down. No form of racism is too intricate for God to untangle, expose and destroy (Hebrews 4:12-13). Nothing is too hard for God (Jeremiah 32:27; Genesis 18:14). God has spoken His Word of victory over your life and is not about to change His Mind (Zephaniah 3:15-17; Isaiah 41:13). God is not human that He will go back on His Word and promises (Numbers 23:19)—know this and believe it without a shadow of doubt in your mind.

God will not go back on His Word and promises.

You must always resist the devil even when he comes in a subtle form, including the loathsome spirit of racism and racist actions that are perpetrated against you. God's Holy Word promises us that if we submit ourselves to God and resist the devil that he will flee from us (James 4:7). The demon that you must resist in this case is the vile spirit of racism and it will flee from you!

Resist the devil even when he comes in a subtle form.

∞∞∞∞∞∞∞∞∞∞ ♦ ♦ ♦ ♦ ♦ ∞∞∞∞∞∞∞∞∞∞

Chapter Quiz

1. What spiritual and scriptural foundation is true faith built on?

___

2. How can you apply Luke 1:37 to gain daily victory over racism and the spirit of racism?

___

3. According to Numbers 13:33, how must you not view what seems like a goliath such as racism or the evil spirit of racism in order to defeat it?

___

4. According to Isaiah 59:1, 16-19, how can you apply this Holy Scripture to move God's Hand

on your behalf to gain daily victory over racism or the foul spirit of racism?

_____

5. How must your faith be grounded? On what spiritual principles must your faith be grounded?

_____

6. How do you make the despicable spirit of racism flee from you?

_____

∞∞∞∞∞∞∞∞ ♦ ♦ ♦ ♦ ♦ ∞∞∞∞∞∞∞∞

Reflections:

_____
_____
_____
_____

∞∞∞∞∞∞∞∞ ♦ ♦ ♦ ♦ ♦ ∞∞∞∞∞∞∞∞

CHAPTER 9 – The Power of Faith Fuels Forgiveness

We are all sinners, yet when we ask God for forgiveness through Jesus Christ, He cleanses us of our sins by the precious Blood of Christ (1 John 1:9). God's Word also instructs us to forgive others as we wish God our Father in Heaven to forgive us (Matthew 6:14-15; Mark 11:25). So, to forgive those who direct racism against you is to release your daily blessings from God without interruption and to permanently bind the effect of their wicked actions against you. Then, He, God the Father, will place His spiritual hedge of protection around you and no form of subtle or overt racism will have control over you or bring

The power of faith fuels forgiveness.

harm to you. By your forgiveness, God will nullify the evil plots of your racist offenders that will never prevail over your life (Isaiah 54:17). We must all be absolved of the need to judge others, seek revenge or harbor any negative emotions toward anyone, because such feelings disable our spiritual power and disrupt the flow of God's blessings from His heavenly realm onto our lives.

It is by our own faith we believe that Jesus Christ is the divine Son of God and the Redeemer of all humanity. It is also by faith that we accept Him as our personal Lord and Savior, believing and knowing that He also existed in human flesh as the expression of God's Holy Word, love, salvation, mercy, hope, joy, faithfulness and all goodness enveloped in One. By faith, we accept that Jesus Christ is the Savior of the World Who brought salvation, redemption and victory to everyone by His death and resurrection (John 3:16; Romans 10:9-10; Isaiah 53:4-8). Jesus Christ also came to heal the broken-hearted and give freedom to those in bondage (Luke 4:18-19; Isaiah 61:1-4). By faith, we acknowledge, understand and accept that we are more than conquerors through Jesus Christ, our Lord and Savior (Romans 8:37), Who gives us our daily strength (Philippians 4:13). By faith in God's Holy

> *We are to forgive one another and ourselves.*

Word, we understand who we are through authentic spiritual knowledge revealed to us in His Holy Word, and by His Holy Spirit Who dwells within us (1 Corinthians 2:10-16). God created us in His excellent Image and without charge, offered us eternal salvation by the precious Blood of Jesus Christ, placed His seal of ownership in us by divine deposit of His Holy Spirit, and empowered us by the gift of His Holy Spirit (John 14:16-26).

By faith, we are assured of the very existence and power of God's Holy Spirit, Whom we received through His Son Jesus Christ and Who dwells within every one of us who believes in Christ. By faith, we acknowledge and accept to develop the Fruit of the Spirit, that is, the fruitful gift of God's Holy Spirit—love, joy, peace, patience, kindness, goodness, faithfulness, gentleness and self-control (Galatians 5:22). Like a sponge, we soak up God's Holy Word and its awesome power through Jesus Christ, and like a fresh spring we begin to develop and bring forth the Fruit of God's Holy Spirit, Which God gave us through Jesus Christ Himself.

Let go of the seed of retaliation and vengeance against your racist offender(s).

By faith, we acknowledge, understand and accept that God's enabling grace within each of us through Jesus Christ is more than sufficient for us (2 Corinthians 12:9) to receive the awesome Power of the Holy Spirit for us to overcome evil, including injustice and oppression such as racism. By faith, we are assured that when we forgive others, we, too, are forgiven, and our spirit becomes energized and empowered by the unquenchable spiritual power of God that gives us Christ's victory (John 16:33; 1 John 5:4-5) over trials and tribulations, including racism. So, we must forgive our racist offenders on a daily basis while we release them to God's holy and impartial justice—allow God to invoke His divine and inescapable judgment against our unrepentant racist offenders.

Forgiveness is a form of spiritual cleansing of the soul.

Knowing this, we must act based on our faith that declares God's ultimate triumph in our lives. Faith becomes the foundation of our spiritual and physical courage, because it defeats the seeds of fear, anxiety, anger, frustration, hate, bitterness, unforgiveness, vengeance and all other negative emotions, thoughts, actions and words that the foul spirit of racism attempts to plant within us. By faith, we will forever believe God's Word and His sovereign rule over our lives through Jesus

Christ. By faith, we stand on God's grounds of integrity (Ephesians 4:1), knowing that as we forgive all those who assault us and those who subject us to the injustice of racism and other forms of wickedness and oppression, we release them to God's judgment, for vengeance is His and not ours to execute (Leviticus 19:18; Deuteronomy 32:35; Isaiah 34:8). The seed of vengeance, when planted within our hearts and minds, binds up and holds back victory in our lives because it is contrary to God's Word, where the ultimate triumph lies. We must let go of the seed of retaliation and vengeance against our racist offender(s) and release the flow of God's holy victory in our lives. Now, let the Footprints of Jesus Christ lead you onto the sure paths of victory over racism as you offer daily forgiveness to your racist offenders.

Let the Footprints of Jesus Christ lead you onto the sure paths of victory over racism.

∞∞∞∞∞∞∞∞ ♦ ♦ ♦ ♦ ♦ ∞∞∞∞∞∞∞∞

Chapter Quiz

1. Can unforgiveness keep your blessings from God from manifesting in your physical environment? Why? How?

2. Will God forgive your own sins if you hold grudges against racists and refuse to forgive them?

3. As you deal with your racist offenders, explain one way that you can ensure that your blessings from God are not withheld.

4. How can the power of your faith in God's Holy Word give you sure victory over racism?

5. Why must you forgive your racist offenders?

∞∞∞∞∞∞∞∞ ♦ ♦ ♦ ♦ ♦ ∞∞∞∞∞∞∞∞

Reflections:

∞∞∞∞∞∞∞∞ ♦ ♦ ♦ ♦ ♦ ∞∞∞∞∞∞∞∞

Chapter 10 – God's Kingdom Power in Us

By accepting Jesus Christ as our Lord and Savior, we receive also the power of God's Holy Spirit within us—we receive God's Kingdom power in us. Now, children of the Most High God, we should walk in obedience to God's Holy Word, opening our hearts and minds to the guidance of the Holy Spirit, to help us live a Christ-rooted life of holiness. God's supernatural power and grace has been established in us by His divine relationship with us through Jesus Christ. Christ revealed and manifested God's awesome character, which embodies love, mercy, faithfulness, kindness, patience, forgiveness, peace,

> *With God's Kingdom Power within us, our faith becomes a fortress against racism.*

understanding and all other Christ-like qualities that transform us into a brand new person in Him; but first we have to *truly* accept Jesus Christ in our hearts as our Redeemer and Lord (2 Corinthians 5:17). Spiritually, we become born again in our spirit when we *truly* receive Jesus Christ as our Savior and Redeemer in our hearts. However, while the renewal of our spirit is immediate once we *truly* accept Jesus Christ in our hearts as our Lord and Savior, the full manifestation of Christ-like qualities in our soul is a dynamic process and a work in progress, which God has made perfect in us only through Christ.

The renewal of our minds by God's Holy Word (Romans 12:2; Ephesians 4:23-24) is not instant; rather it is an on-going, enduring process. Our carnal self, our soul, does not automatically become renewed in Jesus Christ. Apostle Paul acknowledged that our carnal self sometimes resists our Christ-like spiritual nature (Galatians 5:17). The process of daily renewal of our minds is gradual as we hear, read, believe and apply God's Holy Word in our daily living, spend prayer and worship time with God, grow our faith, and declare the power of God's Word over our lives.

God's Kingdom Power has supreme authority over all things.

When the incorruptible Seed of God, Jesus

Christ, and His Holy Word through Him take root within us, the Kingdom of God within us begins to yield a harvest that starts to overflow in our life (Mark 4:30-32). Jesus Christ is the Way, the truth, and the life, and no one can get to God the Father except through Him (John 16:6). Christ is the only true Way to God's Kingdom and His Kingdom Power; for He, Christ, is the Kingdom of God that lived as Flesh on Earth and Who now dwells within us believers who have accepted Him as our Lord and Savior—and as He promised us, we have also received God's Holy Spirit (John 14:6; Luke 17:21).

Our holy harvest comes as God reveals the mysteries of His Kingdom to us through His Holy Word and Holy Spirit within us (1 Corinthians 2:6-12; Psalms 25:14). It is in the secret place where God reveals Himself to us through the Holy Spirit (Psalms 91:1; Daniel 2:22; Deuteronomy 29:29; Isaiah 45:3). When you allow God's sovereignty to rule within you through Jesus Christ and the Holy Spirit, and allow the Triune God to take charge of every aspect of your life, you activate the power of the Kingdom of God within you. This Kingdom and its supreme Authority is not seen by human eyes but perceived spiritually by faith in Jesus Christ and through God's Holy Spirit Who dwells within

> *Our faith in God's Word is a fortress against racism.*

us. God's Holy Spirit guides, enlightens, quickens, empowers and drives our spirit and soul. Through Jesus Christ the Kingdom of God establishes in us God's love, righteousness, mercy, peace, faithfulness and joy in our lives despite societal ills like racism that may surround us.

Again, faith is a necessary spiritual ingredient for receiving, establishing and releasing the power of God's Kingdom within us. It is our faith in Jesus Christ that becomes the foundation of our spirit that propels our soul into victorious living. By faith we become armed with true spiritual knowledge once we have embraced the Kingdom of God that resides within us, and our minds are continually renewed by the Holy Word of God (Romans 12:2). When we embrace God's Kingdom power within us, our Holy-Word fueled faith also becomes a fortress against evils like racism. When we believe that God is always with us and that no one can be against us (Romans 8:31), then no weapon fashioned against us, including racism, will ever become victorious in our lives (Isaiah 54:17). God's excellent purpose for our existence remains intact. We can discover and rediscover our authentic self through Jesus Christ, and then gradually understand and walk in Him toward God's perfect purpose for our lives (Jeremiah 29:11). Then,

The Holy Spirit tunes out the noisy world around us.

God's glory will begin to appear within and through our lives, and in time, we will achieve our goals, desires and life's ambitions, making racism and its negative effects practically of no consequence in our daily lives.

When we embrace faith in God, His Holy Spirit and Jesus Christ, our Lord and Savior, we embrace God's Kingdom that is the solid Foundation of our spirit and life. We have to listen to the voice and guidance of the Holy Spirit within us and not to the untruthful racist voices that surround us. To hear the voice and guidance of the Holy Spirit within us, we must tune out the noisy world around us and tune into God's Holy Spirit Station, hear His voice and follow His guidance. We must be still and quiet in prayer, worship and thanksgiving to God our Maker, and know that He is truly the Lord our God (Psalms 46:10)—and we shall see manifestation of His glory (John 11:40). His voice and guidance may come as a still, small, soft and clear voice (1 Kings 19:12) of intuition, ideas, knowledge or directives on how to solve a problem; and this births material success. His guidance is clear and will give us words to say; tell us how and when to say those words; and show us how to respond or what and how to prepare in and

Tune out the noisy world us and be still and quiet in prayer, worship and thanksgiving to God our Maker.

for every racist situation that we encounter (Luke 12:11-12).

By our faith in Jesus Christ, God establishes His Kingdom in us and begins to mold us into the person through whom He can act, show-up and "show-out" for a higher purpose in order to glorify His Holy Name. Within His Kingdom, God is the sovereign King to Whom we must submit our spirit, soul and body through Jesus Christ. So when we become Christ-rooted and centered through our belief and faith, obedience and submission to the Word of God, and through a deep prayer life and thanksgiving, and holy worship to Him in spirit and truth (John 4:24), we become God-centered and empowered by His Holy Spirit. Then we begin to understand and communicate with God on higher grounds—always in spirit and truth (John 4:24), trusting and obeying Him in all aspects of our daily lives—and immediately repenting when we falter and sin. We open our hearts to His Kingdom of love, joy, peace, patience, mercy, kindness, forgiveness, faithfulness, goodness, virtue, integrity, and spiritual prosperity, to dwell and rule within us.

> *Seek first God's Kingdom and righteousness.*

Our faith assures us that God's enabling grace—Jesus Christ—His Kingdom Power within us, is enough for us to defeat life's adversities, including racism (2 Corinthians 12:9; Luke 10:18-19). Daily, this becomes our applause of  the power of God's awesome Kingdom within us. Therefore, now and always, we are to seek first His Kingdom and righteousness, fully convinced that He will add all other things that we seek or desire (Matthew 6:33)—including our daily victory over the foul spirit of racism.

Meditate on Matthew 6:33.

∞∞∞∞∞∞∞∞∞∞ ♦ ♦ ♦ ♦ ♦ ∞∞∞∞∞∞∞∞∞∞

Chapter Quiz

1. What is God's Kingdom Power in us as believers in Jesus Christ?

   _____

2. Can the spirit of racism corrupt the incorruptible Seed of Jesus Christ, Who dwells in believers who have accepted Him as Lord and Savior?

   _____

3. What spiritual "Factor" is necessary for you to receive, establish and release the Power of God's Kingdom within you?

_____

4. How can your faith become a fortress against any form of evil, including racism and the vile spirit of racism?

_____

5. What must you do to hear from God and receive His divine guidance against racism and the foul spirit of racism?

_____

6. When you allow God's sovereignty to rule within you, can the vile spirit of racism take over God's sovereign rule in you? Explain your answer.

_____

∞∞∞∞∞∞∞∞ ♦ ♦ ♦ ♦ ♦ ∞∞∞∞∞∞∞∞

Reflections:

_____
_____
_____
_____

∞∞∞∞∞∞∞∞ ♦ ♦ ♦ ♦ ♦ ∞∞∞∞∞∞∞∞

CHAPTER 11 – God's Kingdom Power Against Racism

The Kingdom of God "shall never be destroyed" (Daniel 2:44). The Kingdom of God established within us through Jesus Christ, is the divine Government of God with His sole sovereignty ruling within and around our lives (Daniel 4:3; Psalms 103:19; Luke 17:21; John 3:5-7; Matthew 6:33,19:23). Through our faith in Jesus Christ, the Kingdom of God within us establishes God's spiritual power within us, which magnifies in our lives (Mark 4:30-32). His Holy Word is loaded into spiritual missiles, His Holy Power, which helps us detonate and defeat all adversities, oppression and injustices that we encounter. Racism is

You can apply God's Kingdom Power against racism.

orchestrated by the foul spirit of racism. It is an adversity, wickedness, oppression and injustice that you must defeat and overcome in your daily life with the awesome power of God's Holy Word—the Sword of the Spirit (Ephesians 6:10-17; Hebrews 4:12-13).

It is important for you to recognize that when you seem beaten down by oppression and injustice of racism, your spirit may be temporarily broken, but through such experiences you will be remolded spiritually into a stronger, improved, mature and Christ-rooted person, if you present your case to God in prayer with thanksgiving and worship (Psalms 68:9; Isaiah 40:31; Isaiah 57:10; Lamentations 5:21; 2 Corinthians 4:16; Ezekiel 37:4-6). Through Jesus Christ, you have been moved onto higher spiritual grounds, above the evil spirit of racism, and you can and will be used for God's higher purpose and glory, first on Earth and then in everlasting life.

Through Jesus Christ, you are above the evil spirit of racism.

God is a consuming fire (Hebrews 12:29). If you trust God and submit to His Word and will, He will consume the evil activities of the foul spirit of racism against your life. Through Jesus Christ, God's Kingdom within us establishes His spiritual power within us, and this power will become the fire that consumes the adversities that we face. In accordance with God's Living Word, if we seek first His Kingdom and righteousness—His virtue, morality, justice, decency, uprightness, rectitude, and honesty—then everything else that we desire will be given to us (Matthew 6:33).

Even your desire to overcome racism and spiritual battles against it must be secondary to establishing and sustaining a close relationship with God. Child of the Most High God, it is a marvelous thing to dwell in the secret place of the Most High God, in the Name of our Lord and Savior Jesus Christ (Psalms 91:1). It is your relationship with God through Jesus Christ that anoints and fortifies you to overcome the despicable spirit of racism and its evil fruit racism. Regardless of the challenges that you have in your life, God should be your number-one priority. Then, His Kingdom will provide for your needs and desires in accordance with His will and purpose for your life. Let the unseen power and glory of God empower you for triumph over the obnoxious spirit of racism (2 Corinthians 4:16).

Give your emotional and physical burden to Christ.

You must first seek for the values of the Kingdom of God in Heaven to be established within you and not the values of the kingdom of man on Earth. If the values of the kingdom of man on Earth are set in accordance with the Kingdom of God, then God would also sanction such values. Your God Kingdom powered-faith gives you certainty that even as you may be temporarily broken by your negative experiences, hurt, pain and suffering, you would be raised again above such adversities by God's sovereign love (1 Peter 5:10).

If you continue to abide in His Holy Word and allow His sovereign rule in and over your daily life, you will receive God's answers to your prayers (John 15:7). Even as you abide in God's Word and walk in obedience, you also need to offer forgiveness within your heart to those who offend you; this includes your racist offenders (Mark 11:25). The power within the promise of the Kingdom of God has no limitations except for the limitation imposed by our lack of faith and belief, disobedience of God's Word, unrepentance, unforgiveness, and ignoring the directions and guidance of His Holy Spirit.

God's Word refuels us when we run out of "Spiritual Gas."

Our human abilities are limited without God but limitless with God through Jesus Christ (Matthew 19:26). Our human capabilities and spiritual power should be 100 percent reliant on God. God's power fuels our own, and without Him, we simply run out of "spiritual gas" that fuels our human strength. We must come to the realization that without God through Jesus Christ "we can do nothing" (John 15:5). This does not mean that we should simply sit and do nothing and wait for God to help us do everything without us working hard. It only means that whatever we do, we must seek God's guidance and direction, and when we reach the end of our human strength, by faith we must rely on God to carry us across His "Holy Bridge" over our troubled waters or terrain.

God is the "super" over our natural, carnal self and nature.

God only does for you what you cannot do for yourself. He is the "Super" over our natural, carnal self and nature. You must lay your emotional and physical burden at the "Feet" of Jesus Christ or such burden would hold you captive and you become a slave to it; that is what racism has done to so many individuals who have tried to tackle it all on their own. The negative power of racism can burn you out emotionally if you don't lay down its daily burden in prayer at the "Feet" of Jesus Christ.

Within the Kingdom of God lies the limitless power of God. So, to gain ultimate spiritual, mental and physical victory over any obstacle, challenge or adversity, including racism, the Kingdom of God must first dwell within you through Jesus Christ. God's sovereignty, and not that of humans or their racist activities, should define and govern your daily state of love, joy, peace, patience, kindness, faithfulness, goodness, gentleness and forgiveness. When the Kingdom of God dwells within you through Jesus Christ, your life becomes God-centered and focused. Through Jesus Christ, by trusting God and His Holy Word with undoubting faith and belief in His omnipotent power and omnipresence, you release the awesome glory of God to reign within your spirit, to direct your soul (John 11:40).

> *We must exercise our faith to believe the promises of God's Holy Word.*

Many of us ask how we could possibly defeat the power of racism over our lives, especially when we continue to suffer daily due to many racist acts of oppression and injustice. I say we must all believe and trust in God's ultimate supernatural dominance and power over all evil, including racism (Psalms 18:1-3; Psalms 16:1). We must exercise our faith to believe the promises of His Word that He will never leave or forsake us (Deuteronomy 31:6; Joshua 1:7-9) and will always fight and win our battles (1 Samuel 17:45-47), and this includes the challenges that we face daily with the evil spirit of racism. We must come to believe that Jesus Christ has obtained victory for us over the world and racism that exists in it (John 16:33).

By faith, we must continue to applaud God's Kingdom power within us. Even as individuals, we need to make positive affirmations such as: 'I affirm that the powerful radiance of God's Kingdom glows within and through me daily. His rays of victory empower me daily through Jesus Christ and the Holy Spirit. Daily, I see the manifestation of God's glory and power in my life, clearing my paths of any roadblocks, obstacles and challenges placed by racism. Daily, I am more than a conqueror of any form of racism through Jesus Christ. I affirm boldly and with the power of the Holy Spirit of God within me that through Jesus Christ, I am under God's daily guidance. God's warring angels keep vigilant watch over me and daily, I am protected from the foul spirit of racism. I affirm that His guidance through the tough roads of my journey will take my honest, hard and sustained labor to great heights of success, irrespective of racism. I know that by the precious Blood of Jesus Christ, I am able, I can and I have won the ultimate spiritual, mental and "physical"

> *I affirm that through Christ the powerful radiance of God's Kingdom glows within and through me daily.*

fight over racism. Thank You, Father God, for Your limitless power within me, through Jesus Christ, Amen!"

Chapter Quiz

1. What do you understand to be God's Kingdom and His Kingdom Power?

    ___

2. What kind of missiles can destroy the evil spirit of racism or racism itself? Carnal or spiritual missiles? Explain your answer.

    ___

3. How can you apply Matthew 6:33 to gain victory over the wicked spirit of racism or racism itself?

    ___

4. Between 0 and 100, what percentage of reliance or dependence should you have on the Triune God (God the Father, His Son Jesus Christ and His Holy Spirit), and His Holy Word? Explain your answer.

    ___

5. What does Joshua 1:7-9 reveal to you about God's role in your personal battles with the challenges that you face in your life, such as

racism?

6. How can you apply God's Kingdom Power, His sovereign rule over your life to gain daily victory over the evil spirit of racism and its nasty fruit of racism?

∞∞∞∞∞∞∞∞ ♦ ♦ ♦ ♦ ♦ ∞∞∞∞∞∞∞∞

Reflections:

∞∞∞∞∞∞∞∞ ♦ ♦ ♦ ♦ ♦ ∞∞∞∞∞∞∞∞

Chapter 12 – God's Illuminating Rays of True Spiritual Knowledge

True knowledge of yourself is the knowledge that you have of your authentic spiritual identity in Jesus Christ. The whole entity of "you" or "me" encompasses our spirit, body and soul that are created by God, although in the natural, "self" is often used to refer to our body and soul. Our spirit is also created and activated by God and is what gives life to our "inner person—our spirit man" that is expressed through the soul and body (Genesis 2:7). You and I were created in the excellent Image of God, our Creator. As children of God through

God gives life to our inner person— our spirit man (Genesis 2:7).

Jesus Christ, He, God, has placed His Holy Spirit within us to help us live a life of holiness and achieve the greatest heights that He has set for our individual lives (2 Corinthians 1:22; 2 Timothy 1:14; Ephesians 1:13-14).

The Person of God's Holy Spirit inhabits and searches our "inner self" and reveals the truth to us—not just some truth but all truth (John 16:13). It is He, the Person of God's Holy Spirit, Who dwells within our inner spirit and reveals the deeper meaning of God's Word to us (1 Corinthians 2:13). The Holy Spirit of God helps us to activate our inherent measure of faith (Luke 17:15; Romans 10:17), drive our creativity through the core of our spirit and soul, inspire us to spring into faith-driven action (2 Corinthians 5:7), direct and redirect our plans and paths, and navigate us through life, if we allow Him (Psalms 37:23-24; Psalms 40:2; Proverbs 16:9).

God has vested His power and Holy Spirit within you!

Knowledge of who we are starts with true knowledge of God (Psalms 111:10; Matthew 16:15-18). Through Jesus Christ, revelation knowledge of God's Holy Word comes alive in us through His Holy Spirit Who dwells in us—and our true person becomes revealed to us (Matthew 16:17; 2 Corinthians 4:6). Knowing and understanding who you are in spirit, your authentic identity and nature in Jesus Christ, is the gateway to knowing God's purpose for your life. Thus, true spiritual knowledge in Jesus Christ is a heavenly key to the well-being of your spirit, soul and body. True spiritual knowledge, that is, pure and undefiled knowledge of God's Holy Word, also becomes your spiritual wisdom for psychological resistance against racism and its evils.

Racism still remains deeply rooted within the hearts, thoughts, minds, motives, and actions of millions of individuals. Racism is a byproduct of the demonic spirit of racism, which inhabits the souls of many who let it into their hearts. As a result, racism is deeply entrenched within the everyday culture of society, Therefore, wise and prudent knowledge is needed to tackle it (Proverbs 8:12, 14:18,16:21,18:15). Racism is not a product of one's imagination. It is also not a mere perception; it is very real to your inner spirit, soul and body. It is a scourge from the odious spirit of racism that is designed to plague those it is directed against and also those perpetrating it (1 Peter 5:8-9). Racism is one of the devil's multiple designs of evil originating from "spiritual wickedness in high places" (Ephesians 6:10-18) that

Racism is real and not a figment of your imagination.

manifests in one individual being against another.

It is not racism by itself that corrodes our heart and mental shield; rather, it is our own spiritual complacency, or lack of spiritual preparation to defy and resist it, that makes our souls (hearts, minds, thoughts, emotions, will, motivation, resolve) and actions, vulnerable to its evils. Through authentic spiritual knowledge, your spirit and soul can be become fully equipped with the awesome power of God's full armor to defeat any and all of the negative effects that racism could potentially have on you. Our reliance solely on our natural self to respond to racism and its negative, potent, destructive effects makes our soul defenseless against it.

We have to apply spiritual warfare—the power of 2 Corinthians 10:3-6 against racism: "For though we walk in the flesh, we do not war after the flesh for the weapons of our warfare are not carnal, but mighty through God to the pulling down of strong holds; casting down imaginations, and every high thing that exalteth itself against the knowledge of God, and bringing into captivity every thought to the obedience of Christ; and having in a readiness to revenge all disobedience, when your obedience is fulfilled." We are spiritually minded so we

Racism attacks your psyche like a ferocious beast.

understand that the vile spirit behind racism is not carnal; it is a demonic spirit whose evil racist activities can only be dismantled by the power of God through Jesus Christ (Romans 8:6; Ephesians 6:10-18).

You need the enabling and empowering Spirit of God to take you to higher spiritual grounds of God's supernatural protection (Psalms 23, 27, 91). You need God's Word to protect you from the foul spirit of racism and its human hosts (that is, those who perpetrate racism against you). Without the empowering of God's Holy Word and Holy Spirit, you won't be victorious against the evil activities of the vile spirit of racism and its willing human hosts. If you are "naked" without spiritually wearing the full armor of God, you will suffer long life defeat by the odious spirit of racism and its human recruits.

True self-knowledge in Christ pushes back against racism.

Only a fool with a death wish would attempt to confront a lion without having the skills and weapons to defend him or herself. A hunter who travels the forest without a loaded gun runs the risk of not returning home intact, or losing his or her life. If you challenged or confronted racism without God's spiritual protection, it would devour you like a wild beast tears up its prey. To deal with the demon spirit of racism, you need God's spiritual protection, knowledge and wisdom that starts with the reverence of Him and His Holy Word, which are both inseparable (John 1:1-2). Spiritual warfare and divine wisdom from God are the most powerful forces and ammunition to help you deal victoriously with racism.

Racism attacks your psyche like a ferocious beast that tries to devour your heart, mind, thoughts, emotions, will, resolve, dreams and aspirations, leaving you wounded, broken, frustrated, defeated, angry, embittered, hostile, defenseless, helpless and hopeless. This is because unrelenting racist attacks can turn you into a wounded soul, if you allow them. True spiritual knowledge in our Lord and Savior Jesus Christ is a silent gear that pushes back against racism until racism is permanently stalled and unable to attack or burrow into your psyche. You have to resist the foul spirit of racism; otherwise, if you succumb to it, it could transform you into a wounded spirit.

Only God's Holy Spirit is authorized to inhabit your spirit and being through Jesus Christ.

A wounded spirit has unresolved emotional hurt that has settled deep in his or her heart and has taken possession of his or her mind, emotions, will or entire soul. A wounded spirit becomes crushed under the weight of an obstacle or challenge and no longer believes it can be victorious. Racism can turn you into a wounded soul (Proverbs 18:14) if you allow it; or you can opt to believe God, stand by His Word in the Name of Jesus Christ, and breakdown the stranglehold that racism attempts to wrap around you—and its treacherous claws that clamp your mind. Mental resistance is effective against racism when your spirit and soul are fortified with the power of God's Holy Word. With such fortification, resisting and defying racism with your mind becomes both a conscious and subconscious process that is not brain-energy demanding.

So, tune into God's spiritual station; His Holy Word, to hear His voice and instructions through His Holy Spirit, Who will give you the key to a firm psychological resistance, which is Christ-rooted spiritual resistance against racism.

You are wonderfully and fearfully made by God (Psalms 139:14).

This will reveal authentic spiritual knowledge to you and become your daily opposition to the potential destructive effects of racism. Then you would know that in reality, no one has real power over your spirit except God—and He alone can and will direct your spirit, soul, actions and behavior, if you allow Him, rather than the world and racism in it to control you. You would understand that only God's Holy Spirit is authorized to inhabit your spirit and being through Jesus Christ; every other contrary spirit is unauthorized and does not have legal authority or access to you. However, you can grant a contrary spirit access to your soul. Only you can give unauthorized, illegal access to the negative spirit of racism or any other evil spirit that is contrary to God's Holy Word to possess your soul.

God's wants you to be on a spiritual mountain top of victory and not at the bottom of a carnal valley of spiritual defeat, and God's grace is sufficient for you to achieve this (2 Corinthians 12:9). All you need to do is to love God above all things, with all your heart, mind and strength (Deuteronomy 6:5; Matthew 22:37); hold on to Jesus Christ and His power in you (John 15:1-8); stay focused on God's Holy Word (Joshua 1:7-9) and immovable love for you (Romans 8:35-39); and continue to harness the power of God's Holy Word and His Holy Spirit within you through Christ. Regardless of racism that may surround you, if you are Christ-centered and Holy Word-focused, God will attend to your desires, acknowledge and reward your

God's Holy Spirit will lead you to authentic spiritual truth, knowledge and understanding.

earnest hard work, and make you succeed in accordance with His will and purpose for your life (Matthew 6:33; Jeremiah 29:11).

As you obtain and exercise the revelation power of the Holy Spirit given to us by God through Jesus Christ, you will recognize clearly that your earthly image is beautiful in the eyes of God, in Whose excellent Image you were made. Then, accepting who you are becomes a natural, easy, normal and positive attitude for you.

Through the view of authentic knowledge, which comes from God's illuminating rays of true spiritual knowledge, your mind can open up to the fundamental truth that, yes, you are wonderfully and fearfully made by God (Psalms 139:14), and your spiritual image in Jesus Christ is also in His divine Image (Genesis 1:27; 2 Corinthians 4:4).

God's Holy Spirit will lead you to liberating truth.

The evil spirit of racism may rear its ugly head against you; but as the Holy Spirit of God illuminates your spirit and soul, it becomes crystal-clear to you that there is absolutely no room for self-hate or hate for others within your heart, the seat of your soul. The Holy Spirit of God will lead you into a whole new, liberating world of authentic spiritual truth, knowledge and understanding in Jesus Christ.

Chapter Quiz

1. Which is superior to the other: carnal or spiritual knowledge? Explain your answer.

   _____

2. If you didn't know who you were in Jesus Christ, could you have true self-knowledge and could you apply true spiritual knowledge against racism or the spirit of racism? Explain your answer.

   _____

3. True or false: Self-knowledge is only true and complete with the authentic knowledge of God through Jesus Christ. Explain your answer.

   _____

4. How can you identify if your experiences with racism have caused you to develop a wounded spirit?

   _____

5. How can you resist racism's attack on your mind or psyche?

   _____

6. Discussion point: Applying the power of God's Holy Word against racism and the foul spirit of racism. From what you have learned so far,

   _____

discuss how you can apply God's Word against any form of racism you may face.

◆ ◆ ◆ ◆ ◆

Reflections:

◆ ◆ ◆ ◆ ◆

CHAPTER 13 – Power of God's Grace Over Racism

Our Lord and Savior Jesus Christ is God's awesome and divine grace to us. God's grace through Christ to us is His boundless and limitless divine favor (Psalms 30:5; Proverbs 12:2), which redeems, blesses, empowers, fortifies, shields, protects and shelters us, teaching us through His Holy Spirit, Who shows us new ways and strategies for our well-being (1 Corinthians 2:10-16). Through Jesus Christ and the Holy Spirit Who dwell in us, abiding in God's Holy Word empowers our spirit and soul to live in holiness and to stand in Christ's victory over evil, including racism (Colossians 2:14-15). Individual victory over racism does

God's grace fortifies, shields, protects and shelters us.

not mean that you as an individual can eradicate racism around you or racism in the world. What it means is that you will gain positive control over racism in your daily life, have a positive spiritual strategy for defying, resisting and ultimately diminishing or eliminating its potent poisons that attempt to place physical or psychological limitations and strongholds on you.

If you can retain your inner joy and peace and become highly successful in all areas of your life—career, relationships, family and health, despite your daily encounters with racism, then you would have transcended it victoriously. On the other hand, when you allow racism to begin devouring your being, to corrupt and subdue your heart, mind, thoughts, emotions, will and resolve, make you angry, frustrated, bitter and hateful, undermine your belief in yourself, and place visible or invisible barriers around you and so on, then you would be living a life defeated by racism. If the latter is the case, you lack true spiritual knowledge in Jesus Christ and have not activated God's Kingdom Power within you—and the power of God's awesome grace—Jesus Christ in you. Your true spiritual person is still lying dormant within you. The key

God has power to break the yoke of any physical or mental burden in your life.

to the mantle of spiritual victory over racism lies within you and me. The power of God's grace in us—Jesus Christ, His divine favor within and over our lives, dictates our paths of justice, and racism lacks the power to interfere with the beautiful roads to success that God has paved for each of us (Jeremiah 29:11).

Your role is to submit your spirit, soul and body completely to God through Jesus Christ our Savior and Redeemer, without resistance, doubt or questioning the awesome power of God. Your job is to harness God's grace, Jesus Christ in you, and allow your spirit and soul to be illuminated by His holy light of wisdom and understanding, and to be brought into His paths of equity and justice (Psalms 7:11; 9:8; 118:8). Never look to your fellow man or woman to execute justice on your behalf; rather, look unto God, Who is the greatest and most just Judge. He alone can and will always deliver true and impartial justice to you and on your behalf, for He is a God of righteousness, impartiality, equity, even-handedness, just-dealing and integrity—He is a Holy God Who can never align Himself with any form of unholiness, injustice or oppression, including racism (Psalms 37). He delivers the oppressed from the clutches of the wicked (Psalms 9:9-

> *God has given us the power to pull down strongholds.*

10; 7:1, 11; 11:5-6) and also delivers justice to the oppressor (Psalms 37; 109). All of His Ways are illuminating paths of righteousness and justice and His grace—His divine favor of goodness and mercy through Jesus Christ. His brilliant rays radiate all holiness in One—God Himself.

What do God's illuminating paths of grace mean for our individual battles with racism? His grace paves divine paths for the manifestation of His righteous truth and justice on our behalf. His grace determines that His everlasting goodness will overcome any evil that we encounter. God is just and impartial and He will accept and protect anyone who believes in Him through Jesus Christ, regardless of their race, ethnicity or nationality (Acts 10:34-35). God has given us the power to pull down strongholds in the Name of Jesus Christ (2 Corinthians 10:3-6), and racism is no exception. It is a stranglehold that can and must be broken down by the power of the Word of God, and you can break down racism in your own world.

God is impartial—He is a God of righteousness, even-handedness, fair dealing, justice and integrity.

In the workplace, God may want you to oppose racism by doubling your efforts and doing the best job ever. If you continue to encounter racist attitudes, despite your effort, He will show you the power of His righteousness, grace, justice and might in the quietest and most mysterious ways.

I have seen God suddenly reorganize departments, removing the very stumbling blocks that were the racist attackers of His anointed children. God may even want you to take your valid case of racism to a court of law, and with God's grace and backing, be assured that the final verdict will be in your favor. So, like King Jehoshaphat did (2 Chronicles 20), before you oppose a vicious army, like racists you may face in your workplace or elsewhere, first go in prayer before God—call upon His invisible and invincible spiritual army to go ahead of you so that the opposing or defensive strategy that He reveals to you will be the most effective against specific racist situations in the environment you are in. Surely, God will send His powerful warring army that will overrun your racist enemies (2 Kings 6:16-17). Let God's Word loaded with the power of His Holy Spirit move ahead of you in your daily battles against racism (Psalms 35; 37; 91; Ephesians 6:11). Put on the whole armor of God that you may be

God's Word declares His holy love for you and His excellent plans for your future (Jeremiah 29:11)

able to stand against the evil attacks of the vile spirit of racism!

The Holy Word of God is the most powerful replacement of the garbage that racism attempts to place in your conscious and subconscious mind (John 8:31-32, 36). If you receive God's Word in your heart, meditate on it day and night and let it be the truth that you believe, His power prevents, blocks, reverses or deletes any attempt by the vile spirit of racism and its human recruits to defile your heart and mind.

God's Word declares His holy love for you and His excellent plans for your future (Jeremiah 29:11). God has declared His stand against any form of oppression (Exodus 3:7-10; Proverbs 22:22; Psalms 27; 35; 37; 103:6), and racism is one such oppression. God has the power to break the yoke of any physical or mental burden in your life (Isaiah 10:27), and to re-infuse you with love, power and a sound mind (2 Timothy 1:7)—and provide you with every positive reinforcement that you need to purge your soul of fear of racism and its lies. God's awesome grace is more than sufficient for your daily victory over racism—and His strength is made perfect in your weakness (2 Corinthians 12:9).

The Word of God is the most powerful replacement of racist garbage.

So, there you go! You have the upper hand over the loathsome spirit of racism.

Chapter Quiz

1. Why should you always defy and resist racism and the foul spirit of racism?

   _____

2. Based on God's Holy Word, explain your positive spiritual strategy for defying and resisting racism and the evil spirit of racism.

   _____

3. How does God's holy grace cover and protect you from racism and the nasty spirit of racism? Explain your answer.

   _____

4. In your workplace, how can you apply God's Word to oppose and defeat racism and the wicked spirit of racism behind it? Explain your answer.

   _____

5. How can you apply Isaiah 10:27 to break down and remove the physical and mental burden that

racism and the loathsome spirit of racism try to impose on you?

∞∞∞∞∞∞∞∞ ♦ ♦ ♦ ♦ ♦ ∞∞∞∞∞∞∞∞

Reflections:

∞∞∞∞∞∞∞∞ ♦ ♦ ♦ ♦ ♦ ∞∞∞∞∞∞∞∞

CHAPTER 14 – Resist the Spirit of Racism

If you allow the despicable spirit of racism to reside in your heart, you can become a vehicle through which racist actions will be perpetrated against others from your heart (Proverbs 4:23). Likewise, if you allow yourself to be overtaken by evils such as racism and its negative effects, it can transform you into a spiritually and mentally defeated person. Such a person cannot and will not have the faith in God's Word to claim their legal status as an "overcomer" in Jesus Christ (Romans 8:37), or become a vessel through whom God's conquering power in Jesus Christ would appear to

Submit to God and His Word, and resist the evil spirit of racism.

positively touch others. You have only one godly valid option, and that is to always submit to God and resist the evil spirit of racism and all that it stands for with the power of God's Holy Word (James 4:7). Your other option would be to submit to the vile spirit of racism and its willing human recruits and be defeated. However, that option is not God's design for your life—so, reject it! Know and believe that Jesus Christ has redeemed you from the evil source of the vile spirit of racism, the devil who is the father of all lies (John 8:44). Christ has cancelled the effect of racism in and on your life; He, Christ, has cancelled the charges of racism against you (Colossians 2:14).

God's Word protects you from the abusive storms of racism.

God is for you so the odious spirit of racism that is behind racism cannot be against you (Romans 8:31). Jesus Christ "stood in gap" for you—He shed His Blood for you, so racism has lost its power over you—and He cancelled all wicked charges that the evil spirit of racism drummed up against you. Therefore, the devil and his racist schemes have no authority over your life (Romans 8:31-34, Colossians 2:14-15). Yes, I repeat: Jesus Christ has nailed racism to the Holy Cross on your behalf; and

He has cancelled all charges against you (Colossians 2:14-15). Jesus Christ has overcome the world on your behalf (John 16:33) and you too have overcome the world through Him Christ (1 John 5:4-5). God's power to overcome evil is in you through Jesus Christ, so you, too, can overcome the world and racism that exists in it (John 16:33; Luke 10:18-19). Yes, indeed, through Jesus Christ, you can override and overcome racism and the wicked spirit of racism behind it, because His power in you is greater than the power in the world (1 John 4:4).

You must become an impenetrable shield of God's Word against racism.

If the despicable spirit of racism is trying to gain illegal entry inside you or build a fortress in and around you, by faith in Jesus Christ, rebuke it with the Sword of the Spirit, that is, God's Word (Ephesians 6:17). God has outlawed and barred any spirit of wickedness, oppression or injustice, including the obnoxious spirit of racism, from operating in and around your life; and He despises injustice (Amos 5:21-24; Psalms 10:12-18; Micah 6:8; Isaiah 1:17). Therefore, you too should abhor any form of wickedness, injustice, inequity, or racism.

Spiritual resistance against racism requires mental and verbal affirmations to yourself about the sovereign authority of God's Word in your life and His awesome power against racism. God's Word empowers your spiritual resistance against racism. It gives you a new mindset in Christ and becomes a holy shield that gives you psychological resistance against racism, its tricks, lies, intrigues, unlawful schemes and evil plans directed against all areas of your life, whether mental, physical or spiritual. You must become an impenetrable shield of God's Word (Ephesians 6:10-18), which protects you from the abusive assaults and storms of racism.

By faith in the powerful Blood of Jesus Christ, your total resistance against racism must include bolstering your spirit and soul with the Word of God by always reading and meditating on it; fueling your heart, mind, emotions, thoughts, words, will, resolve and actions with God's Word, prayer, thanksgiving, worship, and spiritual fasting, to keep the evil spirit of racism subdued and powerless; taking a Christ-rooted stand against racism and frequently speaking God's Word against it to yourself as guided by God's Holy Spirit within you; declaring spiritual and mental victory over racism through Christ; and believing and affirming this victory in your heart, mind and thoughts even before it begins to appear in your physical environment.

Let God bulldoze through racist paths and barriers on your behalf.

Now is the time for you to acquire and apply God's enabling spiritual ammunition through His Holy Spirit, Who dwells inside of you. Let God bulldoze through racist paths and barriers and take you from faith to faith and from glory to glory—to His awesome victory for you. You were born and created rich, having access to God's grace through Jesus Christ to heal your wounded spirit and turn your defeat, real or imagined, into spiritual and material victory. You are endowed with great gifts, talents and abilities for success. Through Jesus Christ, the spirit of racism has lost any power or stronghold over your life.

You are endowed with great gifts, talents and abilities for success.

∞∞∞∞∞∞∞∞ ♦ ♦ ♦ ♦ ♦ ∞∞∞∞∞∞∞∞

Chapter Quiz

1. How can you apply John 16:33 to overcome and defeat the different forms of racism that you face?

   _____

2. How can you apply 1 John 4:4 to overcome and defeat any form of racism that you encounter?

   _____
   _____

3. According to Ephesians 6:10-17, in your workplace or elsewhere, how can you apply God's Word as a spiritual missile to demolish any form of racism that you face? Explain your answer.

_____

4. What does your spiritual resistance against racism require? Explain your answer.

_____

∞∞∞∞∞∞∞∞ ♦ ♦ ♦ ♦ ♦ ∞∞∞∞∞∞∞∞

Reflections:

_____
_____
_____
_____

∞∞∞∞∞∞∞∞ ♦ ♦ ♦ ♦ ♦ ∞∞∞∞∞∞∞∞

Chapter 15 – Remain Steadfast Against the Spirit of Racism

The enemy of your soul, the devil, originated the unclean spirit of racism—and through a human heart he fuels this abhorrent spirit against your soul. The devil tries to use racism to kill, steal and destroy you, but Jesus Christ has given you life more abundantly (John 10:10)—the power to overturn and overrun racism and trample the demon-spirit behind it (Luke 10:17-19).

The devil tries to use racism to kill, steal and destroy you.

The despicable spirit of racism uses "spiritual terrorism" against your soul—it seeks to devour your soul (1 Peter 5:8-9). Racism can negatively affect anyone, so you must not allow racial prejudice to take root within your heart (Proverbs 4:23). You must stand firm against racial bias with the knowledge of God's Holy Word.

> *Christ has given you the power to overturn and overrun racism.*

Don't let the devil, the father of all lies (John 8:44) use racism to fool you into believing anything that is contrary to the Word of God; and racism is definitely opposed to God's Word. Don't allow the vile spirit of racism, the evil spiritual force that perpetrates and perpetuates racism through humans, to have either brief or prolonged residence within you. Don't allow the odious spirit of racism to distort your mind and thoughts about your true identity and nature in Jesus Christ.

Part of your walk in and with Jesus Christ requires never allowing the enemy of your soul to affect you through your daily experiences with racism or any of its evil machinations. If you submit to God and resist the evil spirit of racism long enough, it will cease from pestering your heart, mind and thoughts and your entire soul—and cease to have any negative impact on your emotions, attitude, actions, will, resolve, behavior, dreams and aspirations (James 4:7).

In one of the letters (1 Peter) of encouragement that Apostle Peter wrote to Christian believers who resided in Pontus, Galatia, Cappadocia and the Province of Asia and Bithynia, and at the time were being persecuted under Emperor Nero, he, Peter, emphasized the importance of fruitful growth of their faith and its empowering spiritual strength that is deeply rooted in the power of God through Jesus Christ. Peter reminded them that the adversities they faced were a test of their faith that they must endure and persevere so that they may overcome the "fire" (that is, the adversities) that they encounter. Peter told them that the firmness of their faith must reflect praise, honor and glory of Jesus Christ even in the face of such trials (1 Peter 1:3-9).

Apostle Peter's words are as real today as they were then; so you, having been empowered by God's Word within you, should remain clear-minded and calm, watchful, guarded and vigilant (1 Peter 5:8-9) against the evil spirit of racism. Your unwavering faith in the power of God to demolish any form of racism on your behalf through Jesus Christ must also be reflected through your continuous and unending praise, honor and glory of God through Jesus Christ, even in the face of the daily challenges that racism and other adversities present to you. Simply resist racism and refuse to swallow, gobble up or consume the lies that the devil, the enemy of your

Your unwavering faith in God demolishes the vile spirit of racism.

soul, tells you about yourself through racist individuals, situations or circumstances. Maintain a firm, unchanging and unwavering Christ-rooted stand against the spirit of racism. Why? Simply because racism is wrong and you posses the power of Christ in you and have declared His victory over the vile spirit of racism (1 John 5:4).

Put on the full armor of God (Ephesians 6:10-18) so that He will empower you, the target of racism, and you can repel and conquer its negative effects on you. Faith, righteousness in Jesus Christ and the truth of God's Word are absolute requirements for Christ-rooted empowerment. Cancel and delete from your mind the lie that the vile spirit of racism has any power over your career and life's success.

Put on the full armor of God (Ephesians 6:10-18) so that you are empowered!

This is a lie of the devil. Reject it! Even in a racist environment, society or country, God has the ultimate power to give you abundant success in all areas of your life (Deuteronomy 8:18). So don't wait for racism to be eradicated in your society or in the rest of the world before you fire God's Word against it.

Through Jesus Christ, God's Kingdom Power within you is the only authentic Power that will help you gain your individual triumph over the wickedness, lies and deceit of the foul spirit of racism. It is the only authentic power that will guide you to God's excellent plan for your life's success (Deuteronomy 8:18, 28:1-14; Jeremiah 29:11).

You just need to remain focused,
God has excellent plans for your life!
follow the guidance of God's Holy Word and Holy Spirit. Also, you need to work hard and stay honest in all the things you do, walking worthy and upright before God, and showing Christ-rooted integrity in your daily business and personal conduct (1 Thessalonians 2:12; Ephesians 4:1-3). Then after you have done all that God's Word and Holy Spirit has instructed you to do, just stand strong (Ephesians 6:13), don't give up (Hebrews 10:35-36, 12:1-4) and watch God bulldoze racism out of your way!

∞∞∞∞∞∞∞∞ ♦ ♦ ♦ ♦ ♦ ∞∞∞∞∞∞∞∞

Chapter Quiz

1. What must you keep doing to remain steadfast against racism and the evil spirit of racism?

_____

2. What must you keep doing to ensure that you do not allow the evil spirit of racism either temporary or permanent residence in your soul?

_____

3. How must you continue to strengthen your faith against the "Emperor Nero" that comes against your life in the form of racial or ethnic prejudice, discrimination or racism?

4. If racism is a test of your faith, like your faith being put through a "fire," how do you plan to endure, persevere and overcome the "fire" and come out victorious against the despicable spirit of racism?

5. According to 1 Peter 5:8-9, how must you remain vigilant against the wicked spirit of racism?

∞∞∞∞∞∞∞∞ ♦ ♦ ♦ ♦ ♦ ∞∞∞∞∞∞∞∞

Reflections:

∞∞∞∞∞∞∞∞ ♦ ♦ ♦ ♦ ♦ ∞∞∞∞∞∞∞∞

Chapter 16 – Jesus Christ in You is Greater than the Spirit of Racism

Daily experiences with racial prejudices and discrimination are quiet killers and destroyers of lives. They can capture and imprison your heart, mind, emotions, thoughts, will, resolve, aspirations and dreams, placing strongholds and limitations on your mind, if you allow them. Then, through your own negative mind, emotions and thoughts, they can attack your own perception of your self-respect, self-regard, self-acceptance, self-appreciation, self-worth, self-esteem and ultimately your self-confidence and belief in your dreams (that is what you aspire for and can achieve). Racism is a negative spiritual weapon that originates from

Jesus Christ in you greater than the evil spirit of racism

unseen "principalities, dark powers, rulers of the darkness of this age and spiritual hosts of wickedness in high places" (Ephesians 6:12), and it comes against you daily through its willing human hosts, that is, other people in your environment who are inhabited and influenced by the loathsome spirit behind it. For this reason, you must always prevent, defy, or offset the negative impact of racism on your heart and mind and in your life, by embracing the truth of God's Holy Word.

Racist practices are everywhere, and through them the devil seeks to devour, demolish, dispose of, or gulp down your mind. The devil plots to distort your view of your self-respect, self-regard, self-worth, self-determination, self-will, self-esteem, self-love, self-acceptance, self-confidence, self-competence, dreams, hopes and aspirations. The devil roams around looking for someone to devour (1 Peter 5:8)—with the vile spirit of racism and its willing human recruits (racists). Racism comes against you and me as a brutal, wicked, undermining, overwhelming and unrelenting force, but we must remain steadfast in our faith, knowing that through Jesus Christ, God's power in us which strengthens us is greater than its negative influence

Racism is contrary to God's will and purpose for your life.

(Isaiah 41:10; 1 John 4:4). Yes, the power of God within you through Jesus Christ is greater than any evil (including racism) that may exist round you (1 John 4:4). Racism did not overcome Jesus Christ; He overcame it on behalf of you and me (John 16:33). Knowing this, you must protect your heart and mind from the despicable spirit of racism (Proverbs 4:23). You should always submit to God and resist racism (James 4:7)—with your heart and mind empowered with the truth of God's Word—and with your faith in Jesus Christ that through Him, you are victorious over racism, and not a victim of it (Romans 8:37). It is through Christ's victory on the Cross that you can and will transcend all challenges that racism sets before or around you (1 John 5:4).

Jesus Christ has given you life more abundantly.

Racism is contrary to God's Holy Word and is beneath God's will and purpose for your life. The devil comes in many forms, including racist practices and activities designed to kill, steal and destroy you (John 10:10a), but Jesus Christ has given you life more abundantly (John 10:10b), which is yours if you *truly* receive and believe Him in your heart (John 7:38). The awesome power of Jesus Christ in your life must remain your focus rather than racism, which comes to distract and disorganize your journey through God's charted paths of victory for us (Jeremiah 29:11). So now the choice is yours—you can either allow racism to kill, steal and destroy your life, or you can allow Jesus Christ to give you abundant life. Which one is your choice today?

Despite racism that exists around you, allow God to give you abundant life through Christ!

∞∞∞∞∞∞∞∞ ♦ ♦ ♦ ♦ ∞∞∞∞∞∞∞∞

Chapter Quiz

1. Without God's Word in your life, in what ways can the foul spirit of racism bring destruction upon your life? Explain your answer.
   _____

2. Why must you never see yourself as a victim of racism?
   _____

3. Why must you always see yourself as a victor over racism?
   _____

4. How can you apply John 10:10 to gain daily
   _____

victory over the evil spirit of racism?

∞∞∞∞∞∞∞∞ ♦ ♦ ♦ ♦ ♦ ∞∞∞∞∞∞∞∞

Reflections:

∞∞∞∞∞∞∞∞ ♦ ♦ ♦ ♦ ♦ ∞∞∞∞∞∞∞∞

CHAPTER 17 – Feeling Under-represented, Outnumbered and Overpowered?

Do you sometimes feel outnumbered, under-represented, overpowered and marginalized? Are you outnumbered and overpowered by those who rule you in your workplace or elsewhere? Are you being oppressed by them as the Egyptians did to the Israelites, as it is written in the Book of Exodus? Do you sometimes feel overwhelmed by the injustices and oppression of the "Egyptians" (racists) who surround you and wonder where God is? The good news is that because you love

Christ in you is greater than the foul spirit of racism.

God and acknowledge His Holy Name, He will protect, rescue and deliver you from racists, the "Egyptians" that you face whose carnal strength may be greater than yours (Psalms 18:17; Psalms 35:10; Psalms 91:14-15; Exodus 3) and who may outnumber you in your environment (Exodus 14:13-14).

> *If you believe God, the power of His Holy Word will transform you into a victor over racism!*

With God's help in the Name of Jesus Christ, you will be able to overcome the "troop" (2 Samuel 22:30) of racists ("Egyptians") who have come against your life and career. With God's help through Christ, you will scale over the walls of prejudice and discrimination that the obnoxious spirit of racism has erected to constrain and restrict your boundaries (Psalms 18:29).

Sometimes as an individual, as you experience racism or any other form of injustice or oppression, you may feel isolated in your daily battles. Know that God is *always* with you, although you may not always feel His holy presence. His Holy Word promises that He will never leave or forsake you and that He will be with you wherever you go (Joshua 1:7-9). Also, know that you are not the only person who is facing daily challenges with racism, as so many others are under similar oppression, and our Lord God will deliver and honor you and all others who love Him and acknowledge His holy Name, and put their faith and trust in Him (Psalms 34:17, 91:14; Isaiah 26:3, 12).

As a child of God, your name is written in God's eternal Book of Life (Daniel 12:1; Revelation 20:14-15). You have full representation in God's Kingdom and you are a chosen one and a royal priesthood (1 Peter 2:9-10) set apart for God's holy and awesome work. You have attained full citizenship of God's Kingdom through Jesus Christ (Philippians 3:20; Ephesians 2:19). Therefore, you are not a minority, but the majority, because the power of the Kingdom of God in you overrides the human power of the "Egyptians" who surround you (Psalms 18:30-35); their power over you has been

God's anointing will run you over with His spiritual blessings.

cancelled by the authority and power of the precious Blood of Jesus Christ (Colossians 2:14-15) which has redeemed you from any kind of bondage, bullying, intimidation or harassment that is orchestrated by the foul spirit of racism (Galatians 5:1; Colossians 1:13-14; Isaiah 61:1-3). Do not let the devil, the father of the foul spirit of racism and the enemy of your soul, to convince you that you are a minority in a world that Jesus Christ has already overcome for you (John 16:33, 8:44).

Through Christ, God has made you his heir and co-heir with Christ (Romans 8:17), and a full citizen and majority "shareholder" in His awesome eternal Kingdom, which has all power over any earthly kingdom. Through Jesus Christ, God has elevated you above all evil, including racism (Ephesians 1:19-23, 2:4-6). Knowing all these things is to be armed with true spiritual knowledge. Do not be moved by the inherent lies of racism! Christ has set you free from the bondage of racism (John 8:32,36)!

Know that through some of the worst acts of oppression and injustice have come some of the greatest acts of freedom, justice and love. When through you a positive action valiantly and courageously overcomes a negative action, then the voice of God would have been spoken through you. When you overcome the odds of adversities and ride the rough waves long enough to see God's victory appear within and through you, then you would have allowed God's grace and power to radiate through you. His grace is sufficient for your victory over the vile spirit of racism.

Get ready to be blessed, broken and multiplied like Jesus was.

Before your eyes, God would disarm, scatter (Psalms 68:1) and remove your racist attackers just as He did the ancient Egyptians who were oppressing the

Israelite slaves in Egypt (Exodus 14:22-23, 15:19)—and just as He allowed a divide between the north and south of a nation and bloody civil war that ensued to end slavery and the evil plots of wicked slave masters. The same God, the Triune God, our God and Heavenly Father, orchestrated events that led to ending an evil plan to exterminate an entire group of people (Book of Esther). So, you need to trust in the power and might of God (Psalms 18:1-16), and then stand strong wherever you are experiencing racism, and see God transform you and the situation.

If you would believe God, He would make you victorious over racism (John 11:40; Romans 8:37), and you would become one of God's illuminating vessels to others who may be experiencing the same adversity that you had overcome.

God would set a banquet of victory before you in the midst of your racist attackers (Psalms 23:5).

You would take your rightful, victorious position in Jesus Christ, become God's anointed ambassador, and victor over evil, including racism. God would set a banquet of victory before you in the midst of your racist attackers (Psalms 23:5). God's anointing would overrun you with His spiritual blessings that are sure to manifest in the physical realm. Holding on to God's Word and promises when you are in the deepest valleys of trials and tribulations is your preparation to receive the miracles of the promises of His Word, which never fails (Psalms 23:4-6).

When you are experiencing the pain, suffering, injustice or oppression of racism of any kind or of any other adversity, through prayer, praise, worship and fasting, you must never cease to call upon the Name of God Jehovah in the Name of Jesus Christ, asking for His deliverance. To Him you can always cry "Abba Father" and He will surely hear your cry and deliver you (Romans 8:15; Galatians 4:6; Psalms 91:14-15; Jeremiah 33:3).

> *God has the power to rescue you from racists and He will.*

God understands our cry for help in time of need. He sacrificed His only Son Jesus Christ for our sins and salvation (John 3:16). He watched while we humans lied against His Son, brutalized Him and eventually crucified Him, after He, Christ, did nothing but good for us. Why did God allow all the humiliation and cruelty against His Son Jesus Christ? He had a higher and greater plan through that process. First, all of humanity became reconciled to Him through Christ. Second, we now have the opportunity to receive salvation and eternal life by grace when we accept Christ as our Lord and Savior (Romans 10:9-10). Third, we who have become believers in Christ have received the promised Holy Spirit. The Holy Spirit has empowered us to live a life of holiness, for victory spiritually and here on Earth, and He leads us to all truth (John 16:13).

As part of our Christian walk, God will allow us to experience difficult situations to break our carnal nature; not to destroy us, but to remold us, to anoint us, and to empower us for greater victory in our lives—first for spiritual victory and then for material victory in our physical environment.

> *You, too, can boldly declare that through Jesus Christ, you have overcome racism and it did not overcome you (John 16:33).*

As a child of God through Jesus Christ, God will bless you first, then "break" you, and then give "you back" to the world a changed person with Christ's spiritual nature and renewed mind to do great exploits in His holy Name (Matthew 26:28; Luke 24:29-31).

The good news is that God first blesses us before He allows us to start going through the breaking process. This was what He made His only Son Jesus Christ to go through—first, God blessed Him; then God broke Him and then God gave Him to all humanity as a Holy Sacrifice for our eternal salvation (Matthew 26:28). Do you want to be used by God to do great exploits in His holy Name? Do you want to be a blessing to others? If your answer is "yes" then get ready to be blessed, broken and multiplied like Jesus was?

Get ready for God to allow in your life difficult situations and experiences, including your experiences with racism. Life trials and tribulations that will break down your carnal nature and remold you into the spiritual power house—His battleaxe against evil domination, including the vile forces of racism.

Through my daily experiences with racism—of hurt, pain, suffering, oppression and injustice, God released on me His beams of radiance and rays of victory where His power resides (Habakkuk 3:4). First, He blessed me and then He allowed my "carnal nature" to be "broken into many pieces" by my negative experiences with racism. These very pieces became the same pieces that God used to remold me into His spiritual child in Jesus Christ, and I became spiritually stronger than I was before I was broken—now with a renewed nature in Christ. The power of Jesus Christ and God's Holy Spirit radiated within and through me and the brilliance of His radiance transformed me into His

God will allow us to experience difficult solutions to break our carnal nature.

illuminating vessel of light and hope for others through Christ. His light radiated through me, penetrating others around me and starting a cycle of "breaking" and "remolding" them.

Then, once I was in the stillness of the night, through the inspiration of the Holy Spirit, it became clear to me that my daily experiences with racism—which caused me pain and to hurt—and its injustice and oppression that made me experience emotional suffering, were for a greater purpose in God's Kingdom, which now dwelt within me. Through God's Kingdom power within me, the Rays of Victory book series was birthed. Now, I can boldly declare that through Jesus Christ, I overcame racism and it did not overcome me (John 16:33). I received God's holy victory over racism in Jesus' Name—and so have you, Amen.

> *You can boldly declare that through Jesus Christ, you have overcome racism.*

∞∞∞∞∞∞∞∞ ♦ ♦ ♦ ♦ ∞∞∞∞∞∞∞∞

Chapter Quiz

How can you apply the following Scripture to overcome

the wicked spirit of racism, especially when and where you seem to be outnumbered, underrepresented, overpowered or marginalized?

    1. Psalms 18:1-17, 29-30

_____

    2. Psalms 23:4

_____

    3. I John 5:4-5

_____

    4. Exodus 14:13-14

_____

    5. Psalms 91:14-15

_____

    6. Psalms 35:1-10

_____

    7. Psalms 37:1-15, 27-40

_____

    8. Psalms 27:1-6, 11-14

_____

∞∞∞∞∞∞∞ ♦ ♦ ♦ ♦ ∞∞∞∞∞∞∞

Reflections:

_____

_____

_____

Chapter 18 – Discouraged by Experiences With Racism?

Are you discouraged by your experiences with racism? You are not alone. Millions of people all over the world are dealing with the oppression and injustice of racism on a daily basis; it is a scourge that has been around for many centuries. So you, too, should be encouraged by the words of the Apostle Peter that even after you have suffered for awhile, through God's divine favor He will support, perfect, restore, establish, root out the attacks against you, strengthen and settle you and have you well-rooted in Him to triumph over racism (1 Peter 5:10-11). God

God will never leave or abandon you.

will never leave nor abandon you; His awesome and glorious grace and power is large enough to give you victory over racism.

The foul spirit of racism is designed to discourage you and render you ineffective and unable to achieve God's purpose for your life. On the contrary, the redeeming power of the precious Blood of Jesus Christ has freed you from the clutches of the vile spirit of racism. Now, with a renewed mind that is empowered by God's Holy Spirit, you can soar far beyond the limitations that racism has placed in your mind through negative activities of its willing human hosts (Romans 12:2; Ephesians 4:23-24; Deuteronomy 28:13).

God reveals to us that at any point in our lives when we become discouraged or weary because of our experiences with difficult and negative situations like racism, we can always draw inner strength from Him through Jesus Christ. He, Christ has invited all whose burden is heavy to lay those burdens down, for He is there to lighten our load and give us rest (Matthew 11:28-30). Knowing that the abiding love and power of Jesus Christ dwells within you, you can declare that His strength will renew your strength (Isaiah 40:28-31)—His strength is

It is not the will of God for racism to discourage you

made perfect in your weakness (2 Corinthians 12:9), when you are temporarily weakened mentally, emotionally and physically by racism. Only when you lay down your burden for Jesus Christ can you truly declare in your spirit that you are strong, even when your flesh is weak and tired, and because He, Christ, gives you strength when your heart, mind and body feel weakened by your experiences with racism.

The devil uses his human racist recruits to perpetrate racism against you. Whatever the enemy of your soul plots against you in the form of racism, God has cancelled it through Jesus Christ and will use it for your own good (Romans 8:28). Racists may gather and conspire against you, but they will fail—God is with you and He will deliver you

Racists may gather and conspire against you, but they will fail.

from all evil activities of the foul spirit of racism (Jeremiah 1:19; Isaiah 54:15; Psalms 18: 16-17, 28-30, 46-47; Psalms 34:19-22). Know that it is not the will of God for racism to discourage you and dominate your life. God's will for your life is for you to triumph in your spirit, soul and body (and health) (3 John 2) and have a successful family and career (Jeremiah 29:11; Deuteronomy 8:18). Your spirit will be empowered, your soul will be healed; and you will be exalted by God's divine mercy and justice. The power of God's Holy Spirit lives within you through Jesus Christ, so the radiance of God's awesome glory will always reside and glow within you, nullifying the effects of racism. "...God is light; in him there is no darkness at all" (1 John 1:5); therefore, since racism is all darkness, God's holy light will always suffocate it on your behalf. Do you believe this?

God's Holy Spirit lives within you through Jesus Christ.

∞∞∞∞∞∞∞∞∞ ♦ ♦ ♦ ♦ ♦ ∞∞∞∞∞∞∞∞∞

Chapter Quiz

1. As the passage above says, "the redeeming power of the precious Blood of Jesus Christ has freed you from the clutches of the nasty spirit of racism." If you believe this statement, explain your understanding of it.

   _____

2. How can you apply Matthew 11:28-30 to get rid of the physical and mental burden that racism tries to place on you?

   _____
   _____

3. If your experiences with racism have caused you much pain and hurt, what does Romans 8:28 say about God's ultimate plan for you—despite the evil attacks of racism on your life?

_____

4. How can you apply Romans 12:2 to deliver your mind and psyche from the evil spirit of racism?

_____

∞∞∞∞∞∞ ♦ ♦ ♦ ♦ ♦ ∞∞∞∞∞∞

Reflections:

_____
_____
_____
_____

∞∞∞∞∞∞ ♦ ♦ ♦ ♦ ♦ ∞∞∞∞∞∞

Chapter 19 –

Forgiveness—A Form of Spiritual Cleansing

Experiences with racism can be very painful, especially because it attacks your humanity. Nonetheless, as you face racial prejudices and discrimination, your own actions must always remain right and just, and in line with the Word of God. You must continue to walk on God's grounds of integrity (Ephesians 4:1), because it is easy for the oppressed to become like the oppressor while fighting oppression. A powerful spiritual weapon against your racist offenders is to forgive them. When you pray, report

Forgiveness is a form of spiritual cleansing.

your offenders to Jesus Christ and then forgive them (Mark 11:25). God has promised to fight for all who are oppressed and unjustly treated, and He does (Exodus 3:7-10; Jeremiah 30:8-9; 17:16-24; Psalms 37:14-18, 20). When your cause is just and your actions are right, God will fulfill His Word, which promises you that He will fight for you and win your battles.

When you obey God's Word, He takes on your battle, and those who oppose you can never win—God will become an Enemy to your enemies (Exodus 23:22)—and victory will be yours to claim (Psalms 18:30-35).

God will open new doors, byways and highways for you.

In the awesome Name of our Lord and Savior, Jesus Christ, declare a prayer of help: "Contend, LORD, with those who contend with me; fight against those who fight against me. Take up shield and armor; arise and come to my aid. Brandish spear and javelin against those who pursue me. Say to me, "I am your salvation." (Psalms 35:1-3) Then, forgive your racist offenders so that God will oppose their wicked actions against you. By forgiving the actions of your racist offenders, as God forgives your own sins daily through Jesus Christ, God will nullify any racist actions against you. God's Holy Word has instructed us to forgive those who "trespass" against us

(Matthew 6:12). Therefore, we should forgive our racist offenders and others who have wronged us so that we will be right with God.

As you extend the spirit of forgiveness to your racist offenders, the deliberate obstacles and challenges that they set before you will become the stepping stones and building blocks that God will use to take you to His mountaintop of victory. God will open new doors, byways and highways for your career to soar like an eagle's flight. God will take you from faith to faith, indignity to dignity and from glory to glory—never backward, always forward. God will make you the head over racism and not the tail—He will place you on top over racism and never at the bottom (Deuteronomy 28:13). Such is the boundless and limitless power of God, Who is the only true God of justice and equity, and Who hates oppression against the innocent, regardless of ethnicity, race or nationality. He asks only that you have sustained faith and remain in obedience with His Living Word. To have God on your side, you must always act with spiritual integrity (Ephesians 4:1) as you experience any form of racism.

> *When you forgive your racist offenders, you leave the Heavens open above you for blessings.*

When you forgive your racist offenders, you leave the Heavens above you open and ensure that the flow of your daily blessings from God remains uninterrupted by the sin of unforgiveness. When you forgive your racist offenders, even if they remain unrepentant and their negative actions towards you do not change, your relationship with God remains in good standing through the righteousness of Christ. Forgiveness of your racist offenders does not absolve them of their sin of perpetrating and perpetuating racism—only God has the power to pardon anyone of their sins, when they *truly* repent through Jesus Christ and turn from their wicked ways (2 Chronicles 7:14; 1 John 1:9; Ezekiel 18:21-22; Acts 3:19). Release your racist offenders in your heart by forgiving them, and then release God's supernatural protection against any form of subtle or overt racism that is being perpetrated against you (Psalms 91:1-3; Psalms 23; Mark 11:23-25).

"Vengeance is mine; I will repay, saith the Lord." (Romans 12:19)

Pause for a moment and decide to forgive specific individuals, others who direct or have directed racist actions against you, as well as other distant racists whom you may not know personally. For example, forgive the racist pastor who spews vitriolic hate against your race, ethnicity or nationality. Forgive the radio talk show host whose words are hateful and virulent against others. Forgive the politician who uses racial divide to try to get votes from those of similar minds and hearts—and so on. Yes, forgive all of them and let God be your avenger! God has declared: "Dearly beloved, avenge not yourselves, but rather give place unto wrath: for it is written, Vengeance is mine; I will repay, saith the Lord." (Romans 12:19) Believe Him—He meant every word He said! To offer forgiveness does not mean you should not take righteous, constructive actions to right the wrong that has been done (Amos 5:23-24).

Release your racist offenders in your heart by forgiving them.

In the future, if you recall any of your experiences with racism and the names of the individuals who were responsible, remind yourself that you have forgiven them and have handed them over to God. Pray for these individuals every time their names come to your mind. Do not expect that because you have forgiven these individuals that any major, observable changes will instantly take place in their lives. In fact, these individuals may never change at all. However, because you have released them from the debt of their offenses against you, God will protect you daily from their negative actions. In the glorious Name of Jesus Christ, no evil schemes that they have fashioned against you will ever succeed (Isaiah 54:17).

Your focus should then be your continuous offer of true and complete forgiveness to your racist offenders. When you think about these individuals without feeling anger, bitterness, resentment, vengeance or any other negative or hostile emotions, then you will know that you have offered them true and complete forgiveness. Let your daily forgiveness of your racist offenders be spiritual cleansing to your soul. Allow God to oppose, defeat and disgrace your racist offenders—Let Him fight those who fight against you; and let Him cause those who set racist traps for you to become victims of their own evil gallows (Psalms 35:1-8). Yes, let the spirit of Haman against your life be swallowed up by its own evil gallows (Esther 7).

Let God fight those who fight against you!

∞∞∞∞∞∞∞∞∞ ♦ ♦ ♦ ♦ ♦ ∞∞∞∞∞∞∞∞∞

Chapter Quiz

1. How is forgiveness a form of spiritual cleansing?
_____
_____

2. By your own understanding, explain the spiritual power of forgiveness.

_____

3. Why must you forgive all your offenders?

_____

4. Why must you forgive your racist offenders?

_____

5. Does God's Holy Word permit you to be vengeful against anyone, including your racist offenders?

_____

∞∞∞∞∞∞∞∞ ♦ ♦ ♦ ♦ ♦ ∞∞∞∞∞∞∞∞

Reflections:

_____

_____

_____

_____

∞∞∞∞∞∞∞∞ ♦ ♦ ♦ ♦ ♦ ∞∞∞∞∞∞∞∞

Chapter 20 –

Dismantling Negative Effects of Racism

The vile spirit of racism is a lying and abusive spirit, and when it inhabits a person, it seeds its lying spirit of racial hostility and hate in him or her.

Racism is designed to stifle your potential, abilities, gift and creativity.

Manipulated by the obnoxious spirit of racism, prejudiced and racist actions are usually motivated by evil intentions to debase a person's humanity and strip them of their sense of worth and dignity. Racism is designed to stifle your potential, abilities, gifts and creativity. It uses lies and negativity to pollute your mind to convince you that you are unacceptable, unequal, unworthy, inferior, and are of less, little or no value. Don't be fooled for even a split second, for this is a trick and are wicked lies of the devil, the enemy of your soul (John 8:44).

God knows the thoughts of humans, which fuel racism against others (Psalms 139:1-4; Jeremiah 17:9), and He knows that the thoughts of man are futile (Psalms 94:11). So if you trust God, He will turn racist thoughts, words and actions against you into foolishness before your eyes. God will also use you, who was once labeled "foolish" and "inferior" by your racist offenders, to shame them. "He chooses the foolish things of this world to shame the wise; He chooses the weak things of this world to shame the strong" (1 Corinthians 1:27). In the presence of your enemies and racist offenders, God will promote and honor you and set a banquet for you, anoint your head with oil and give you an overflow of blessings (Psalms 23:5). God's spiritual power which has absolute supernatural dominion over everything on Earth will breakdown all racial barriers set before you, and this will become a daily occurrence for your own testimony of the glory of God (1 Chronicles 29:11-12; Psalms 103:22, 145:13; Daniel

God has supernatural dominion over everything.

7:14; Matthew 28:18; John 17:2). Every evil action planned against you will be demolished in the mighty Name of Jesus Christ. Every trap set for you will fail in the mighty Name of Jesus Christ (Jeremiah 1:19; Psalms 35:7-8). God will bind the hands of your oppressors and use the evil that they planned against you to bring triumph and victory in your life (Jeremiah 1:17-19, 30:16-17).

God will release your mind from the invisible chains of lies and distortions that have been planted in your thoughts through your experiences with racism (John 8:32,36,44). He will flood you with His spiritual light so that you can hold any and every negative thought captive to the obedience of Jesus Christ (2 Corinthians 10:4-5) and breakdown any racial barriers against you (Jeremiah 51:20). Your heart and mind will become illuminated with the floodlights of God's grace through Christ, which will break through all clouds of limitations and move you onto His glorious paths of spiritual triumph for you (Jeremiah 30:8-9, 22-24). Then each day, subtle or overt mockery, criticisms and rejections of prejudiced and racist people will cease to have any effect on you, because the Holy Spirit of God

> *You must believe that nothing, absolutely nothing, is too great for God to accomplish in your life.*

will move your own spirit onto higher spiritual grounds and elevate your soul above racism. Now, your daily knowledge of the Holy Word of God and His promises will arm you with the stones of David for precise spiritual targeting and defeat of racist activities forged against your life (1 Samuel 17:47-49).

God will demolish any effects that racism has had upon your life.

The key to God's victory over racism for you is undoubting belief and faith in His power and grace through our Lord and Savior Jesus Christ, through Whom God makes all things possible in our lives. You must believe that nothing, absolutely nothing is too great for God to accomplish in your life and on your behalf in the Name of Jesus Christ (Jeremiah 32:17). You must believe that each day, God will demolish any effects that racism has had upon your life, because through Christ and with Him all things are made possible in your own life (Matthew 19:26; Luke 1:37).

∞∞∞∞∞∞∞∞∞∞ ♦ ♦ ♦ ♦ ∞∞∞∞∞∞∞∞∞∞

Chapter Quiz

1. What are some of the negative spin-off or lingering effects of racism that you may still have

in your life?

2. How can you apply God's Word to rid your life of the negative spin-off or lingering effects of racism?

3. How can you apply Mark 11:22-25 against the wicked spirit of racism?

4. What did Jesus say about the devil in John 8:44 and how does this Scripture apply to racist lies against you or those who may share the same racial identity with you?

5. John 8:44: The devil is the father of all lies as Christ declared to us in John 8:44 and the originator of all lies and wickedness. How can you apply this Scripture against racism and the evil spirit of racism?

∞∞∞∞∞∞∞∞ ♦ ♦ ♦ ♦ ♦ ∞∞∞∞∞∞∞∞

Reflections:

∞∞∞∞∞∞∞ ♦ ♦ ♦ ♦ ∞∞∞∞∞∞∞

CHAPTER 21 – Are You Sick and Tired of Racism?

Racism is everywhere. It exists in the secular world and in the church. The evil seed of racial hostility and hate has been seeded deep in the soil of the hearts of many who have willingly or by ignorance received it from the vile spirit behind it. Are you sick and tired of racism? Are you sick and tired of being sick and tired of racism? Are you being buried deeper in more areas filled with hidden "land mines" of oppression and injustice of racism? The moment you realize how much of a burden you've been carrying is when you finally release your experiences with racism to God in the Name of Jesus Christ. Then, it will dawn on you how unrealistic you

God is always faithful.

have been to think that on your own you could resist, defy and defeat all forms of racism that you've ever experienced or are currently facing. A new variation of covert racism appears in your environment daily with finely polished and subtle new dimensions that are more technologically advanced like silent missiles with more destructive effects. You will eventually run out of carnal strategies and tools to cope with racism. You will become sick and tired of feeling angry and frustrated about your experiences with racism.

A friend who is a registered nurse told me that she once worked at a medical clinic where she worried constantly and feared about what her colleagues planned to do to her. She believed that their negative attitudes and actions against her were racially motivated. I don't know about you, but I too have often feared constantly that I could step on one of the "land mines" hidden by racists at any time. I needed to do something, because I had nothing to detect and detonate the mines of hostility that were being directed at me. I felt like I was at war armed with sticks and pebbles while my racist "enemies" had "automatic rifles and machine guns" and were sustained with a steady backup of "ammunition and armored

Embrace the truth of God's Word against racism.

vehicles." At this point, no human could help me. I needed a supernatural force and I chose the Triune God, the only true God Who is the only ultimate divine and holy Force Who created and gave me life in the first place. God didn't disappoint me, because He is always faithful.

God gently took my hand and cradled me in His arms. First, He began to heal my hurt and pain, and He cleansed me of my fear of racism (Proverbs 3:25-26; 2 Timothy 1:7; Psalms 46:1; Psalms 55:22; Psalms 91:4-6; Nahum 1:7).

> *The power of God breaks down racism and racist barriers.*

At the same time, He filled me with new revelations that gave me a whole new understanding and wisdom about who I am in Jesus Christ, what I am, the reason for my being where I was and a peek into His new horizons for my life (Hebrews 4:12; Psalms 119: 105,130; Joshua 1:8; Isaiah 2:3; 2 Corinthians 4:6). At the same time, His grace and power started to change things in my natural realm. Racial barriers began to break down and in some cases the human hosts of the obnoxious spirit of racism began to be removed from my path in the quietest and most mysterious ways.

Now, I sat back in awe and praise as I watched my God, the Great I Am, the Alpha and Omega, the

Beginning and the End, the First and the Last (Revelation 1:8) take each of my battles with racism first through spiritual triumph and then into physical victory (Job 22:28; Psalms 20:6; Psalms 44:3,6-7; Psalms 60:12; 1 Chronicles 18:6,13; Psalms 108:13; Psalms 129:2; Psalms 118:15). He removed the racist "land mines," detonating them without a sound. Suddenly, my eyes were opened and I realized that a Christ-rooted approach to gaining personal victory over racial prejudice and discrimination, especially subtle racism, is the most effective and efficient way.

God's holy approach to demolishing the activities of the foul spirit of racism is the most effective way because His ways are more than adequate to produce the exact intended outcome—which is to obscure or eliminate such activities, and prevent, reverse or cancel the intended or unintended negative consequences in your life. God's approach to eliminating the evil

Trust God and see His awesome power manifest.

intrigues, schemes and machinations of the loathsome spirit of racism is also the most efficient—far more efficient than yours or mine, which is to exterminate the foul activities of the evil spirit of racism with minimal or no effort or waste of time and energy. You see, finally, I saw the futility of my carnal battles against racism. How crazy it was for me to battle racism solely on my own without God backing me! It is impossible to defeat a wicked spirit such as the odious spirit of racism without the power of God on your side. "What shall we then say to these things? If God be for us, who can be against us?" (Romans 8:31 KJV)

So as you experience racism, embrace the truth of the power of God's Word against racism and gain spiritual and material triumph over racism. Let your spiritual eyes become opened to the light of the

Trust God and His Holy Word!

Gospel of Jesus Christ that shines brilliantly and radiates in and through all who are willing to receive it. Wherever you are, whatever form of racism you may be experiencing, know that God can take care of it. There is nothing—and I mean absolutely nothing—that is too hard for God to do (Jeremiah 32:17,27). From this very moment, in the Name of Jesus Christ, stop trying to battle racism solely by your carnal power, because you cannot gain personal victory over racism without God. From this very moment, acknowledge to God and to yourself that your daily battles with hidden or blatant racism are no longer yours but His (1 Samuel 17:47-49; 2 Chronicles 20:15b).

Trust God and His Holy Word and you will see His awesome power begin to take control of the racist situation in the quietest and yet mightiest ways in your daily life (John 11:40). He is faithful and His Word stands forever (Isaiah 40:8; 1 Peter 1:25)—and He does mighty things with great and quiet splendor (Psalms 118:15). The strength of even the mightiest man, woman or army on Earth is less than a speck of dust when compared to the power of God, Who created them. When God takes on your racial battles, be assured without any doubt in your mind that you will emerge victorious (Jeremiah 30:1-4,8).

> *He is faithful and His Word stands forever.*

∞∞∞∞∞∞∞∞ ♦ ♦ ♦ ♦ ∞∞∞∞∞∞∞∞

Chapter Quiz

1. Are you sick and tired of being sick and tired of racism? If you are, what strategies based on God's Holy Word must you apply to rid your soul of the spirit of weariness from your experiences with racism?

2. Matthew 11:28; Isaiah 40: 28-31: How must you

apply these Scripture verses to overcome physical and spiritual weariness caused by your experiences with racism?

---

3. What does 2 Timothy 1:7 say about fear? How must you apply this Scripture against your fear of the evil spirit of racism?

---

4. What does 1 Samuel 17:47-49 and 2 Chronicles 20:15b tell you about your personal battles? How can you apply these passages of Scripture against racism and the evil spirit of racism?

---

5. 2 Timothy 1:7: How can you apply this Scripture to banish your fear of racism, especially when you face racist individuals or groups, or institutionalized racism?

---

6. Matthew 11:28-30: At your workplace or elsewhere, when you are made weary by your experiences with racism, how can you apply this Scripture to rejuvenate your spirit and soul?

Reflections:

_____
_____
_____
_____

Chapter 22 – False Beliefs Perpetuate Racism

You have to reject the false beliefs and tradition of lies of those who perpetrate and perpetuate racism against you. Never forget that the foul spirit of racism and its evil product racism originate from the kingdom of darkness. The loathsome spirit of racism is an ancestral spirit that originates from the devil who is the father of all lies (John 8:44). So, now that you know the origin of racism, you have to always reject the negative words and actions that prejudiced and racist individuals direct against you. You should only dwell on the truth of God's Holy Word. You should dwell on whatever is true, noble, right, pure, lovely,

> *Reject the false beliefs, wicked actions and lies of racists.*

admirable and praiseworthy (Philippians 4:8-9), and remember that racism is none of these things. You must leave no room for the negativity of racists and racism within your heart and mind.

A negative spirit can harbor negative words, either self-generated or from others, which bring about negative thoughts, and such thoughts can breed negative imaginations in your mind, which can breed negative actions and attitudes through your soul. Therefore, negative thoughts originate from negative spiritual influences that can produce negative imaginations in our minds. Negative imaginations produce negative visions in our minds and can bring forth major strongholds in our lives. This is what the lingering effects of racists' words and actions can do to us, if we let them.

God cancelled the power of the evil charges of racism.

Therefore, when you experience *rejection*, you must counteract such *rejection* by *rejecting* the words and actions of prejudiced and racist individuals. By *rejecting* the *rejection* of racism, you *reject* the lies of racism that the devil tries to deposit in your heart and mind through his human hosts. You can only achieve this by being and remaining empowered by God's Holy Word, which is sustained in you and revealed to you by His Holy Spirit Who dwells in you, by God's grace through Jesus Christ

(John 14:15-17). Let God's Holy Word be the truth, the Sword of the Spirit in you—and your shield and buckler (Psalms 91:4; Ephesians 6:10-18). This will enable you, empowered by the armor of God, to overcome any and all negative effects of racism. (Ephesians 6:10-18). The Holy Spirit of God will empower you with true spiritual knowledge that will become your daily buffer against destructive effects of racism that targets your mind (John 14:26).

Authentic spiritual knowledge gives rise to true self-knowledge that opposes and stifles evil spiritual lies that cultivate self-dislike, self-hatred or self-condemnation. Self-condemnation or condemnation by others only becomes real in our minds through negative and destructive thoughts, words and actions, when we receive them. Romans 8:1-2 (NIV) tells us that "...there is no condemnation for those who are in Jesus Christ." When we condemn others with negative words like "unintelligent," "inferior," "cracker," the N-word, N-head, "R-neck" "fools," "W-thrash," "clueless," "ignorant," "damned folks," "monkey," "animals," "chimpanzees," "savages," Akata," "Kunta Kinte," "Koon or Coon or Raccon," "Punk ass," and so on, we

You must affirm who you truly are in Jesus Christ.

also condemn ourselves (Matthew 7:1-2). The only truth is that there is no truth to any of these derogatory, manmade labels. These are false labels received only by a mind that is not renewed by God's Word (Romans 12:2; Ephesians 4:23-24; Hosea 4:6). It is only when we choose to reject God permanently by rejecting His Holy Word—His Holy Seed, His Son Jesus Christ Who is our Redeemer and Savior—that we condemn ourselves and lose our souls. Those who are lost are those who try to "damn" others by their oppressive actions, and wicked words, and who in their carnal arrogance have refused to ask for forgiveness from God through Jesus Christ, Who was offered as the holy sacrifice for our eternal salvation (John 3:16; Titus 3:5-6; Romans 3:22-24).

> *God declares to me that "I can" through Christ.*

Therefore, before you speak such words like "punk ass," "all those damned folks" or "ignorant folks" or any other bad name to anyone, stop and think, because your own words may become your own self-condemnation. Likewise, when we accept condemnation from others, we buy into their carnal lies and limit God's truth and power acting within and through us, and by so doing we limit God's power in us through Jesus Christ. We exchange God's holy truth with lies of the devil which he presents to us in the form of racism (Isaiah

28:15; John 8:44)—and yet through Jesus Christ God cancelled the power of the evil charges of racism over our lives (Colossians 2:14).

Are you living a Christ-rooted, centered and focused life? Make a commitment today to begin to live a Christ-rooted, centered and focused life, if you are not already doing so. Through your words and daily living you need to affirm that you are in Jesus Christ; thereby rejecting the vile spirit of racism. This was and still is my own daily affirmation against racists: "My racist offenders told me that "I can't" but God declared to me that "I can," because I am more than a conqueror through Jesus Christ, my Lord and Savior Who gives me strength. They told me that "I am unable," but God revealed to me that in the awesome Name of Jesus Christ, I am more than able through His enabling and empowering Holy Spirit. They told me that I don't belong to their "club," but God declared to me that I belong to His Club, the best Club ever —the mighty Kingdom of God. I am a full citizen of God's Kingdom. They lied about me and called me "lazy" and "unintelligent;" but God already called me intelligent, smart and wise, energetic, effective and efficient and

If you trust God and stay close to Him through Christ, He will make your racist enemies your footstool.

victorious through Jesus Christ. They told me that I missed their boat, but God revealed to me His special Boat for me that no one could take away. They tried to place their limitations on me and called it a 'glass' or concrete ceiling;' but God removed all ceilings and revealed to me that through Jesus Christ, my limit is beyond the skies. They told me that I am finished, but God declared to me that I have just begun the journey of my life's success and His excellent purpose for me. They tried to sink me into their carnal valley of defeat, but God lifted me up onto His spiritual mountaintop of success and confirmed to me that I can and I am able to reach the ultimate heights of success that He has set for me (Jeremiah 29:11). In the wonderful Name of my Lord and Savior Jesus Christ: Thank You, Father God, for Your awesome promises, revelations, declarations and confirmations in my life; Thank You for cleansing my soul of frustration, fear, anger, vengeance, hopelessness, helplessness, resentment, bitterness and unforgiveness, and of any toxic deposit from my experiences with racism, Amen."

Daily, you must affirm who you are in Jesus Christ.

As I experience daily acts of racial prejudice and discrimination, I declare that: I possess God's enabling Holy Spirit through His holy grace to us—Jesus Christ,

Who empowers and energizes my spirit and soul, and I claim the hidden power of God's rays of victory within me (Habakkuk 3:4). I declare the victorious power of Jeremiah 30:8,16-17 over my life and I urge you to do the same. Child of the Most High God, as you draw nearer to God daily by investing in a loving spiritual connection with Him, through reading and meditating on His Word daily, and offering thanksgiving, prayer, praise and worship, He too, will draw nearer to you (James 4:8; Hebrews 10:19-22).

Through Jesus Christ, God has already guaranteed that triumph and victory is surely yours to claim over racism (John 16:33; 1John 5:4). If you believe God and His Holy Word, then: you will see your daily reward appear above human boundaries and limitations (John 11:40); and you will never again be deceived by any illusion of the power of racism over your life. Through Christ, God has given you the final victory over the foul spirit of racism (Isaiah 41:10,13; Isaiah 54:4a; Psalms 27:1,3; Zephaniah 3:15,17; Psalms 46:10; Luke 12:4-7; 1John 5:4).

God has given you the final victory over the foul spirit of racism through Jesus Christ.

Apostle Paul said this to the church at Ephesus (and to us who are today's believers in Christ): "And what is the exceeding greatness of his power to us who believe, according to the working of his mighty power, which he wrought in Christ, when he raised him from the dead, and set him at his own right hand in the heavenly places, far above all principality, and power, and might, and dominion, and every name that is named, not only in this world, but also in that which is to come: and hath put all things under his feet, and gave him to be the head over all things to the church, which is his body, the fullness of him that filleth all in all." (Ephesians 1:19-23 KJV) Do you believe in the power of Ephesians 1:19-23 in your life? If you do, then stand still and see the salvation of God, your Lord God—for your racist enemies you see today, you shall see no more (Exodus 14:13). If you trust God and stay close to Him through Christ, He will make your racist enemies your footstool (Psalms 110:1-2).

> *If you trust God and stay close to Him through Christ, He will make your racist enemies your footstool.*

Chapter Quiz

1. How can you apply Philippians 4:8-9 to repel any

form of negative thinking, including the negative thoughts that racism or the odious spirit of racism tries to imprint upon your mind?

2. Why is self-condemnation or condemnation by others not of God?

3. Why is condemnation of others also self-condemnation?

4. What does Romans 8:1-2 tell us about condemnation?

5. Why does the devil try to use racism to deposit in you the lying spirit of self-condemnation or condemnation of others?

6. Based on God's Holy Word, explain some of the ways that you can dispel the negative thoughts of racism from your mind or psyche.

∞∞∞∞∞∞∞∞ ♦ ♦ ♦ ♦ ∞∞∞∞∞∞∞∞

Reflections:

∞∞∞∞∞∞∞ ♦ ♦ ♦ ♦ ∞∞∞∞∞∞∞

Chapter 23 – Are You Bound By Seeds of Hostility?

The seeds of racial prejudice and discrimination bind many people. Such seeds breed racial hostility that is deeply embedded within a person's heart, and that spring forth as attitudes and actions of racial prejudice and discrimination, and this becomes a way of life for them. Racism is perpetuated by wicked tradition (Matthew 15:3; Mark 7:13; Colossians 2:8). Racist attitudes originate from the seed of racial hostility within the hearts of many individuals. Racial hostility can reside in the hearts of those who use racist activities to target others as well as those who are the targets of racism. Such a seed is deeply planted and rooted within one's heart and brings

Racist attitudes can originate from the seed of hostility.

forth unhealthy fruits that can yield resentment, anger, bitterness, a superiority or inferiority complex, and acts of oppression, injustice or retaliation, in those who are targeted by it.

Racial prejudice—the seed that germinates racial hostility and discrimination—binds one's heart and gives rise to hatred. Racial hatred becomes watered daily by a culture that has for centuries offered fertile grounds to nurture and grow racial hostility.

The seed that germinates hostility binds one soul.

Daily, a seed of racial hatred bears new, unhealthy fruits of negative thoughts, beliefs and actions. The seed of hatred becomes deeply planted in the soil of the heart, where it is nurtured and grows. It germinates into acres of unfruitful fields of resentment or anger, superiority or inferiority, oppression, injustice or meanness within the hearts of many (Jeremiah 17:9). Either as the person who harbors a seed of racial hostility or as the person targeted by such hostility, Jesus Christ can set and make you free from the bondage of racism (John 8:32,36; Isaiah 61:1-3).

Discrimination based on a person's own prejudice is both a conscious and subconscious cultural habit. Over many centuries of accepting individual, group and cultural practice of racial prejudice and discrimination, racism has become a generational spirit, passed down from one willing generation to another. The seed of racial hostility has been planted in the soil of the hearts of so many people. It has germinated and become deep-rooted, consuming their conscious minds and rational reasoning, and have settled in their subconscious minds as well.

Some individuals or groups of them also consider racist practices to be profitable, and for them to change in a positive direction seems too great an endeavor to conceive of, an affront to his or her culture and societal privileges, a culture that was handed down to them by their forefathers. Others are constantly in fear of losing or at least having to share their sustained power in society. This fear is so intense

A seed of hostility can give rise to self-condemnation and condemnation of others.

that it fuels hostility towards individuals of other races and appears as negative and often destructive words and actions towards others who are not like them. So many have had their minds programmed over generations to mistreat individuals of other races through learned false belief of superiority. Many who follow such an impious tradition do so without a single thought or care about what they do, why they do it or the devastating impact it can and does have on other individuals.

In some cultural and social settings, racism has an unspoken and unwritten stamp of approval in many circles, and there are no penalties, especially for subtle forms of it. In such circles, there is an unspoken acknowledgment when one is a part and beneficiary of an age-old tradition. This age-old tradition of subtle racism has often handed down condemnation to many and convinced them that they are unworthy, unequal and unacceptable in society. This condemnation has succeeded in destroying the self-confidence, self-determination and will of those who accepted such condemnation instead of rejecting it and fueling their hearts and minds with God's Holy Word (Romans 8:1). Such condemnation has caused many people to be and remain in a state of condemnation, even though Jesus Christ has freed us all from any and all condemnation (Romans 8:1-4). According to the Word of God, the truth is that no human creation of God is condemned, only if we reject permanently God's salvation through His Living Word that was made Flesh in Jesus Christ, our Lord, Savior and Redeemer.

Jesus Christ has freed us all from any and all condemnation (Romans 8:1-4)

Unfruitful fields of resentment or anger, superiority or inferiority, oppression, injustice, retaliation and meanness, produced by the seed of racial prejudice, bring forth acts of racial hostility and discrimination and become spiritual weapons of evil against one another. Regardless of your race, ethnicity or nationality, if you allow a seed of racial hostility or hatred to settle and germinate within your heart, you run the risk of becoming a carnal weapon of the loathsome spirit of racism against another individual.

When fear of individuals or groups of other races or ethnicity, or a seed of racial hostility takes root within your heart, it can give rise to anger and unhealthy fruits of blatant or hidden aggression towards them. We humans tend to "attack" who and what we fear, or be in a defensive state anticipating attack from them. Therefore, we are ready to transition into an offensive state of attack, verbally, by other legislative actions, or even physically by using deadly weapons such as guns in situations that do not warrant such an extreme or harsh response. Fear can also breed anger and cultivate in us the seed of racial hostility; this can also manifest in words or actions of condemnation of such individuals or groups of people. When you condemn

A seed of racial hostility can take root in your heart and give rise to anger and unhealthy fruits of blatant or hidden aggression.

anyone, you are quick to judge them and assume the very worst about them.

A mother "Susan" of a young man once told me that she and her husband "Mike" considered their race as the "preferred" race that needed to be "protected" from individuals of other races, whom she considered the "non-preferred race" in the state where she resides in her country. Susan confessed that it was prejudice and racial hostility towards those she considered the "non-preferred" race that caused her to vote in favor of a law that was named "three strikes law." This law, she explained, mandated that their state courts impose twenty-five years to life sentences on persons convicted of three or more serious criminal offenses, and this law was extended to include drug addicts caught with small amounts of any illegal drug substance such as cocaine, crack or heroin which they were using themselves. At the time that Susan voted in favor of the "three strikes law" she had no idea that one day, her own teenage and only son "Bobby" would become a drug addict. Her son was soon arrested and upon his third arrest, he was given a life sentence. Susan said that she and her husband Mike were devastated by the harsh sentence handed over to their dearly beloved son whom they knew needed

God loves all people—regardless of race, ethnicity or nationality.

medical help and not a life sentence in prison. At the time I met Susan, she her husband Mike had spent their life's savings paying lawyers to appeal their son's conviction and Mike had subsequently died of a heart attack. She believed that it was his heartbreak about their son's situation that caused his health to deteriorate to the point of the fatal heart attack. Perhaps, had Susan and Mike voted for a more constructive law that required medical treatment and rehabilitation for drug addicts caught with illegal drugs they were using, their own son would not have received a life sentence under the same law they were once in favor of. While Susan and Mike were not responsible for their son Bobby's bad decisions and the wrong paths he took that ultimately led him to his drug addiction, Susan believed that she and her late husband contributed to their son's harsh life sentence.

Are you harboring racial prejudice or hostility in your heart?

You see, the evil spirit of racism seeds racial hostility and hate in our hearts. It puts a veil over our minds, blinding us from the truth that God loves all people; regardless of race, ethnicity or nationality. He created all humans equal and in His perfect Image; no one is inferior or superior to any other person; and no one deserves unjust treatment, no matter what they have done.

The seed of racial hostility is an ungodly seed of enmity that feeds hatred for self and others. It is opposed to our true image in the Likeness of God, Who has asked us to love one another as He has loved us (John 13:34-35). Racial fear, anger, prejudice and hostility fuel racism and are opposed to Oneness in Jesus Christ (Galatians 3:25-26). Are you afraid of individuals of other races, ethnicity or nationality? Are you harboring racial fear, anger, prejudice or hostility in your heart? [Only you can answer these questions and God also knows the true answer.] If you are, this is the time—I mean this very moment, that you need to ask God for forgiveness by His enabling grace through Jesus Christ, and to cleanse your heart of any and all racial fear, anger, prejudice or hostility.

> *The seed of racial hostility is an ungodly seed of enmity that feeds hatred for self and others.*

∞∞∞∞∞∞∞∞∞ ♦ ♦ ♦ ♦ ♦ ∞∞∞∞∞∞∞∞∞

Chapter Quiz

1. Do you have any seeds of racial fear, anger,

prejudice or hostility? If so, list them.

___

2. How can you apply God's Holy Word to rid yourself of any lingering seeds of racial fear, anger, prejudice or hostility?

___

3. Do you exhibit actions of racial discrimination? If so, list them.

___

4. How can you apply God's Holy Word to rid yourself of any lingering unfruitful seeds of racial prejudice or hostility?

___

5. Why must you never allow any seeds of racial fear, anger, prejudice, hostility or hatred to settle within your heart?

___

6. Galatians 3:25-26: Can you use this Scripture to explain this statement? "Racial fear, anger, and prejudice hostility fuel racism and are opposed to Oneness in Jesus Christ."

___

Reflections:

_____

_____

_____

_____

CHAPTER 24 – The Spirit of Racism and Self-Deceit

The evil spirit of racism is also a spirit of self-deceit and it veils your mind to the truth of God's Holy Word (2 Corinthians 4:3), if you allow it. The odious spirit of racism plants the seeds of racial prejudice and hate within those

Are you harboring the spirit of racial prejudice or racism?

who are willing to receive them. This foul spirit, a lying, wicked spirit, also helps its willing human recruits and hosts to devise ways to conceal and deny that they have beliefs of racial prejudice or that they are racist.

Are you harboring the loathsome spirit of racial prejudice or racism? If you are, it will pervert your heart and corrupt your mind with self-deception and deception by others (Galatians 6:3-5). A former work colleague of mine once told me that feeling superior to others of another race came rather naturally to her, because in many unspoken ways she was taught that and has always believed that her race is superior to others. She said it was not something that she tried too hard to think about, but it was simply a part of her "normal" reasoning to believe that people of her race are superior to others. She truthfully acknowledged that she would find it very hard to be supervised in the workplace by someone of another race. I felt offended by what she said, but at the same time I admired her truthfulness, because many people would not have admitted such things. However, someone like her simply cannot unlearn the lies she has been told for most of her life. She would need the grace of God to break down the stronghold that she considers her "normal way of thinking" to build up the truthful way of thinking (Romans 12:2; Ephesians 4:23-24). What she considers to be her normal way of thinking is actually a negative stronghold of a superiority complex. A carnal state of a superiority complex is a signal of spiritual corrosion, and to believe in superiority of race is self-deception (Galatians 6:3; Romans 8:7). The truth is that she has not come to know

To believe in superiority of race is self-deception.

God's truth, which says that she is neither superior nor inferior to anyone—for every human being is created in the awesome Image of God and we are equal in humanity and dignity. Also, whatever we possess, and I mean everything we have, we received from God and by His grace (1 Corinthians 4:7).

Without God, we are unprepared or at best ill-equipped to deal with issues concerning racism. Consequently, we suffer tremendous mental or physical damage that impact our adult life and, sometimes, the rest of our lives. Yet if we were asked, most people would simply say we have "learned to deal with racism." The reality is that most prejudiced and racist individuals and those of us who have been discriminated against have learned to accept such attitudes as the way things are and always have been. We have not learned to make changes with a Christ-rooted mindset, a positive spiritual attitude. Such an attitude would empower and enable us to gain victory over the mental and physical battles against racism. Unfortunately, many of us have fallen prey to the deceit behind racism and its traditions. In many ways, we have believed the lies of the traditions of racism and have allowed them to invade our hearts

> *Many of us have fallen prey to deceit behind racism and its traditions.*

and minds (Matthew 15:3). We have not turned to God's Holy Word for true spiritual knowledge, to uncover the truth about our authentic identity and nature in Jesus Christ. We are yet to exercise the authority that God has given to us through Christ to shatter the serpent and scorpion spirit of racism, that is, the wicked tradition of racism perpetrated and perpetuated by human hosts of the foul spirit of racism (Psalms 91:13; Luke 10:18-19).

God has given you and me the power to trample and defeat the despicable serpent and scorpion spirit of racism through Jesus Christ (Luke 10:17-19; John 16:33). It's up to us to exercise our spiritual authority over racism through Christ—no matter what, we never have to submit to the foul spirit of racism.

> *It's up to you to exercise your spiritual authority over racism through Christ.*

∞∞∞∞∞∞∞∞∞∞ ♦ ♦ ♦ ♦ ♦ ∞∞∞∞∞∞∞∞∞∞

Chapter Quiz

1. Are you harboring any racial prejudice in your heart? Explain your answer.

2. Do you have a superiority complex? Explain your answer.

_____

3. If you believe that you are superior to anyone of another race, please explain why and how God's Holy Word supports your belief. Please cite a Scripture that states that your race is superior to another race.

_____

4. Do you have an inferiority complex? Explain your answer.

_____

5. If you believe that you are inferior to anyone of another race, please explain why and how God's Holy Word supports your belief. Please cite a Scripture that states that your race is inferior to another race.

_____

∞∞∞∞∞∞∞∞ ♦ ♦ ♦ ♦ ♦ ∞∞∞∞∞∞∞∞

Reflections:

_____
_____
_____
_____

∞∞∞∞∞∞∞∞ ♦ ♦ ♦ ♦ ♦ ∞∞∞∞∞∞∞∞
_____

Chapter 25 – Are You Passing On the Tradition of Racism?

Racism is a generational spirit. As a cultural practice it is perpetuated as parents teach their children the falsehood of racial superiority and inferiority. As if this is not enough, children also learn racial bias and dominance through the power structure in society. Growing up with this mindset, they become adults who accept and continue the system. As adults, they go on to have children and once again pass on the tradition of racial bias as their means of racial preservation, so they think, and the cycle goes on and on.

The spirit of racism pollutes children through adults.

While many will not admit it, racism is taught in homes in a subtle or overt manner. In some cases, derogatory comments about people of other races are made while children listen and learn that it is fine to make such comments. In other cases, there may be an understanding in the family that they are not allowed to mingle with or bring home certain kinds of people. In many ways, racism at home is also reinforced by negative media stereotypes and images about races other than the dominant group or preferred race. Regardless of the sources that fuel and validate racism in our homes, if we opened our doors to such negative influences and allowed them to take solid root within our families, we would invite their strongholds into our homes and our lives. In the same manner, we can also validate the words or actions of racists in our homes by accepting their lies about our race, ethnicity, or our person. Let your children know the truth that God did not create either a superior or inferior race, and that your race or ethnicity, whatever it may be, is an added blessing to the world. Declare to your children the truth that God created all people in His excellent Image, and equal in humanity and dignity, regardless of race, ethnicity or nationality. He created

God did not create a superior or an inferior race.

each and every one of us for a unique purpose, so that we can achieve whatever God has called us to do through Jesus Christ, Who strengthens us (Philippians 4:13). God's thoughts for us are good and not evil; He has awesome plans for us to have hope and a great future (Jeremiah 29:11).

Racism is infectious and spreads like a deadly contagious disease that is hard to contain or cure once it spreads; so it becomes like a chronic disease that hangs around for a long time and in many cases never seems to go away. The odious spirit of racism pollutes children as it operates through adults whom they respect and who have influence on them; or through other children who themselves are already tainted by other adults.

God has His Eyes on every good and evil.

Just as adults can pick up the vile spirit of racism by being influenced by racist individuals and other elements within a racist culture, children are also "infected" by adults or other children. In many cases, the fear of being labeled an "outsider" or not belonging to the "in" crowd causes individuals to receive and practice racism, even when they are not fully convinced that they should. Race-based peer pressure and institutionalized racism can cause fearful invididuals who may not necessarily be racist to accept traditions of racism. Blind loyalty to one's race can result in the adoption of "herd mentality" or "herd behavior." The term "herd mentality" describes how individuals are influenced by their peers or mates to adopt certain attitudes and behaviors, and exhibit actions that they would not normally endorse in the absence of peer pressure. In other words, a person who is being influenced by a "herd mentality" adopts a "group mentality" to be accepted. There are many individuals who may not be racist, but who adopt a racist mentality when they are in the midst of other racist persons. They are afraid to stand up and declare that racism is wrong for fear of reprisal against them. For self preservation they temporarily adopt the group's racist mentality.

Racism is infectious and spreads like a deadly contagious disease.

Perhaps Peter was not prejudiced against the Gentiles, for he had been eating with them and also teaching that any separation between Jews and Gentiles had been brought down and broken by the Blood of Jesus Christ. Yet when certain Jews came from Apostle James, Peter became fearful and withdrew from any fellowship with Gentiles.

Was Peter prejudiced or racist, or was he fearful of what other Jews might think of him? Remember that Peter was already a baptized follower of Christ and yet he still managed to harbor prejudicial sentiments against the Gentiles which he did because he feared what other Jews would think of him if he was found communing with Gentiles. God confirmed to Peter in a vision that He (God) had never declared anyone or group of people to be inferior, unclean, lower class or of less value. Peter learned the truth that what God has made clean cannot be impure (Acts 10:13-15). God also made it clear to Peter that He did not sanction prejudice and racism (Acts 10:9-15, 27-34). In Acts 10:27-29, in Peter's own words to Cornelius in verse 28, Peter now admitted that while tradition expected him to foster prejudice against the Gentiles, he now knew better because God had taught him the truth, which was to go against tradition to obey God. There is certainly a lesson for all of us to learn from Peter's experience, especially if you are one who perpetrates or perpetuates racism, or one who has accepted the tradition of racism.

> *God has never declared anyone or group of people to be inferior, unclean, lower class or of less value.*

For those who have been targets of racism, let your children know that racism has no real power over their lives because through Jesus Christ, they have become more than conquerors of it (Romans 8:37), and He has defeated all the evil machinations of the devil on their behalf. Jesus Christ has defeated the world and the vile spirit of racism that exists in it (1 John 4:4). Let your children know that they can defy racism with the power of the Word of God; and they can weaken racism's strongholds and melt down its foundations.

Let no one fool you into thinking that evil will overcome God's holiness. His grace to us, Jesus Christ, is available to you for conquering the adversities that you face with good deeds (Romans 12:21). The fiery darts of racism that are aimed at God's shield and protection around you will break down into jumbled pieces that can never rise again to fire at you in the same manner. God has His Eyes on every good or evil deed that occurs in our lives and in the world; and He will expose and destroy evil, including racism, even when it is hidden, and every one of us will account for our actions before Him (Hebrews 4:12-13).

> *Let no one fool you into thinking that evil will overcome God's goodness and holiness.*

Chapter Quiz

1. If you have children or grandchildren, have you taught them or are you teaching them that racial prejudice, hostility, hatred and discrimination are wrong? If not, explain your answer.

   _____

2. Do you believe it is your responsibility not to pass on any tradition of racial prejudice, hostility, hatred and discrimination to your children or grandchildren? Explain you answer.

   _____

3. How can you shut the doors of your home to the obnoxious spirit of racism?

   _____

4. Do your children and grandchildren know that that racial prejudice, hostility, hatred and discrimination are wrong and are against God's Holy Word?

   _____

Reflections:

_____

_____

∞∞∞∞∞∞∞∞ ♦ ♦ ♦ ♦ ∞∞∞∞∞∞∞∞

CHAPTER 26 – The Spirit of Racism Infects Children

Negative reinforcement can permeate our natural conscious mind and solidify in our subconscious mind. Every child, regardless of race, ethnicity or nationality, is born totally devoid of any beliefs about racial or ethnic differences or inequality. A child acquires racial prejudices from grown adults, and later as he or she gets older, from their peers who are also negatively influenced by other tainted adults. Some children have been taught that they are superior and they have acquired their belief by watching and listening to adults they respect, especially in their families or other places. Other children have been made to believe that they are inferior because of their race, ethnicity or nationality; also, they have been negatively

The spirit of racism infects children.

influenced by spiritually defeated adults in their families or by the racist structure within the society they live. For example, if any child is told daily that he, she or another child of a different race or ethnicity is inferior and ugly, he or she begins to register this information in their natural conscious and subconscious mind. This is called the power of negative reinforcement, which is what racism bombards our children's minds with daily. Through racist individuals the devil lies to our children about who they are (John 8:44), and if their hearts and minds are unguarded by the truth of God's Holy Word, they will receive such lies which will settle in their hearts and minds.

As the child continues to see adults speak or act in a racist manner, his or her belief in the inferiority or superiority of race starts to solidify in their natural subconscious mind. By the time this child becomes an adult, it becomes quite hard and sometimes virtually impossible to convince this adult that all races really are equal in God's eyes. Whenever he or she confronts this issue, their natural subconscious mind will retrieve negative beliefs, thoughts, words or actions. This is why any successful and sustained change in our thought patterns and belief system must originate in our spiritual

Children can easily pick up both good and evil.

conscious and subconscious mind as we are being renewed by God's Holy Word. This means that our mind needs to be reprogrammed by the truth of God's Word as it is constantly being revealed to us by God's Holy Spirit.

This is positive reinforcement with the power of God's Holy Word, which renews our mind (Romans 12:2; Ephesians 4:23-24), and cancels every lie of racism (Colossians 2:14; Isaiah 54:17). When subtle or blatant lies and untruth that we have been exposed to over many years have messed up our natural minds, we need the Holy Word of God and the Holy Spirit of God in our lives, to cleanse and train our hearts and minds, and to reverse the effect of such lies on our lives.

When we harbor the loathsome spirit of racism and then pass it on to our children, either by our words or actions, we become agents for the perpetuation of racism in our family tree or lineage. On the other hand, when we teach our children God's holy truth that racism is wrong, we begin to shield their hearts and minds from the despicable spirit of racism and plant God's Holy Word, His Holy Seed of truth, Jesus Christ, which will in time grow into a fruitful harvest in their lives (Psalms 94:22;

The truth of God's Word reprograms our mind.

Ephesians 6:14; Psalms 91:4). Children learn fast—they can easily pick up both good and evil as they watch or listen to their parents, other adults and peers who may have influence over them.

The foul spirit of racism is seeking to enter your children's hearts and minds at a very early age so that it can crystallize lies within them as they get older. It is seeking to devour your children (1 Peter 5:8). If you sow the evil spirit of racial prejudice in your children's hearts and minds, you will also reap acts of racism from them.

You are a beautiful creation of God made in His perfect Image.

The parents of a teenager who committed a hate crime by killing another teen of a different race paid the price by witnessing their beloved son sentenced to life in prison. Both the family that lost their son to death and the family that lost their son to life imprisonment were victims of the foul spirit of racism. On the one hand, the wicked spirit of racism influenced one son, corrupted his heart and mind, and propelled him to murder and to take an innocent life. The son who was the murderer was motivated by racial hostility and hate. On the other hand, the evil spirit of racism mounted a vicious attack on an innocent young man (the murder victim) by possessing the mind of another young man (the killer). Could the family whose son murdered an innocent young man have prevented this tragic incident if they had taught their son to love and respect all people, regardless of their race, ethnicity or nationality? While a parent or parents should not be blamed or held responsible for every single action of their children, especially their adult ones, nonetheless, one could ask some basic questions: 1) Did the parents engage in making racial comments to their son? 2) Did the parents fail to speak truthfully to their son about the equality of all races or ethnic groups? 3) Did the parents ignore racial comments that were made by their son, or adults in the presence of their son, instead of correcting them? 4) Did the parents sow a spirit of racial hostility or superiority in the heart of their son?

To teach your children to resist and oppose the negative effects of racism on their hearts and minds, you must first teach them who they are spiritually, which means they must first understand who they are in Jesus Christ, our Savior and Redeemer (Proverbs 22:6). For sure, Christ would not have killed anyone, regardless of race, ethnicity or nationality. It is important for us to begin teaching our children who they are in Jesus Christ because true knowledge of God and

When we harbor the loathsome spirit of racism, we can pass it on to our children.

His Holy Word guards and protects their hearts and minds from the lies of the devil, and sets them on the path of holy and victorious living. God's Holy Word is God and God is His Word which transcends natural knowledge in the physical world—it is the Foundation of true love (John 1:1; 1 John 4:8). God's holy love is the spiritual basis for Christ-rooted love (Romans 8:35-39).

A child should know and believe that they and everyone else were made in God's excellent Image (Genesis 1:26-27). A child should know that God is multiracial, and this means that all races are one in Him through Jesus Christ (Galatians 3:28-29; 1 Corinthians 12:12-14). A child should know that God chose to birth their spirit in a body with a specific and peculiar racial and ethnic makeup, hence their parents and family lineage—so they never need to be ashamed of, explain or apologize for their race or ethnic makeup.

Your children are victors and not victims of racism (Romans 8:37).

This means that a child should know that their spirit preceded their race and ethnicity, and that their spirit is one with God through Jesus Christ, Who is the Name that is above any other name—their Lord and Savior. This knowledge will bolster within the child the right spiritual foundation to resist and oppose racism and its negative effects as they encounter them. Teach your children to make affirmative statements such as "I am a beautiful creation of God. I am made in His perfect Image (Genesis 1:27) and with His excellent purpose (Jeremiah 29:11), so racism will never destroy or deter me from the wonderful paths that God has designed for my life's success."

In simpler text you must begin to teach your children such affirmative statements during the early stages of their innocent lives, since a good number of them are likely to encounter racism from a very young age and possibly throughout the course of a lifetime. Start teaching your children that they are victors over racism; teach them that thinking they are victims of racial prejudice and discrimination brings thoughts of defeat and signifies a lack of true spiritual and self-knowledge (Hosea 4:6). Such thoughts are false and do not come from God, Who is the Originator of our true person, our renewed spirit in Jesus Christ (Galatians 2:20; 2 Corinthians 5:17; Romans 12:2).

Your children are victors over racism.

Let your kids know that thoughts of defeat of any kind are the devil's design to scatter their positive spiritual energy and disorganize the core of their heart and mind, trying to entice them to give up God's rays of victory within their lives. They must hold on to God's glorious rays where His power is hidden (Habakkuk 3:4). Your children are victors over racism and not victims of racism (Romans 8:37). Crystallize in them the truth that God did not give them a spirit of defeat or fear, but a spirit of power, love and a sound mind (2 Timothy 1:7), which triumphs over racism or any other challenge that they may encounter. A sound mind has the clarity of God's purpose for his or her life and cannot be shaken by racism or it elements.

Christ-rooted spiritual opposition offsets the negative effects of racism and should become part of our daily spiritual warfare; both in our conscious and subconscious mind, against the fiery darts of racism and its well-crafted evils. Let your kids receive, believe, know and understand God's holy truth, which states that through Jesus Christ, He has already made them free from every form of evil, including the unclean spirit of racism (John 8:32, 16:33; Isaiah 61:1-3).

Christ-rooted spiritual opposition offsets the negative effects of racism.

Chapter Quiz

1. Do you believe that we are born prejudiced or racist? Explain your answer.

　

2. If you believe that we are not born prejudiced or racist, how do we acquire our prejudices and the vile spirit of racism? Explain your answer.

　

3. Explain one way that you can use God's Holy Word to protect your children's hearts and minds from the evil spirit of racism?

　

4. Cite one verse of Scripture that shows that God opposes oppression, wickedness or any form of racial prejudice or discrimination.

　

5. Explain one way that you can apply God's Holy Word to ensure that the foul spirit of racism does not infect and pollute your children's hearts and minds through the wicked tradition of racism?

Reflections:

_____
_____
_____
_____
_____

Chapter 27 – A Spiritual Mind – A Guarded Gate Against Racism

If you know and believe who you are in Jesus Christ, then you should never allow yourself to become spiritually complacent and accept the negative effects of racial prejudice and discrimination—you should never allow racism to condemn you (Romans 8:1).

You should never allow racism to condemn you.

Racism is degrading and should never be accepted by anyone, regardless of race, ethnicity, nationality or any other distinction. In our conscious mind, we must constantly stage a "spiritual fight" (Ephesians 6:10-18) against such attitudes through prayer, fasting, worship and reading and meditating on God's Holy Word. We must constantly subdue any racist or other thoughts, arguments or knowledge that is contrary to God's Holy Word before they establish a stronghold in our hearts and minds (2 Corinthians 10:3-6). Our spiritual conscious mind would then become a positive guarded gate into our subconscious mind, keeping us protected, calm and wholesome in our earthly environment. At the same time, when our conscious mind is constantly being renewed by God's Word, our subconscious mind is able to wage a constant spiritual battle for us against the falsehoods, untruth and negativity of racism. In time, this would become the permanent state of both our spiritual conscious and subconscious mind.

Racism is designed to keep you on the outskirts and exclude you from mainstream society. It is designed to create a feeling of self-rejection within your heart and mind, and a rejection of others who may share a racial or ethnic identity with you. However, based upon God's Holy Word, this strategy of rejection and exclusion is meaningless, because your membership in any human "clan" or "club" is less important than your membership in God's Kingdom. Quite frankly, you do not need to belong to any man-made club, organization, mainstream or "other

You are in the world but not a part of it (John 15:19).

stream"—you are already a citizen of the highest Kingdom, God's Holy Kingdom. You are in the world but not a part of it (John 15:19, 17:15-16), and the highest honor that you should strive to attain first is a full citizenship in God's Kingdom (1 Peter 2:9-10)—which you have attained through Jesus Christ. Luckily, access to this citizenship has been given freely to us through the death and resurrection of Jesus Christ, the Son of God (John 11:25).

The only acceptance that you should seek is the acceptance of Jesus Christ as your Savior, Lord and Redeemer in your heart, through Whom we receive God's Holy Spirit. Never allow your heart and mind to get used to accepting the negative, evil and wicked words or actions of racially prejudiced individuals. Rather, acquire and get used to a Christ-rooted, spiritual plan of action, which will enable your heart and mind to reject and counteract the negative effects of racially prejudiced individuals' words and actions.

Racism is designed to create a feeling of self-rejection within your soul.

The Lord God will prepare you, empower you and fortify you for constant spiritual warfare (Ephesians 6:10-18), and prevent your soul from being discouraged, beat down, destroyed or defeated (Joshua 1:9; Proverbs 18:14). The Lord God will prepare a holy table of harvest before you in the presence of your racist offenders and attackers (Psalms 23:5). He will anoint you by His Holy Spirit Who dwells within you (Psalms 23:5), and His anointing will equip you with holy power (Psalms 91:5) for your daily victory over racism.

To maintain this permanent state of spiritual warfare, you must fortify your spirit and soul by the power of God's Holy Word through Jesus Christ. Then your heart and mind will be free of any toxicity from any assault and can remain focused on the infinite possibilities of the limitless and boundless power of God in your life (Luke 1:37). Within your spirit lies a greater Spirit—God's Holy Spirit, Whom you have received through Jesus Christ and Who gives you revelation knowledge, understanding, and wisdom that comes from God. God's Holy Spirit leads you to all truth (John 16:13). This is the authentic spiritual truth that your Creator, God Almighty, has embraced you and that you are made worthy, able and holy through His Son Jesus Christ.

A spirit that is deeply rooted in Christ becomes like a fortress that can weather all storms.

Your spirit and soul deeply rooted in Jesus Christ, become like an impervious, inviolable, impenetrable shield and fortress for your heart and mind that can weather all storms (Psalms 91:1-2; Ephesians 6:10-11; Matthew 7:24). God has promised to raise a standard for you against any storm, including a racist tempest that rages against your life (Isaiah 59:19b). He is faithful and keeps His Word!

So, on the days when your heart becomes weary and your mind weakens and you seem overwhelmed and bombarded by racist assaults, you must cry out "Abba Father" (Romans 8:15; Galatians 4:6), and call upon the Holy Spirit of God to fortify your own spirit and renew your strength (Isaiah 40:31). God will breathe His fresh new breath into you (Genesis 2:7), revitalize and strengthen your heart, mind, emotions, thoughts, will and resolve, all of which make up your soul. Now, you are able to ward off the attacks of racism on your heart and mind and its lingering effects—and you are able to declare victory through Jesus Christ (1 John 5:4).

God has promised to raise a standard for you against any racist tempest (Isaiah 59:19b).

Chapter Quiz

1. Do you know who you are in Jesus Christ? Explain your answer.

   _____

2. Why must you always stage a spiritual fight against racism and the abhorrent spirit of racism? Explain your answer.

   _____

3. As a child of God who has received Jesus Christ as your Lord and Savior, are you a full, first-class citizen of God's Kingdom? Explain your answer.

   _____

4. If you are a full citizen of God's Kingdom and if Jesus Christ has conquered the world for you (John 16:33), does that mean that you, too, have conquered the world (1 John 5:4)? Explain your answer.

   _____

5. According to John 16:33, if Jesus Christ has conquered the world for you, does that mean that He has conquered racism on your behalf as well? Explain your answer.

   _____

   _____

∞∞∞∞∞∞∞∞ ♦ ♦ ♦ ♦ ♦ ∞∞∞∞∞∞∞∞

Reflections:

_____

_____

_____

_____

∞∞∞∞∞∞∞∞ ♦ ♦ ♦ ♦ ♦ ∞∞∞∞∞∞∞∞

Chapter 28 – True Spiritual Relationship – A Pivotal Force Against Racism

God meticulously designed components of the entity called "You" (Psalms 139:14). So who are "You"? As a born again believer, do you and I know who the "I" or "You" in us is?

Without God through Jesus Christ we can do nothing.

(John 15:1-8) Each of us is a spirit and we possess a soul, both of which are encased within a physical form, our body. Therefore, our outermost being is our body, and our intermediary and outer-inner being is our soul.

The innermost and deepest part of our being is our spirit, and this is what gives us access to God through Christ. Our spirit is reborn through Jesus Christ and is connected to God through Him (John 3:16; Romans 10:9-10; 2 Corinthians 5:17). When we receive Christ as our Lord and Savior, we are justified—made blameless and righteous through Him, and we receive and become baptized by the Holy Spirit. Then, our soul begins to undergo a process of sanctification. This is the process of being set apart for God's work and being conformed to the Image of Christ, and this process requires your participation with the help of God's grace made available to you through Christ. If you submit to God's holy will for your life, dwell on and in His Holy Word, resist deliberate sinning and make daily effort to walk closely with God through His Word, His anointing increases in your life and the manifestation of His sanctification process begins to show in your life through daily renewal of your soul.

God has given us the Holy Spirit through Jesus Christ.

Our soul can simply be defined as a combination of our heart, mind, thoughts, emotions, will and resolve. Our soul through our heart and mind expresses the thought, power and action of our spirit. God created us in His excellent Image (Genesis 1:27) and justified our spirit through our Lord Jesus Christ. As we remain obedient to His Holy Spirit Who dwells in us, He continues to guide our soul to walk and live in the holiness of Jesus Christ (1 Corinthians 1:2, 6:11; Hebrews 10:10). God's Holy Spirit and Holy Word beam His true light of holiness in Christ in your spirit and soul which then reflects His holy light in your life (Psalm 119:105). God's rays of light are like the gentle touch of His powerful fingers on you! Therefore, your spirit, empowered by God's Holy Spirit and Holy Word, can be likened to the electricity that powers a light bulb or fuel that powers the engine of a car. If the energy that originates from either the source of electricity or fuel dissipates or is not funneled in the right manner or direction, neither the light bulb nor car would function well.

> *The Holy Spirit teaches us all things.*

We deceive ourselves if we think that our soul and body would ever be whole and functioning well if God's Holy Word and Holy Spirit did not power our inner man, our spirit being. Really, without God through Jesus Christ, we can do nothing (John 15:4-5). Our Lord Jesus Christ promised that He would ask our Heavenly Father to give those of us who receive Him the free gift of the Holy Spirit; and this promise He has already fulfilled (John 14.16-17; Acts 1:7-8). Through Jesus Christ, God's Holy Spirit is the energizing spiritual Source of "electricity and fuel" that powers our own spirit and soul. This drives our actions through our body when we are led by the Holy Spirit. When we allow God's Holy Spirit to enlighten our spirit and power the heart and mind of our soul, we will be guided and guarded by Him as sons and daughters of God (Proverbs: 1:23; Isaiah 42:6; Psalms 32: 8; Psalms 73:23-24).

> *Our true worth is not determined by any material possession.*

Our spirit communicates with God our Heavenly Father through His Son Jesus Christ, our Lord and Savior, and His Holy Spirit, Who is our Helper that is promised by Christ, to stay with us through eternity (John 14:16-17; 1 Corinthians 2:12). The Holy Spirit guides us into all truth (John 16:13)—He teaches us all things—He teaches us about spiritual things of God, and these things have the power to drive our natural self, first into spiritual victory for our eternal triumph, and then into material success while we are still here on Earth. We must first become spiritually-minded in order for us to begin to grasp authentic spiritual truth that changes situations and circumstances in our physical world.

Through daily thanksgiving, prayer and praise, and worship in spirit and in truth (John 4:24), we maintain a true spiritual connection with God through Jesus Christ, our Mediator (1 Timothy 2:5). For us to be spiritually protected and whole, our spirit must always remain in close communication with

God must always remain "Numero Uno" in our lives.

God. God is Spirit, and we can only worship Him in spirit and in truth (John 4:24). We can communicate with God in spirit and in truth through prayer (thanksgiving, praise and worship), and prayerful spiritual fasting as our Lord Jesus Christ did. My sister Maryanne, a humble, Holy Spirit-led woman and prayer warrior, once said that: "if you don't know who you are in Jesus Christ, the world will interest you." Yes, I do agree with her. If we allow our natural and carnal self to dominate our soul, we will not follow the leading of the Holy Spirit of God; rather we will obey the external world around us. In John 17:15, Christ in His prayer to God the Father said: "I pray not that thou shouldest take them out of the world, but that thou shouldest keep them from the evil." So, we are in the world but we are not to be controlled by the world.

When we are in Christ, by the help of the Holy Spirit, dwelling in God's Word and meditating on it daily, we develop a wholesome and healthy spirit that directs properly our soul (1 Thessalonians 5:23), which in turn defines what's in our heart, mind, thoughts, emotions, will and resolve—and is expressed through our body, which is in close contact with the physical world. Thus, making true spiritual connection with God through Jesus Christ and maintaining it is most crucial, because it sustains our spirit, soul and body, and holds the key to the true foundation and essence of our creation and existence. When our spirit is under the direction of God's Holy Word and Holy Spirit, He shapes the state of our thoughts, emotions, will and resolve through our heart and mind.

"If you don't know who you are in Jesus Christ, things of the world will interest you."

God has given us free will; so if we opt to, we can choose to be under the direction of His Holy Spirit (Romans 8:14). The Holy Spirit dwells within each and every one of us who are God's children, adopted through Jesus Christ (Ephesians 1:4-6). If we choose to come under the guidance of the Holy Spirit, He desires truth, honesty and integrity from our inner person, and will guide us in ways that will keep us on God's righteous path. However, our soul also has the choice to not accept God's Holy Spirit; rather, we may choose to follow directives filtered through our mind from external sources such as racist elements within the physical world. If we choose to be directed by external forces, our soul will express what it learns from the part of us that is not being directed by God's Holy Spirit (Romans 8:7; Romans 8:1-17). When this is the case, the influence of the external sources within the material world will direct our hearts and minds, and will dictate our mindset, thoughts, words, attitude, actions, happiness, self-worthiness, self-respect, self-regard, self-competence, self-confidence, self-esteem, hope, joy, dreams and aspirations, and our overall perception of who we are. When these things are based on external factors, they are not Christ-rooted, not based on God's Holy Word, and not based on authentic spiritual truth that comes from the Holy Spirit of God to our inner spirit man. As such, they are usually not stable and can be shaken or shattered at any point in time by racism or other challenges or circumstances. This is because external factors within the physical world are usually transient, spiritually unfulfilling and unable to fill the spiritual void within us. You need

Our hearts and minds are not to be defeated by racism.

to build your spiritual foundation on the Triune God—the Eternal Rock of Ages, Who is the same today, yesterday and forever (Isaiah 26:4; Psalms 18:31, 90:1-2 ; Matthew 7:24; Hebrews 13:8). You and I must become Christ-rooted to be able to deal with the challenges of the world, including racism.

Being Christ-rooted, Holy Spirit led, God-centered and God-focused also means that as we work hard to get the good things of this life that God Himself created for us, God must always remain "Numero Uno" (Number One) in our lives. In fact, when we pursue God rather than material things, He releases the things we need and desire to us (Matthew 6:33). Simply put, when we prioritize God in our lives, the material things which we seek will begin to pursue us rather than us pursuing them. God must remain the primary motivating Factor in us and in our lives; and seeking Him must be first and everything else must come after Him (Matthew 6:25-34). It is imperative that we do not worship money and other material things and hold them to be more important to us than God (Matthew 6:19-21; 1Timothy 6:10). God is the Giver of life, wealth, and all material things (Deuteronomy 8:18),

Truth revealed to us by the Holy Spirit of God arms us with authentic spiritual knowledge.

and it is wise to give reverence to the Giver above His gifts (James 1:17). As God has promised us, when we put Him First in our lives, He in turn showers us with all the things we desire and seek according to His holy will for us. Our true worth is not determined by money or any material possession or by any institutionalized power structure within society. Our true worth is in Jesus Christ. As Believers, we understand this because we have the mind of Christ (1 Corinthians 2:16).

Worldly possessions are not sufficient to rid us of our daily heartaches, depression or feelings of hopelessness, nor can they permanently fill the void within our inner spirit and soul. Even prejudiced and racist individuals latch onto expressions of hate or a superiority complex as a way of dealing with the void deep in their spirit, the emptiness they feel in their soul, when no real connection has been made with God. Their spirit, soul and body remain in perpetual struggles and conflicts. Such individuals live in a carnal valley of spiritual defeat with a false sense of superiority over their fellow humans. They falsely validate their humanity by perpetrating racist behavior toward others. Only unstable, transient energy and power from their worldly surroundings fuel their inner spirit and direct

God is the Giver of life and all things.

their soul. It takes only a loss of investment, money, property or a job for them to plunge into depths of depression and in some cases resort to illegal drugs or legal addictive medications as an escape route from their material loss. In a flash, their false sense of superiority over other humans vanishes and they sink into a dark valley of unworthiness. Ultimately, some may resort to taking their precious lives because in their minds they feel extreme hopelessness and see no other way out of the pain and emptiness within their soul. And yet God's Holy Word and Holy Spirit validate the only truth

We have been made worthy and righteous through Jesus Christ.

within us—that there is hope in Jesus Christ (Romans 5:2; Ephesians 1:12; Colossians 1:27; Hebrews 3:6). We are already made valuable and priceless by our creation and humanity, regardless of race, ethnicity and nationality. We have been made worthy and righteous through Jesus Christ Whom we have accepted in our hearts as our Lord, Savior and Redeemer (Romans 10:9-10).

Truth revealed to us by the Holy Spirit of God (John 16: 12-13) arms us with authentic spiritual knowledge that our priceless worth has been determined and defined by God through Jesus Christ and remains unchanged in each and every circumstance—and racism cannot redefine you, for God has already defined you in and through Jesus Christ. We are never to let our hearts and minds become defeated by the negative actions of others or situations around us. We should not allow the foul spirit of racism to defile our hearts and minds; rather we should be vigilant and protect our hearts and minds from the odious spirit of racism and its toxic outgrowth racism (1 Peter 5:8-9; Proverbs 4:23). Each and every one of us is a temple of God (1 Corinthians 6:19). We must press forward toward the goal to win the prize for which God has called us through Jesus Christ. (Philippians 3:14) God created us to glorify Him—He has predestined you and I for His glory on Earth and in Heaven—so, despite racism that exists around us, let us bask in His glory for it is ours through Jesus Christ.

> *We should not allow the foul spirit of racism to defile our hearts and minds.*

Chapter Quiz

1. How is your personal relationship with God through Jesus Christ a pivotal and powerful force against racism and the foul spirit of racism? Explain your answer.

---

2. What kind of relationship must you have with God through Jesus Christ on a daily basis that will equip you to defeat all forms of evil, including racism? Explain your answer.

---

3. As a child of God who has received Jesus Christ as your Lord and Savior, are you a full, first-class citizen of God's Kingdom? Explain your answer.

---

4. Does racism have legal spiritual authority over your life? Explain.

---

5. What does Romans 8:37 tell you about your spiritual power in Jesus Christ to conquer any challenge that you face, including racism?

∞∞∞∞∞∞∞ ♦ ♦ ♦ ♦ ∞∞∞∞∞∞∞

Reflections:

_____
_____
_____
_____

∞∞∞∞∞∞∞ ♦ ♦ ♦ ♦ ∞∞∞∞∞∞∞

Chapter 29 – Are You Plagued By the Grasshopper Complex

Have you allowed your experiences with racism to give you a "grasshopper complex" (Numbers 13:17-33). This type of complex means thinking small; always believing that you 'can't'; limiting God's power within you; blaming racism for all your failures; accepting the "inferior" label; and the list goes on. Can you imagine the silliness of the "grasshopper complex"—a human being who thinks small like a grasshopper or believes that his or her abilities to achieve great success are only as small as those of the grasshoppers'?

> *Have you allowed racism to give you a "grasshopper complex"?*

To illustrate this, let's look at the lives of two individuals being raised in the same environment. Based on how they each responded to their individual experiences and environment, their lives had different outcomes. The first individual, "John," accepted and allowed the negative experiences with racism to settle in his mind and define who he is. "John" believed that racism was responsible for all the adversities that he was facing and had power over his life. "John" also received negative reinforcement at home, was influenced by spiritually defeated relatives and friends and was lukewarm about or totally ignored God's awesome power in him by the precious Blood of Jesus Christ. "John" did not know God's Holy Word and did not stand in Christ and declare the Word over his life. The second individual, "Jane," consciously rejected the negative experiences she had in the same environment and refused to allow those experiences to permanently register within her mind. While racism was endemic where "Jane" grew up and lived, she focused on the truth of God's Holy Word about who she is in Christ. She meditated on the Word day and night and chose to ignore racism and racists around her. "Jane" knew and believed in the power of God's Word and she exercised

Have you allowed racism to rob you of your talents and purpose?

the authority of the Word. "Jane" took responsibility for her own actions and did not blame racism for every problem that she was dealing with. She simply believed that racism did not define her true person, worth or future destination. She believed that the only true definition of her worth was in and through Jesus Christ, and she remained focused on her dreams and worked hard and smart towards achieving them with the guidance of God's Holy Spirit within her. She believed and trusted God for success in her life (Deuteronomy 8:18), despite racism around her and negative reinforcement at home and from spiritually defeated relatives and friends.

> *Do not allow the foul spirit of racism to rob you of God's reward.*

As time went on, "John" faced life's challenges with a defeated spirit while "Jane" like Joshua and Caleb (Numbers 13:17-33) faced life with faith in God through Jesus Christ. She faced life (and racism) with courage, determination, and belief in the limitless and boundless power of God and His Holy Spirit within her. "John" remained in the circle of negativity, while "Jane" though in the same environment became spiritually empowered, prepared and ready for success. "John" and "Jane" each had unique talents and purpose, but "John" buried his talents and blamed racism for all his woes while "Jane" invested hers despite racism that existed around her.

What have you done with your own individual talents and purpose from God? Have you blamed racism for your inability to properly invest God-given talents, or have you pressed through the obstacles that racism mounts against you to ensure that your talents are fully invested and vested? Remember "The Parable of the Talents" in Matthew 25:14-28 where the "Master" rewarded only the servants who used their talents well. Have you allowed your experiences with racism to rob you of talents and purpose? Have you allowed racism to give you a grasshopper or limping mentality?

You need to check yourself for any hidden or exposed forms of grasshopper complex that you may have and ask God to help you to get rid of those things. If you believe that good education, success, wealth and complete prosperity in your life belongs only to certain kinds of people, you may have a grasshopper

A defeated spirit is not a conquering spirit and lacks true spiritual knowledge.

complex. If you believe that only certain kinds of people should participate in and win certain sports like ice hockey, ski racing, horse racing, golf, or tennis, then you may have a grasshopper complex. If you believe that attending college is only possible for certain people, you may have a grasshopper complex. If you believe that aspiring to achieve greatness is unrealistic and not possible for you, you may have a grasshopper complex. I can go on forever with more examples that qualify as "grasshopper complex." Basically, negative thinking can crystallize over years of practice to give anyone a "grasshopper complex."

In the case of the two individuals illustrated above, "John" had a grasshopper complex while "Jane" didn't. As a result, "John's" outcome was the exact opposite of "Jane's"—defeat in "John's" case, and victory and triumph in "Jane's". A defeated spirit is not a conquering spirit. A defeated spirit lacks spiritual truth, understanding, knowledge and wisdom. A defeated spirit has not tapped into God's power in His Word by reading and meditating on it day and night, and applying it in his or her daily living. A defeated spirit has not activated the conqueror in him or her through Jesus Christ. A defeated spirit is unable to properly invest and reap from their God-given talents, gifts and abilities. Often, the defeated individual also has a wounded spirit and is now unable to apply the power of God's Word and Holy Spirit, in the Name of Jesus Christ, to enable Him heal the wounds in his or her soul.

Reject a "grasshopper" or "limping mentality."

"A wounded spirit comes as a result of a reaction to negative words, events, actions, or a violation of your person or rights—a reaction that crushes you, knocks you down and from which you cannot rise…we cannot heal ourselves of a wounded spirit…we need someone else to release it in positive, believing prayer."[1] "A wounded spirit is injury to any area of our soul or spirit faculties—mind, emotions and will. It is injury to the unseen areas of our being."[2] If you have a wounded spirit, cry out in prayer to God for help and He will surely deliver you directly, or send a helper, a true believer to pray for your deliverance from a wounded state.

Do not conform to ungodly traditions of the world like racism.

Reject the "grasshopper complex" and its negative effects on you, and let God heal your wounded heart and mind before that complex finds residence within you and brings you prolonged or permanent defeat. Do not allow the foul spirit of racism to deposit a "grasshopper" or "limping mentality" in you. Do not allow the vile spirit of racism to rob you of God's reward for your obedience to His Word—for properly investing your talents for a good return to the glory of His Name (Matthew 25:14-28).

Don't allow your experiences with racism to transform you into a defeated spirit, for there is no victory within defeat. The ball is now in your court. You can receive God's Holy Word and allow it to start the process of daily renewal of your mind (Romans 12:2; Ephesians 4:23-24). You can ask the Holy Spirit of God through prayer to help you to begin the work of cleansing your mind of any junk, falsehood or negativity, and actively guard your mind against the negative assaults of racism with God's Holy Word. You can ask God's Holy Spirit to teach you how to guard your heart and mind with God's Word against any negative impact of racism and its toxic lingering effects. You can ask the Holy Spirit of God to flood your mind with the radiance of God's glorious power.

Reject the "grasshopper complex".

Let the Holy Word of God enrich you with only positive and uplifting information (Philippians 4:7-9). Allow God's Word to continually renew your mind and give you a Christlike mind: So, "Do not conform to the pattern of this world, but be transformed by the renewing of your mind. Then you will be able to test and approve what God's will is—his good, pleasing and perfect will " (Romans 12:2, 21; Ephesians 4:23-24) for your life regardless of racism that you may encounter or that exists around you.

Chapter Quiz

1. What is a "grasshopper" or "limping mentality"?

2. Examine yourself: Do you have a "grasshopper mentality" in dealing with the challenges of life, including racism? Explain your answer.

3. Look at Numbers 13:17-33: What can you learn from Caleb's response in Numbers 13:30 in responding to your fears of racism or the power that you perceive racism and racists to have over your lives?

4. What is a wounded spirit? Explain your answer.

5. What is a defeated spirit? Explain your answer.

6. What must you do on a daily basis to prevent the foul spirit of racism or your experiences with racism from giving you a defeated or wounded spirit?

∞∞∞∞∞∞∞∞ ♦ ♦ ♦ ♦ ♦ ∞∞∞∞∞∞∞∞

Reflections:

_____
_____
_____
_____

∞∞∞∞∞∞∞∞ ♦ ♦ ♦ ♦ ♦ ∞∞∞∞∞∞∞∞

Chapter References:

1. A Wounded Spirit *by* Rodney W. Francis Founder/Director: "The Gospel Faith Messenger" Ministry. http://www.gospel.org.nz/FreeArticles/Rodney'sArticles/A%20%20WOUNDED%20%20SPIRIT.htm
2. Breaking strongholds & healing wounded spirit book 1: Breaking Spiritual Strongholds and Healing the Wounded Spirit ©2008 Eric Gondwe. http://www.spiritualwarfaredeliverance.com/books/08-breaking-spiritual-strongholds-healing-wounded-spirit/html/what-is-wounded-spirit-define.html

CHAPTER 30 – Dealing With Racism in the Workplace

Even in a racist environment, God has the ultimate power to give you success in all areas of your life (Deuteronomy 8:18). God can and will promote you (Psalms 75:6-7), if you trust Him, abide in His Holy Word (John 15:1-7), thank Him with sincere gratitude for His daily blessings and praise and worship His Holy Name (Psalms 107:1, 145:7; 1 Chronicles 29:11-13)—and work hard and stay focused on your dreams and aspirations in accordance with His purpose for your life. Don't wait for racism to be eradicated in your workplace or the world for you to activate God's brilliant

A prejudiced individual is under a negative spiritual stronghold.

light (Habakkuk 3:4)—His rays of victory through Jesus Christ, which will help you to gain individual triumph over racism. Racism, like many other human vices, is a manifestation of evil influences in the spiritual realm (2 Corinthians 10:3-6). There is a demon spirit behind racist practices perpetrated by some individuals. A prejudiced or racist individual is under a negative spiritual stronghold or influence. If those who are targeted by racism are not empowered with God's Holy Word to deal with it, they can also come under the stronghold of the negative influences of racism. Then, they begin to see themselves as victims of racism, rather than victors over it.

There is a demon spirit behind racist practices perpetrated by some individuals.

For many adults, including you and me, workplace experiences with racism, especially injustice of racism, can be very challenging. These include being denied earned promotions and bonuses; being demeaned, disrespected or disregarded in overt or subtle ways; being given a position but stripped of the authority of the position; enduring false verbal charges of poor performance which are never documented because they are fabricated lies; being labeled "angry', a potential "violent" or "disgruntled" employee because you raised a legitimate objection or concern; dealing with false accusations of not being a team player or not having a team spirit because you simply refused to ago along with unfair, unjust and wicked practices; dealing with your manager's disparaging remarks before your peers and subordinates (in your presence or absence); being told constantly that you are not ready for a supervisory or managerial position when the persons of a preferred race or ethnicity you hired and trained on the job have been promoted above you and are now supervisors and managers; and the list goes on.

Such subtle or overt assaults can be overwhelming on your person and can have a profound negative impact on your heart and mind, and then your health. Such negative impact, if you allowed it, could cause you potential lifelong erosion of your self-regard, self-respect, self-appreciation, self-confidence and self-esteem, and the emergence of a pattern of silent self-dislike or self-loathing, self-distaste, self-hate or hate of others that could destroy the core of your very being. Your heart and mind could become eroded and you could become psychologically undermined.

The Power of the Holy Spirit is a positive weapon of destruction of evil.

Even with the enormous negative impact that racism in the workplace can potentially have on individuals, there are only few well-organized professional groups that assist those who are targeted by racism. The few organizations that exist can only fight racism based on overt, evidence-based and documented racism. It becomes harder for them to battle the more subtle forms of racism that attack individuals daily through psychological warfare. This is why you must apply spiritual warfare in your fight against racism (Ephesians 6:10-18), because in the natural realm, the odds are stacked against you. You see, the evil spirit of racism attempts to intimidate its targets. This foul spirit makes people fearful of racism—it makes individuals uncomfortable when the word "racism" is mentioned—it causes society as a whole, including the church, to shy away from dealing with and tackling racism. There are many members in the church, including deacons, elders, pastors and bishops who are racist; so, it is difficult for the church to take on racism in the secular world when it is yet to tackle racism in the church.

There is a huge invisible but well-understood

> *The spirit of racism attempts to intimidate its targets.*

boundary around the issue of racism that is clearly marked as a "no-go" area. The consequences of violating this unwritten but understood boundary could make life intolerable for you in the workplace or elsewhere. In some cases, this may even lead to loss of employment through subtle means. To further complicate matters, the individuals who perpetrate racism have devised rather ingenious ways to present such situations in the workplace as a mere figment of your imagination.

Often, the reality of your experience with racism in the work environment can merely be regarded by the perpetrators as your "imagination" or "perception," and you are told that you "perceived" the experience, which they say in their "reality" never actually happened. You are then consciously and deliberately barricaded within a psychological fortress. Within this fortress, you, the target of racism, are put on the defensive. The perpetrator, "the prejudiced and racist person" and "the system" in the workplace become the "judge" and the "jury." You must now prove to both the "judge" and the "jury" that the vivid reality of your experience with racism is not merely "a figment of your imagination," and as such is not merely subjectively "perceived." You must also prove to

Your spiritual triumph will give you mental victory.

the "judge" and "jury" that they are the ones who have deliberately translated your "reality" to fit their definition of "perception." You must prove that their actions are a deliberate attempt to mask their racist practices in the workplace.

The question is, how can you achieve this while in your physical environment you may be greatly outnumbered and overpowered by both the "judge" and "jury," who may also be biased and desensitized about the problem that you face daily? How can you sensitize your "judge" and "jury," who may never have experienced racial discrimination and may not be able to relate to your situation, or simply don't care about your situation and mental anguish? Quite frankly, in such an environment, you may have close to an impossible task on your hands, because it is not easy for a "blind" man to make a man with "sight" understand what it really feels like to be "blind." The task of the "blind" man is even more arduous when the "blind" man's blindness is and has always been profitable for the man with "sight." Why then should the man with "sight" give up any of his "profit" just for the "blind" man to regain his "sight"?

Thus, in the workplace, the path of greatest

How can you prove to the "judge" and "jury" that racism is not a figment of your imagination?

resistance for you individually is direct confrontation of racism. If you choose this path, you may be like a small fish being swallowed by a large barracuda, and you are likely to be crunched into oblivion. You are sure to lose the daily physical battles, but you will also run the risk of losing the ultimate spiritual war in the process. The path of least worldly resistance against racism is spiritual warfare in your conscious and subconscious mind, a path that will empower you with God's awesome glory (2 Samuel 22:30; Psalms 18:29) for victory. Your spiritual triumph will give you mental victory and prevent buildup of any stronghold and its negative effect on your heart, mind and body. Spiritual direction by the Holy Spirit allows you to understand the game of those who perpetrate and perpetuate racism within the system, keep them in check by the power of God and pull down their stronghold against you (2 Corinthians 10:3-5). Spiritual warfare through prayer and fasting breaks down the evil walls of racism. It causes God to rise up and scatter your racist enemies (Psalms 68:1). It causes God to oppose those who oppose you,

> *Spiritual warfare through prayer and fasting breaks down the evil walls of racism.*

fight them and become an Enemy to them (Psalms 35:1-3).

Armed with the knowledge and full armor of God's Word, you will then place the cryptic and overt practices of racists under guard in both your spiritual conscious and subconscious mind. You will remain cognizant that your reality is not just mere perception, and that a racist's deliberate twisting of your reality to their definition of perception is merely a mind game to mask their racist practices in the workplace or elsewhere. You will know and believe that the success of your career and ultimate destiny is not in the hands of anyone, including a prejudiced and racist individual; but solely in the Hands of God your Maker. God is your ultimate provider—and it is He who gives you the power to become prosperous (Deuteronomy 8:18), not racists or anyone else.

You are empowered by God through Christ to overcome racism.

You will become empowered to deal with your daily reality of racism without internalizing any of its negative and destructive impact. By this, the power of God the Father and His Holy Spirit through His Son Jesus Christ in you will become your fortress and shield against daily assaults of racism, and like an airbag, which is released inside a car upon deadly and violent collision or impact, your spirit will act like a buffer and prevent your soul from sustaining any spiritual wounds. This means that racism may "ruff" you up a little on a daily basis, with a few bruises on the outside, but on the inside you remain untouched by the trauma from the outside (2 Corinthians 4:8-9). This is where your victory lies—protecting your inner peace, tranquility, love, joy, happiness, hope, faith, dreams, visions and aspirations, and determination for your life's success by the truth of God's Holy Word and the power of the Holy Spirit (Philippians 4:7-8), even in the midst of chaos, injustice or wickedness around you.

To gain victory over the negative effects of racism, maintaining an inner spiritual core that is empowered daily by God's Word and His Holy Spirit, is the greatest ammunition ever. It is a silent and powerful spiritual weapon that nullifies the effects of all negative attacks, and shatters all plans that are fashioned to stand in the way of your success (Isaiah 54:17). The fire power of the Holy Word and Holy Spirit of God is a positive spiritual weapon of destruction against evil, inequity, injustice, wickedness, oppression and all forms of negativity that may be fashioned against

Let the ammunition of God's Holy Word power your faith against racism you face.

any child of God who has submitted their spirit and soul through Jesus Christ to the awesome power and glory of God.

Basically, the elements of racism are designed to attack your soul, your heart and mind that dictates your thoughts, emotions, will and resolve, and which ultimately dictates your attitude, actions, personality and behavior, the very core of who and what you are. These elements are designed to capture your minute-by-minute attention and distract you from God's appointed purpose for your life. Such things are meant to become unplanned detour of your God-ordained original course. You should be like Nehemiah when he ignored Sanballat and Tobiah, the wicked elements of destruction whose plan had been to distract and destroy the work that he was focused on doing (Nehemiah 2:10,19, 4:1,7, 6:1,2,5,12,14, 13:27-29).

Let God be your major "distraction" from your experiences with racism.

If the elements of racism can no longer get your attention, having been defeated spiritually by the power of the truth of God's Holy Word in you, with the help of His Holy Spirit dwelling in you, then they would have lost their power over you in the physical environment.

Let God and His Holy Word be your major focus

away from your experiences with racism and its oppression and injustice in the workplace. Have faith in God and let Him fight your battles in the spiritual and natural realms, for though the power of God is unseen, it has supernatural dominion over everything, including the despicable spirit of racism that is battling you in the workplace or elsewhere. Having undoubting faith in God pleases Him (Hebrews 11:6), and He has given you spiritual victory through Christ. Your victory through Christ will shift the dynamics of events and bring them to a positive outcome on your behalf at your workplace (Romans 8:28; 1 John 5:4).

Herein is the secret to altering the negative effect of any word, action or circumstance on your conscious and subconscious mind, your body, and ultimately your physical environment. You must subdue and conquer a problem in your spiritual conscious mind, and this victory will translate positively in your spiritual subconscious mind. It is believed that our subconscious mind only accepts what we really believe in our conscious mind to be the dominant truth. So, the dominant truth in our hearts and minds is what eventually settles in our subconscious mind—that is what is accepted as the truth

Racism exists, but you can become spiritually empowered to conquer it through Jesus Christ.

in our subconscious mind. If you really believe God's Holy Word to be the absolute truth and His promises to be true and unfailing, your subconscious mind will also accept this as the dominant truth it accepts. So, even in your dream, when attacked by demonic forces, you can speak God's Holy Word and plead the precious Blood of Jesus Christ and receive victory over them. This is because in your conscious mind you believe in the power of God's Word and the Blood of Christ, and this becomes the dominant truth in your heart and subconscious mind.

Daily, as you read, receive and meditate on God's Holy Word, your Christ-rooted conscious mind programs and reprograms your subconscious mind with the renewing power of the Holy Word (Romans 12:2; Ephesians 4:23-24). God's Word that you declare verbally and in your conscious mind must be in complete agreement with the truth that is accepted by your subconscious mind for God's power and glory to manifest in your life (John 11:40; John 7:38). Over time, this will become your permanent state of mind and will become your daily reality. So, if you verbally declare

Believe now and always that God has anointed and empowered you through Christ and the Holy Spirit over the vile spirit of racism!

God's Word but do not believe it in your heart, it will not manifest victory in your life. This is why Apostle Paul tells us in his letter to the Romans in Chapter 10 verses 9 and 10 "that if you *confess with your mouth* the Lord Jesus and *believe in your heart* that God has raised Him from the dead, you will be saved. For *with the heart one believes* unto righteousness, and with the *mouth confession* is made unto salvation." So, what you confess with your mouth and believe in your heart must be the same before you receive the manifestation of God's promises. When what you believe in your heart contradicts what you say, God's Word will not manifest in your life. Many of us who are believers in God's Word, in Jesus Christ, tend to confess what we don't believe or believe what we don't confess, and this does not work! God's hands are "tied" and He cannot act on our behalf when our hearts contradict our confession or vice versa, even when we are referencing His Holy Word.

Let God be your major focus away from your experiences

Racism exists, but you are spiritually empowered to conquer it through Jesus Christ. God should be your primary focus; it is He Who sacrificed His only Son Jesus Christ for your eternal salvation; and it is through Christ that His Holy Spirit anoints you and gives you daily training and guidance on how to live holy and deal with daily challenges, including racism. With a daily spiritual connection with God by His Holy Word in you through Jesus Christ—and by your daily praise, worship, prayer and spiritual fasting, and empowerment by His Holy Spirit, you gain spiritual fortification and are able to apply spiritual ammunition against adversities like racism. Let the ammunition of God's armor power your faith against racism you face (Ephesians 6:10-18).

Spiritual fortification and empowerment by God's Holy Spirit through Jesus Christ gives you godly authority, control and power over the world that will enable you to make the right decisions, act positively and become divinely creative in dealing with a negative force like racism (1 John 4:4; 1 John 5:4; John 16:33; Luke 10:17-19). Only God has the supernatural power to uproot the foul spirit of racism from the heart of a person, and from the hearts of millions of people in the world, because the vile spirit of racial prejudice is rooted in the hearts of many and is hidden as a secret sin. This is expected since the evil spirit of racism is a product of lies and fiery darts of the wicked one—the devil and his evil forces. So when you

Only God has the supernatural power to uproot the foul spirit of racism from the heart of a person.

take up the full armor of God (Ephesians 6:10-18), He will empower you, the target of racism through Jesus Christ, and you can repel or conquer racism's negative effects on you. Faith, righteousness in Jesus Christ, and truth of God's Holy Word, are absolute requirements for this empowerment.

Your victory over adversities like racism will become reality either by a change of your response to the situation, a change in the situation or both. I challenge you to stand firm on the power of God's conquering Holy Word through Jesus Christ—and receive supernatural anointing and empowering of the Holy Spirit of God within you. Yes, child of the Most High God, as a believer in Jesus Christ, if you believe and apply God's Word, you will gain spiritual power and victory over challenges like racism in the workplace, church and everywhere you encounter it (1 John 5:4; John 7:38, 11:40).

God has anointed you through Christ to overcome racism.

Believe now and always that God has anointed and empowered you through Jesus Christ and the Holy Spirit to overcome the vile spirit of racism!

Chapter Quiz

1. Who has the ultimate power to give you victory over racism you face in the workplace or elsewhere? Explain your answer.

---

2. Who has the ultimate power to promote you in the workplace or elsewhere and to grant you success in your daily life? Explain your answer.

---

3. What does Deuteronomy 8:18 say about God's ability to give you the power to get wealth? Can the odious spirit racism, racists, or racist practices take this power from you?

---

4. As a man thinks so is he (Proverbs 23:7a): How can your own mind work against you and cause the evil spirit of racism to defeat you?

---

5. How can Romans 8:31 empower you against racism and the loathsome spirit of racism? Explain your answer.

---

6. How can Romans 8:37 empower you to believe that you are more than a conqueror over racism

through Christ who loved and sill loves you? Explain your answer.

___

∞∞∞∞∞∞∞∞ ♦ ♦ ♦ ♦ ♦ ∞∞∞∞∞∞∞∞

Reflections:

___
___
___
___

∞∞∞∞∞∞∞∞ ♦ ♦ ♦ ♦ ♦ ∞∞∞∞∞∞∞∞

Chapter 31 – No Room for Negative Effects of Racism

To repel the potential negative and destructive impact of racism, you must identify and ward-off its "spin-off effects" or "lingering effects." What are some of these spin-off effects of racism? By my definition, these are negative attitudes, behaviors, thought processes and perceptions of one's self-worthiness. Spin-off effects are lies and fiery darts of the wicked one, the devil, which we receive as by-products of our experiences with racism, and if not dealt with, could become strongholds in our lives. Such spin-off effects include, but are not limited to, wounded soul syndrome, spirit of

You have to identify and ward-off any lingering effects of racism.

defeat, victim mentality, self-dislike, self-disregard, self-hatred (the most self-destructive spin-off effect); disregard for others who share our racial and ethnic identity; extreme mental stress and duress; internal chaos and lack of inner peace and wholeness of the spirit; built-up anger or perpetual anger (unrighteous anger), bitterness, resentment and unforgiveness within; erosion of self-confidence and self-esteem; inferiority complex; increasing feelings of inadequacy; secondary effects at home (e.g., physical, verbal, or mental abuse of spouse and children); a lack of ambition or drive to reach higher levels and accomplish greater things; a lack of zeal for the workplace environment; other manifestations of depression; dislike for other individuals who represent the racial group that is responsible for our experiences with racism; a lack of zeal for life itself; fear of the actions of racially prejudiced individuals; and a negative thought process that ascribes racism as having power over our lives. Bottom line: The list of potential spin-off effects is endless.

Spin-off effects of racism are fiery darts of the devil.

If the prejudiced and discriminatory actions of the perpetrator cannot control your mind and thoughts, cannot predict or control your behavior or lay down foundations of negative strongholds and their spin-off effects on your heart and mind, then their actions would merely translate into a useless waste of energy. This is one of the secrets to your victory, that is, spiritual, mental and psychological warfare against racism in the workplace or elsewhere. Jesus Christ has won the victory over racism (Colossians 1:13). Therefore, you can stand in Christ's victory over racism!

You can transcend racism with the power of God loaded within your heart and mind.

If you can personally succeed in winning the spiritual warfare against racism, you can and will prevent evil domination of the vile spirit of racism over your life—and you can and will avoid the negative spin-off effects on your heart, psyche, (mind) and health. You can and should live a full, productive and successful life despite your daily experiences with racism, an offensive and potentially destructive spiritually-driven cultural attitude and behavior.

Surely, you can transcend racism in the physical world with the power of God's Holy Word loaded within your heart and mind. The Holy Spirit of God within you has supernatural power over your situation, and you have obtained this power through Jesus Christ. The Holy Spirit will retrain your heart and mind to help your thoughts to meditate only on God's truth, and stay positive (Philippians 4:7-9). When you become a moving powerhouse of God's Holy Word, whatever you conquer in your spirit will become conquered in your heart, mind, thoughts, emotions, will and resolve, and ultimately in your physical environment.

You must always remain focused on God and His awesome grace to you through Jesus Christ. God's grace is sufficient for you to gain daily victory over racism (2 Corinthians 12:9). You must constantly seek God first and His righteousness (Matthew 6:33). You must never lose sight of the truth that God is your Creator and that He alone holds the blueprint of your life and is the Master Architect of your life. You must revel in the truth that your existence and life's success are in the Hands of God and not in the control of any human being—and certainly not in the control of any racist person. You must always consciously replace thoughts of fear and anxiety with thoughts of faith in God, Who is your Maker, the Creator of Heaven and Earth and the entire universe, and Who has limitless power within and around you (Psalms 27:1,3; Isaiah 35:4, 41:13; Philippians 4:6-7). You must always consciously denounce any 'spin-off' or 'lingering' effects of racism while declaring the awesome power of God's rays of

His grace is sufficient for you to gain daily victory over racism.

victory within you through Jesus Christ (1 Corinthians 15:57; Philippians 4:8; Habakkuk 3:4).

As you receive God's brilliant light—His rays of victory within you through Jesus Christ—declare that you know that you can and have won the ultimate spiritual, mental and physical victory over racism.

Chapter Quiz

1. Do you have any 'spin-off' or 'lingering' effects of racism in your life? If yes, list them and explain each one.

   _____

2. How can you get rid of each of these 'spin-off' or 'lingering' effects?

   _____

3. What power do you have within you that can help you rid yourself of all 'spin-off' or 'lingering' effects of racism?

   _____

4. What power within you fortifies you against racism and the foul spirit of racism?

   _____

5. In whose excellent Image are you created? Can

   _____

racism change this? Explain your answer.

_____

∞∞∞∞∞∞∞∞ ♦ ♦ ♦ ♦ ♦ ∞∞∞∞∞∞∞∞

Reflections:

_____
_____
_____
_____

∞∞∞∞∞∞∞∞ ♦ ♦ ♦ ♦ ♦ ∞∞∞∞∞∞∞∞

Chapter 32 – Carnal or Unrighteous Anger Against Racism

Is your spirit filled with unrighteous, unholy anger because of your experiences with racism? When one faces racism and in response to it feels angry, it is important to make a distinction between righteous anger and unrighteous anger. Righteous anger is holy anger that is a positive stirring of your spirit and soul against oppression, wickedness and injustice; while unrighteous anger is a destructive and carnal anger that schemes and orchestrates to pay back evil with evil, like the kind of anger Moses acted on when he killed an

The foul spirit of racism can convince you that your carnal anger against racists is justified.

Egyptian whom he witnessed maltreating one of Moses' own people (Exodus 2). You see, in response to the oppressive actions of racists, the foul spirit of racism can fuel you with carnal, unrighteous anger against your racist offenders. The obnoxious spirit of racism can convince you that your unrighteous anger towards racists is justified and cause you to act in a destructive manner against your racist offenders and yourself. Any destructive action that is driven by unrighteous anger can also result in self-destruction. This is why in Psalms 37:8 God cautions us against carnal anger even when directed at the wicked.

Carnal, unrighteous anger is fueled and driven by a demon spirit.

Like the vile spirit of Jezebel (1 King 19:1-2), the odious spirit of racism incites carnal anger and intimidation, and is also a destructive spirit in those whom it uses to perpetrate racism against others. Carnal, unrighteous anger is not part of your "new man" in Jesus Christ. It is fueled and driven by the devil through the demon spirit of anger. It is a self-destructive anger and has the potential to hurt and destroy us and others, including the individual(s) perpetrating racism.

The actions that you see racists exhibit are also driven by their carnal anger, which is why they lash out against others using vicious or malicious words and subtle or overt actions. Likewise, for those who are targeted by racism, the demon spirit of racism can fuel your response to racism with unrighteous carnal anger. This nasty spirit of racism achieves this by making you internalize the hurt from your daily painful experiences with racism and claim this hurt as your own rather than give it up to Jesus Christ (Matthew 11:28-30). The vile spirit of racism causes you to justify malicious anger based on the truth that racism is wrong.

When the devil fills you with unrighteous anger, he plants seeds of negative thoughts, actions and words within your heart that are not in line with God's Word. This is an old, often-used tactic of the devil where he presents you with an unjust situation or action against you, and at the same time, fuels you with unjust actions against the injustice that you face. Remember that the wrath of man does not appeal to the righteousness of God (James 1:19-20). Don't allow the devil to use racism to trick you with his lies. Jesus Christ declared the devil a liar and the father of ALL lies. Christ let us know that no truth can ever come from the evil one, the devil. Racism is one of the many lies of the devil

Carnal anger will cause you to forget God's faithfulness and sovereign power over racism.

against your soul (John 8:44). He, Christ called the devil one who comes to do nothing but to steal, kill and destroy (John 10:10a). Basically, the devil sets you up with carnal anger towards your racist offenders so that you will act in disobedience to God's Word (Romans 6:12)——and what justification does the devil present to you? Racism is wrong and you have every right to respond to it with unrighteous carnal anger. God's Holy Word says a categorical 'NO' to this justification. Racism is wrong, but God's Holy Word instructs you to respond to evil and injustice like racism with just actions backed with holy righteousness in Jesus Christ (1 Peter 3:8-9; Romans 12:17). So your response to racism should not be driven by carnal or unrighteous anger, rather by righteous constructive anger with the understanding that you have God's full backing against the foul spirit of racism. So when God is with you, who can be against you? (Romans 8:31)

The spirit of racism fuels us with unrighteous, carnal anger.

How can you distinguish between righteous and unrighteous anger within you? Unrighteous anger is driven by the negative spirit of anger, fueled by spiritual wickedness in high places, and it gears you up for a physical or verbal fight with negative emotions, thoughts, words or actions that are contrary to the nature of Jesus Christ that resides in you (Proverbs 15:18; Proverbs 22:24-25; Colossians 3:8-10). Carnal anger causes us to sin against God; for example, one may abuse or curse their racist offenders or plot vengeful and retaliatory actions against them; one could stay up all night thinking of ways to get back at their racist offenders (Proverbs 27:4; Proverbs 29:22).

When you harbor destructive anger, you are unable to pray to God or praise and worship Him, perform fasting as led by the Holy Spirit and calm your own spirit to be able to hear His voice, directions or strategies against the demon spirit of racism (Ephesians 4:26-27, 29-32). Carnal anger does not allow your spirit and soul to be calm and peaceful. Why? This is because it is in the calmness of your spirit and soul that God can and will give you a divine strategy for your own individual victory over your racist offenders.

Let go of every spark of anger within you.

We have to learn to be still and know that God is in control of all things, even in the midst of wickedness, oppression and injustice (Psalms 46:10). 2 Kings 6 presents to us the holy winning strategy that God gave to the Prophet Elisha on behalf of the King of Israel when the army of Aram came against them. In verse 15 when Elisha's servant became afraid and intimidated by what seemed like the show of force of the army and allies of Aram, Elisha said in verse 16 that "those" (God's invisible Army) with us (Elisha and his men) are more than "those" (human armies and allies of Aram) with "them" (the army of Aram): "Don't be afraid," the prophet answered:. "Those who are with us are more than those who are with them" (2 Kings 6:15-16). Elisha was referring to God's invisible Army that was warring on their behalf, though his servant could not see them with his natural eyes: "And Elisha prayed, "Open his eyes, LORD, so that he may see." Then the LORD opened the servant's eyes, and he looked and saw the hills full of horses and chariots of fire all around Elisha" (2 Kings 6:17). Elisha did not act in haste or anger; he was not afraid of the intimidating human army and allies of Aram; rather he sought God's divine strategy, which gave Elisha and the King of Israel victory over the army of Aram and his allies. David applied a similar spiritual strategy when he faced Goliath the Philistine (1 Samuel 17:45-47). By faith David relied on the power of God when he faced the giant Goliath—He was not intimidated by Goliath's giant

> *Carnal anger stirs up negative thoughts and emotions.*

stature and carnal strength—and God gave him supernatural power and the resounding victory over Goliath.

Neither the prophet Elisha nor David allowed unrighteous anger to rule them when they faced challenges greater than their human strengths could handle; rather they turned to God and relied on His supernatural strength for their triumph. Unrighteous anger triggers unrest and chaos within you. It is a quick, fiery and self-destructive anger that seeks to retaliate, curse or condemn offenders such as racist attackers. Unrighteous anger makes one forget God's faithfulness and sovereign power to demolish evil, including racism, on behalf of those who love Him (Psalms 91:14-15). Unrighteous anger makes no distinction between the human host of spiritual wickedness that is being used as a tool to perpetrate racism and the demon spirit of racism that is actually orchestrating racism using the human perpetrator.

The wrath of man does not produce the righteousness of God (James 1:20).

Unrighteous anger seeks to attack the human perpetrator of racism by engaging in energy-consuming, self-destructive and antagonistic carnal battles that cannot and will not lead to spiritual or mental victory over racism. When you are in a state of carnal anger, you become completely unreceptive to God's Word (not reassured by God's Word) and you will have no peace of mind; rather, chaos will dominate your

Carnal anger can cause you to act without thinking and double your suffering.

inner spirit and soul. Carnal anger stirs up negative thoughts and emotions and finally makes you get caught up in what seems like a whirlwind of negativity and regenerated and refueled anger. It will cause you to act without thinking through the consequences of your actions, and it will cause you to respond to racism in disobedience to God's Word—and be outside of God's guidance through His Holy Spirit. Again, remember that the wrath of man does not produce God's righteousness (James 1:19-20). Therefore, no form of unrighteous anger can cause God to release His holy power against evil, wickedness or injustice like racism on your behalf; but righteous anger (in prayer, thanksgiving and worship) can and will cause God to rise up on your behalf against your racist attackers (Psalm 68:1).

If you submit to the demon spirit of carnal anger, it will order your steps in response to racism to bring harm through you to yourself or others, including your racist offenders. Such harm could be by your own thoughts, emotions, words or actions. The evil spirit behind your carnal anger presents you with an unforgiving spirit, making you unable to forgive your racist offenders, so you would hold a grudge against those who perpetrate racism and would be unable to let go and let God take care of the racist offenders and the racist situation(s) that they are orchestrating against you (Psalms 46:10).

Unrighteous anger justifies itself and leads to your disobedience of God's Word, making you unreceptive to spiritual renewal by meditating on God's Word;

Racism can destroy your person by depositing carnal anger within you.

and as long as your are disobeying God's Word, you cannot receive Christ-rooted strategies on applying God's Word against racism. You must first be obedient to God's Word and only then will you be able to become spiritually refueled by His Word to resist evil such as racism (James 4:7). The odious spirit of racism will not flee when you too are acting in disobedience to God's Word—when you do not trust His Word and submit to it.

Ultimately, carnal anger makes the situation worse in the physical environment by your own negative carnal response to racism. It achieves nothing positive for you in either the spiritual or physical environment; rather, it fuels more negative response from your racist offenders towards you. Often it derails you from having a Christ-rooted focus, purpose, goals or plans for your own life. Your focus shifts solely to racism and its perpetrators, and they will drain you of your spiritual, mental and physical energy. Your carnal anger will cause delayed resolution of such situations, since God does not act on anyone's behalf when their soul is fueled with unrighteous anger. I emphasize a third time that the wrath of man does not produce or invoke the righteousness that God desires (James 1:20). He, God, waits for us to ask for His forgiveness for our unrighteous anger, and then seek His guidance on what to do about the racist situations we are encountering. Without a doubt, unrighteous anger will eventually lead to you being defeated by racism, both spiritually and mentally, if you remain in that negative state. You will not be able to receive God's awesome power through His Holy Spirit to release your soul from the stranglehold of the spirit of carnal, unrighteous anger.

> *Without a doubt, unrighteous anger will eventually lead to you being defeated by racism.*

When you are loaded with negative emotions, you are unable to acknowledge and trust God's supernatural power above all things. You may become angry with God; become angry with yourself; become angry with others or blame others; become anxious rather than have peace or spend quiet time with God in prayer, thanksgiving and worship; become vengeful and controlled by negative emotions that make you confrontational, judgmental and condemning toward racist offenders; become depressed, unhappy, doubting God's ability to handle racist situations on your behalf, or fearful of racists or racism; develop self-loathing or hatred for others; develop hostility towards racist offenders; become emotionally constrained; have decreased ability to concentrate or focus; manipulate others; become passively or overtly aggressive; detest or hate your racist offenders; become too quick to speak; or exhibit self-withdrawal from your physical surroundings.

Carnal or unrighteous anger will not heal your pain or hurt.

Carnal or unrighteous anger will not heal your pain or hurt and will not resolve or make right your negative experiences with racism. It will only continue to dissipate your positive spiritual energy and fuel your soul with self-condemnation, self-hatred or hatred for others.

It can consume your soul in burning flames of anger and frustration, and stifle your creative skills, and talents and blessings from God. Unrighteous anger can misdirect your soul and occupy your heart, mind, thoughts, emotions, will and resolve, distracting you from your own personal visions, aspirations, dreams, goals and ambitions. Unrighteous anger can sway you from God's awesome journey and blessings that are part of His purpose for your life and existence (Jeremiah 29:11). This is precisely why the foul spirit of racism fuels unrighteous, carnal anger within your soul; it wants to consume your entire physical being.

Be assured that unrighteous anger can double your suffering by keeping you in an aggravated state due to your frequent experiences with racism. Racism can destroy your person by depositing carnal, unrighteous anger within you, fueling

Let God's own vengeance fight for you against racism (Isaiah 66:13-16)

your constant angry responses to the daily challenges it poses for you. No racist action against you should ever be big enough to make you let go of your life's ambitions and God's journey and purpose for your life. Rather, any form of racism that you encounter should fuel you with more determination to become a success and to make God very proud of you. This means that if every racist action that is directed against you could fuel within you more determination to complete your life's journey with success, you could and would achieve your greatest goals.

Therefore, let go of every spark of unholy anger within you caused by racism; rather redirect and transform such unrighteous anger into righteous anger that births spiritual and material victory. When your spirit is in union with God's Holy Spirit, you become empowered and you will not see yourself as a "victim" of racism—and racists won't be able to use their negative actions to trigger or fuel unrighteous anger within you. You are a child of the Most High God—and you are surrounded by God's horses and chariots of fire and warring angels (Psalms 34:7, 35:5-6; 2 Kings 6:16-17; Daniel 10:9-15). Therefore, dark powers of racism will not overtake you because God's chariots of fire will bring His holy light into the darkness and burn up the fiery darts of racism.

Let go of any form of carnal anger and allow God's army of locusts to overtake the wicked activities of your racist offenders.

Let go of any form of unrighteous, carnal anger and allow God's army of locusts to overtake the wicked activities of your racist offenders (Joel 2:1-11). Let God's own vengeance fight for you against racism (Isaiah 66:13-

16). Let God's consuming fire burn up wickedness, oppression and injustice of racism that is fashioned against you (Hebrews 12:28-29). God has declared that vengeance is His, not ours (Deuteronomy 32:25; Romans 12:19), and so know that He will leave no evil and unrepentant deed unpunished. He will leave no unrepentant racist act unpunished.

Let God's consuming fire burn up wickedness, oppression and injustice of racism.

∞∞∞∞∞∞∞∞ ♦ ♦ ♦ ♦ ♦ ∞∞∞∞∞∞∞∞

Chapter Quiz

1. How can carnal, unrighteous anger derail you from God's purpose for your life?

   _____

2. When the wicked spirit of racism engineers racism against you, how can it use your response of carnal, unrighteous anger towards racism to cause you self-destruction?

   _____

3. Why does the evil spirit of racism try to load you up with carnal, unrighteous anger in response to racism?

   _____
   _____

4. If you are the one perpetrating racism against another person, why does the loathsome spirit of racism load you up with a carnal, unrighteous anger against another person or individuals of another race?

___

5. In whose image are you created? Can racism change this? Explain your answer.

___

6. In whose image is your neighbor who is of a different race, ethnicity or nationality created? Explain your answer.

___

7. Why does the loathsome spirit of racism use carnal anger as a negative spiritual tool of distraction against you who is the target of racism? Explain your answer.

___

∞∞∞∞∞∞∞∞ ♦ ♦ ♦ ♦ ♦ ∞∞∞∞∞∞∞∞

Reflections:

___

___

___

___

∞∞∞∞∞∞∞∞ ♦ ♦ ♦ ♦ ♦ ∞∞∞∞∞∞∞∞

Chapter 33 –

Unrighteous Anger is a Self-defeating Emotion

Daily experiences with racism can fuel intense anger within you. Unrighteous anger can fuel hatred, and hatred for even a racist and prejudiced person is wrong and a sin against God. Racism is wrong and is outlawed and overruled by God, and so is unrighteous anger toward anyone, even a racist individual. Ungodly anger, if not resolved or offloaded on a daily basis, can begin to grow roots of bitterness and resentment, and continue to fester within you, leading to a state of hidden and perpetual anger. Unrighteous anger

> *Racism is wrong and is outlawed and overruled by God.*

by itself is not a sin, but when anger is allowed to settle and grow within our soul, it becomes a source of sin: "In your anger do not sin: Do not let the sun go down while you are still angry, and do not give the devil a foothold." (Ephesians 4:26-7) So, we should let go of anger on a daily basis, start a new day afresh, without bearing a grudge against anyone; otherwise the devil will use your anger as a "foothold" to cause you to do what is wrong.

Sustained unrighteous anger gives the devil a foothold, a "place providing support for the foot in climbing or standing or a firm or secure position that provides a base for further advancement."[1] Sustained, deep-rooted, unrighteous, ungodly anger will work negatively on your emotions and can breed chaos, hatred, unforgiveness, bitterness, resentment and other hostile emotions in your soul. In response to racism, unrighteous anger harbored within us can be self-destructive to us and harmful to those who are the cause or targets of our anger. A constant state of unrighteous anger, although it may not always be outwardly obvious, is a serious 'spin-off' effect of racism. The consequences of such unrighteous anger can be destructive to both our racist offenders and to us who are the targets of racism.

God does not do business with an angry spirit.

Daily unrighteous anger can fester within your soul and build up to sustained and perpetual anger. Long-lasting unrighteous anger can transform itself into self-condemnation, self-dislike, self-hatred or bitter hatred for others, especially your racist attackers. A sustained state of anger can also lead to constant inner irritation of your soul. Therefore, sustained anger can leave you feeling conceited over nothing and angry about everything. Such is also the state of your prejudiced and racist attackers; their arrogance stemming from their illusion of superiority and power. Your unrighteous anger, on the other hand, is your belief in the illusion that you are a victim at the hands of a power-struck oppressor, and yet that power is not real since the only true power resides in and with God, your Creator and Originator. The power of God's Holy Spirit resides in you through Jesus Christ. What other power, seen or unseen, is greater than the power of God in you through Christ? Selah! (Pause and think about this!)

Daily unrighteous anger can fester within you.

You, too, could become like your prejudiced and racist attackers if you let anger rule you because of their negative actions towards you. Anger is wasted spiritual fuel and energy that should be directed into spiritually driven productivity through Jesus Christ, Who is the only

Way to God Himself. As you try to cope with racism on your own, the foul spirit of racism can cause you to develop an artificial inflated ego or carnal arrogance which is a false self-esteem and self-confidence. This is a highly self-destructive band aid approach to dealing with the oppression, wickedness and injustice of racism.

You see, the foul spirit of racism does not fuel Christ-rooted self-esteem and self-confidence which is immovable and unshakable in any situation. It is important to know that the degree or extent of your belief of your true worthiness in Jesus Christ fuels your true self-esteem, and this determines your level of true self-confidence. As one saying goes, "confidence of the spirit is far more valuable than arrogance of the flesh." Pride or arrogance of the flesh is not of God (1 John 2:16; Isaiah 2:12, 13:11, 23:9).

Confidence of the spirit is far more valuable than arrogance of the flesh.

Let your knowledge of your true worthiness in Christ become the foundation of your authentic self-respect, self-regard, self-appreciation, self-acceptance, self-esteem and self-confidence and not what your racist offender calls you or thinks of you. Do not allow carnal or unrighteous anger to fuel you with carnal pride or arrogance which in turn drives a false sense of carnal self-esteem and self-arrogance. This is an unfruitful product of the obnoxious spirit of racism which originates from the kingdom of darkness.

Workplace practices like not being hired for a position for which you are qualified, demeaning your achievements and accomplishments, being monitored by a subordinate or overly monitored by your supervisor or manager, not being promoted when you have worked hard and earned it; being denied earned bonuses; or being given unchallenging tasks and functions can be aggravating. Even subtle practices outside the workplace like being followed around in a merchandise store as a potential thief or receiving shabby treatment at a hotel "courtesy" desk can be unsettling and annoying. Experiences with racism are usually not pleasant and unrighteous anger is one of the natural human responses to them. It is your natural response to acts of unfairness, wickedness, injustice or wrongdoing. Nevertheless, though you may think that your unrighteous anger to racism is justified, when it is sustained, it can also be quite destructive of your person. When such anger is not directed towards a positive, creative focus, it can take you down a self-destructive path. Why? Well, misdirected anger keeps you focused on

Unrighteous anger is nothing but a self-defeating emotion.

the daily negative experiences that are the cause of your anger and which you have no control over, rather than on the things that you can control. For example, in the workplace where racially motivated actions can cause you to be denied promotion or career growth opportunities, this can cause sustained and perpetual unrighteous anger to reside within your spirit. Your positive focus should be securing another job, starting your own business or moving in whatever direction that God is leading you.

The spirit of unrighteous anger within your soul can frustrate you, give you a vengeful heart and over time make you embittered. You must understand that God does not align Himself with an embittered soul regardless of the root cause of the bitterness. God does not do business with an angry spirit; rather, you must present your anger to Him and let go of it in your soul. You must allow God to cleanse you of the unrighteous anger, and then He can use you to conquer the evil (racism) that once tried to defeat you through unrighteous anger. If you allowed God to act on your behalf, He would either cripple the actions of your racist offenders in your workplace and promote you despite their actions (Psalms 23:5) or take you to another

God's truth and justice will deliver you from the foul spirit of racism.

workplace where He has placed someone in authority to help you and to promote you (Psalms 23:1-4; Deuteronomy 8:18). In the meantime, your role is to continue to work hard and stay focused on what you ought to do in accordance with God's Word.

The power of unrighteous anger is so destructive to our own soul that God has asked us to release it from within us, hand over to Him the situation that is causing us anger and let Him be the Judge and the One to avenge our racist offenders. Sustained unrighteous anger fuels self-hate and hate for others. Anyone who harbors the spirit of self-hate, or hates another person, has a soul that is in a state of condemnation, though not a condemned soul that cannot be salvaged. So is anyone who allows the spirit of unrighteous anger to be sustained within his or her soul in response to racism.

Remain grounded in the Word of God and let Him minister to you circumstances with His flames of fire.

Now, don't be fooled by the devil. Don't be swayed by the devil's tricks by succumbing to unrighteous anger that is fueled by your experiences with racism. Prolonged unrighteous anger is nothing but a self-defeating emotion that can never give you victory over your situation. It is the power of God's Word and

His Holy Spirit through Jesus Christ that can give you real and sustained victory over any form of racial prejudice and discrimination.

As you face racism, remain grounded in the Holy Word of God and let Him minister to your circumstances with His flames of fire (Psalms 104:3-4; Hebrews 12:29). Let God's Holy Spirit teach you how to use God's Word to wage both defensive and offensive spiritual warfare against evil activities of the vile spirit of racism operating and manifesting through your racist offenders (Ephesians 6:10-18; 2 Corinthians 10:3-6).

God will build a safety net around you and no weapon of racism formed against you will prosper.

Believing and standing on God's Living Word will build a protective (Psalms 121:7-8, 84:11, 119:114, 116:11; Exodus 12:23) and victorious shield around you (Psalms 59:11; Psalms 91:1-3). God's truth and justice will deliver you from the foul spirit of racism and its nasty product racism, and build His spiritual fortress around you (2 Samuel 22:2; Jeremiah 16:19a; Psalms 9:9-10). God will solidify your position against racism and the foul spirit behind it (Jeremiah 17:7-8), and give you triumph over your arrogant racist offenders (Isaiah 2:11-17, Isaiah 3:11,13-15; Psalms 8:6; Psalms 119:134). God will build a safety net around you and no weapon of racism formed against you will prosper (Isaiah 54:17; Psalms 91, 18:10, 21-31, 29-25), because through Jesus Christ, God has already freed you from the power of the darkness of racism and its captivity (Colossians 1:13; Isaiah 61:1-3).

Through Jesus Christ, God has already freed you from the power of the darkness of racism and its captivity.

∞∞∞∞∞∞∞∞ ♦ ♦ ♦ ♦ ∞∞∞∞∞∞∞∞

Chapter Quiz

1. How can you distinguish unrighteous anger from righteous anger?

___

2. How can you counter ungodly or unrighteous anger that racism ignites within you?

___

3. Why is unrighteous anger destructive to your soul?

___

4. True or false: God has the power to free you from the evil spirit of racism and destroy any

___

effect of racism on your life. Explain your answer.

_____

∞∞∞∞∞∞∞ ♦ ♦ ♦ ♦ ♦ ∞∞∞∞∞∞∞

Reflections:

_____
_____
_____
_____

∞∞∞∞∞∞∞ ♦ ♦ ♦ ♦ ♦ ∞∞∞∞∞∞∞

Chapter Reference:
[1] www.thefreedictionary.com

CHAPTER 34 – Righteous Anger Against Racism

Righteous anger against racism is positive spiritual anger against racism. Righteous anger triggers a constructive course of action to right a wrong created by the injustice of evil such as racism. It is God-driven and it prepares your spirit and soul for active spiritual warfare through thanksgiving, prayer, worship, fasting and meditating on the absolute truth of God's Holy Word. It prepares you to take positive, constructive actions against any evil deed. Righteous anger is the kind of anger that Moses had with the oppression of God's people when he received God's instruction to go to the Pharaoh of Egypt to lead the Israelites out of Egypt.

Righteous anger keeps you in line with God's Word.

There was a difference between Moses' state of mind, in righteous anger (Exodus 3:7-21) and the unrighteous anger (Exodus 2:11-13) that he had when he killed an Egyptian. God's Holy Spirit within you can stir up your spirit and soul with righteous anger to keep you sober and vigilant (1 Peter 5:8-9) about racism so that it's evil effects do not permeate and cause destruction to your soul. The same righteous anger keeps you in line with God's Word to always walk on God's grounds of integrity (Ephesians 4:1), to be obedient to His Word and the law of the State as you face racism.

Even when the law of the State is unjust and unfair, your actions of protest against injustice must first align with God's Holy Word, and therefore, they must always be characterized by civil and never violent disobedience. There are many non-profit organizations that fight against unjust law of the State and they do so through intelligently well-organized, peaceful and non-violent protests, such as civil demonstrations and signature protests. Such organizations operate within the boundaries of God's Holy Word and the law of the State and they are able to galvanize the support of millions of people to declare their stand against injustice such as

"Indefinite silence, in the face of evil, advances evil."

racism.

One of the differences between righteous and unrighteous anger is that righteous anger is completely controlled within a person's thoughts, words, actions, and attitudes. It does not appear as malicious words or actions against another person, even against the person who perpetrates racist actions. It is holy anger that recognizes God's justice against injustice based on His Word, and it gives you Christ-rooted courage to resist evils like racism within the boundaries of God's Word and the law of the State.

Righteous anger offers a forgiving spirit while still praying against the foul spirit of racism.

There is a time to respond to evil like racism and there is also a time to be silent (Amos 5:13). During the time of silence you must apply righteous anger in prayer, worship and spiritual fasting, seeking God's divine direction and specific instruction to apply for victory over racism. However, a saying goes that "silence in the face of evil advances evil." This means that you cannot keep silent against racism indefinitely. During the time to act against racism, after you have prayed and sought God's divine instruction, strategy and direction, you cannot and should not be silent against any form of evil, including racism (Habakkuk 1:13). God will give you the right words to say (Exodus 4:11-12; Mark 13:11; Luke 21:14-15) and direct your steps and actions (Psalms 119:133; Psalms 37:23-24). Your actions against racism should be based on God's Holy Word and leading of the Holy Spirit so that you are assured of victory.

How can you distinguish between when you feel righteous or godly anger and when your response to racism is fueled by carnal, unrighteous anger within you? Christ-rooted or righteous anger is driven based on God's Word; it is a stirring of your spirit and soul to gear up for prayer, for spiritual warfare against racism. Spiritual warfare includes your daily reading of God's Word and meditation on it in prayer, praise and worship, and spiritual fasting. To successfully apply spiritual warfare, and by faith, you have to take on the full armor of God for your protection (Ephesians 6:10-18). Always, you have to believe and trust God's Holy Word as the Sword of the Spirit against the vile spirit of racism.

Righteous anger does not derail you from your God focus.

Godly anger does not cause us to sin against God; for example, righteous anger will not cause one to curse their racist offenders or plot vengeful or retaliatory schemes against them. Righteous anger is constructive anger that triggers prayer, worship and fasting, and meditation on God's Word, and it makes us seek to hear God's voice, directions and strategies on how to deal with the racist situations and other challenges that we face (2 Chronicles 20:1-29). Righteous or holy anger triggers constructive actions against injustice created by racism. In the meantime, we stay peaceful knowing that God's power remains in control of the situation (Psalms 46:10).

Righteous holy anger is not a quick and fiery anger (James 1:19) that seeks to cause self-destruction or to destroy others, but stirs us up to rest upon God's faithfulness and sovereign power to demolish racism. It makes a distinction between the human host

Righteous anger focuses you on the power of God's Word.

of spiritual wickedness who is being used as a tool to perpetrate racism and the demon spirit of racism that is actually orchestrating racism. Righteous anger confronts the unclean spirit of racism by taking on God's full armor in spiritual warfare that is activated and orchestrated in prayer, praise, worship and fasting. It is receptive to the calming and reassuring power of God's Word, which then refuels one's inner spirit and soul with peace and faith in God's sovereign ability to take care of the situation. Godly anger will not cause you to respond to racism outside of God's Word and guidance by His

Holy Spirit. Righteous holy anger allows God to order your steps in complete obedience to His Word, and it brings no harm through you to others, including the racist offenders, but relies upon and waits for God's directed holy justice. Holy anger allows you to take Holy Spirit-directed steps and implement God's willing and purpose-driven strategies for your personal victory over the foul spirit of racism. Basically, when you have God's backing, your strategies and plans will succeed (Proverbs 16:3).

Righteous anger offers a forgiving spirit, which is open to praying for the racist offenders, releasing them from the debt of their offense of perpetrating and perpetuating racism, and handing them entirely to God. When you are in a state of righteous anger, you

God has supernatural dominion over all things, including the foul spirit of racism.

are open to spiritual renewal by meditating on God's Word; to being spiritually refueled with God's Word; and to receiving Christ-rooted strategies for applying God's Word, His holy fire power against racism.

Righteous anger does not derail you from your God focus, purpose, goals or plans for your life. Your focus remains on God and His sovereign power to give you triumph through Jesus Christ over any adversity, including racism (1 John 5:4). Righteous anger applies a Christ-rooted approach, which usually leads to God demolishing the racist situation(s). His judgment of racism appears quickly—God either calms the spirit and soul of the racist offenders by casting out the demon spirit of racism in them if they are repentant, or if they are unrepentant He would remove such human hosts of the odious spirit of racism from the path of His children, and you are a child of the Most High God (Psalms 37, 91).

Righteous anger is constructive and always leads you to gaining spiritual and mental victory over racism, with no prolonged negative emotions or damaging effect on you. Righteous anger allows you to always acknowledge and believe that God's supernatural power has authority over all things, including racist practices and other offenses that are orchestrated against you. With righteous anger, you are not angry with God—you are able to praise Him; you are not angry with yourself; you can declare by faith God's

Righteous anger is constructive.

victory on your behalf over the racist situation(s); you are not angry with others (nor do you blame others); you are not anxious but very calm about the outcome of the situation; you are able to pray and spend quiet time with

God; you are not vengeful, controlled by negative emotions or confrontational; you would not judge or condemn your racist offenders—you are able to pray for them to be convicted by God for a positive change in their lives; you would not become depressed or unhappy; you would never doubt God's ability to handle racist situations on your behalf; you are not fearful of racists or racism; you would not develop self-loathing or hatred for others; you would not develop hostility towards the racist offenders; you would not be constrained emotionally; you would not experience a decrease in your concentration, or lack focus; you would not manipulate others to get your way; you would not become passively-aggressive; you would not become too quick to speak; you would not withdraw from your physical surroundings in fear, distaste or hatred of your racist offenders; or be defeated by your racist offenders. You will stand firmly on God's Word knowing that He, Christ Who is in you is greater than racism that exists around you (1 John 4:4). He has supernatural dominion over all things, including racism. You will believe that through Jesus Christ you have complete victory over the unclean spirit of racism and its nasty outgrowth racism (1 John 5:2-5).

Stand firm on God's Word!

Chapter Quiz

1. How can you apply James 1:19-25 when your encounters with racism cause you anger?

2. How can you distinguish between when you feel righteous or godly anger and when your response to racism is fueled by carnal or unrighteous anger within you?

3. How can you apply righteous anger to wage a spiritual battle against racism?

4. True or false: Righteous anger is not a quick and fiery anger that seeks to self-destroy or to destroy others. Explain your answer.

5. Why must you never be vengeful against your racist offenders?

6. True or false: God's supernatural power is above all things, including racist practices and offenses being orchestrated against you. Explain your answer.

Reflections:

_____

_____

_____

_____

CHAPTER 35 – Turning Unrighteous Anger into Righteous Anger

Is it possible for us to have a mixture of righteous and unrighteous anger? Absolutely—because we are a spirit expressed through a soul, both of which are encased within a physical form, a body, so our flesh sometimes fights against what God's Holy Spirit and His Holy Word directs us to do, that is, what is right before God: "For the flesh lusteth against the Spirit, and the Spirit against the flesh: and these are contrary the one to the other: so that ye cannot do the things that ye would" (Galatians 5:17 KJV).

God wants us to convert unrighteous anger to righteous anger.

Our experiences with racism can cause us legitimate anger, but God wants us to redirect such anger when it is unrighteous and carnal, to positive prayer, thanksgiving and worship, and actions. God wants us to convert any form of unrighteous, carnal anger we feel to righteous, holy anger, if we are to witness His divine victory. If the intensity of your unrighteous anger were so great that you were unable to pray, professing continuously the power of the Name and precious Blood of Jesus Christ in, around and over your life would break that anger and release your soul from it. When you feel unrighteous anger and cannot pray, you can recite Psalms 23 continuously until you feel the bout of unholy anger lift off your heart and mind. For those who are able to pray and also perform spiritual fast, this is a powerful and constructive way to break unrighteous anger, and if any anger remains at all, it would be righteous anger.

Racism can cause us legitimate anger.

If discussing racism makes you uncomfortable, it is a check for you to search deep within your heart for hidden fears, prejudices and racist beliefs, or unhealed or unresolved hurt inside you against others. Such negative emotions may be due to your past or present experiences with racism. Ask God's Holy Spirit to reveal these hidden or suppressed sins to you. On the other hand, if discussing racism brings out unrighteous anger from within you, this should be a check for you to ask God in prayer to cleanse your soul of the spirit of anger, unforgiveness, pain and hurt due to your experiences with racism.

God will fight your battles against racism.

Regardless of whether discussing racism makes you uncomfortable or angry, these are signals for you to begin to bolster God's Word within you to help you gain a spiritually renewed mind (Romans 12:2; Ephesians 4:23-24) so that the odious spirit of racism no longer controls your soul: your heart, mind, thoughts emotions, will and resolve; and your actions, behavior and personality.

God will give spiritual light to your eyes so you can see beyond racism (Proverbs 29:13; Psalms 119:105). If you are a target of racism, acknowledge before God that you are unable to battle racism by your own carnal power; acknowledge that without Christ you can do nothing (John 15:5). Once you acknowledge this, you will become open to receiving God's spiritual light of the truth of His Holy Word that will empower you to triumph over racism through Jesus Christ. Just as God gives illumination through Christ to those targeted by racism, He can give spiritual light to the eyes and minds of those who are perpetrating and perpetuating racism (Proverbs 29:13), so that they can begin to abhor their own racist attitudes. If we were racist and willing to repent and change, God would cleanse our souls of any remnants of the abhorrent spirit of racism and impart in us spiritual light, knowledge and wisdom to reject it always. As sinners, whenever we are willing to repent of our sins and turn from our wicked ways by the redeeming Blood of Jesus Christ, we receive forgiveness from God (2 Chronicles 7:14; Acts 2:38, 3:19).

Jesus Christ has given you the authority and power in His awesome Name to break the spirit of unrighteous anger. First, through Him, acknowledge in prayer before God

Christ has given you the authority to break unrighteous anger.

that your experiences with racism are stirring up unrighteous anger within you. In the powerful Name of Jesus Christ, ask God for forgiveness because you have allowed unrighteous anger to settle within you. Ask God to help you identify, through His Holy Spirit, all other hidden aspects of the unrighteous anger that you feel inside. In the precious Name of Jesus Christ, reject the unrighteous anger that you have toward prejudiced and racist individuals; your soul will begin to register your rejection of the unclean spirit of racism and not its human host. Renew your heart and mind with God's Holy Word through reading and meditating on it daily.

Through Jesus Christ, you have received forgiveness for your own sins and a spirit of forgiveness, so that you can extend forgiveness to your racist offenders.

Acknowledge the power of the precious Blood of Jesus Christ to release your soul from the stranglehold of unrighteous anger in response to racism. Thank God for giving you spiritual authority through Jesus Christ to bind unrighteous anger and loose it to destruction by His precious Blood (Matthew 18:18). Thank God for taking over the racist situation, delivering you from its clutches and giving you His victory and triumph over it.

God will fight your battles for you as He transforms you into a daily conqueror of racism.

God will fight your battles for you as He transforms you into a daily conqueror of racism (Exodus 14:14; Deuteronomy 1:30, 20:4; Romans 8:37). God will empower your spirit and direct your steps to His mighty purpose for your life's journey (Jeremiah 29:11). Through Jesus Christ, He has given you abundance of love, joy, peace and hope. You have His redeeming beams of light (Habakkuk 3:4), the glorious radiance of His rays of victory over every form of evil. If the spirit of anger, hostility, bitterness or resentment is in your soul, you must ask God to help you release it. If hatred is building up within your soul, you must ask God to help you get rid of it. If vengeance is seething within you, you must hand it over to God, as vengeance belongs to Him alone (Hebrews 10:30; Romans 12:19, Deuteronomy 32:35; Psalms 94:1). If unforgiveness lurks within your spirit, you must

In the Name of Jesus Christ, reject unrighteous anger.

ask God to help you to completely forgive all those who have offended and hurt you, including your racist attackers (Mark 11:25). Ask God's Holy Spirit to help you offer daily forgiveness to your racist offenders and He will empower you to do so.

We should pray daily and consciously work hard to rid our minds of thoughts of dislike, distaste, vengeance or even hatred, and any negative emotions created by our daily experiences with racism. If our soul is laden with negativity, we are unable to receive God's holy light, His brilliant rays of victory that smother the darkness of racism. It is God's awesome rays of victory, His beams of glory where His power is hidden (Habakkuk 3:4), that are the very key for our daily conquest of any form of evil, including racism.

Chapter Quiz

1. Is it possible for you to have a mixture of righteous and unrighteous anger? Explain your answer.

_____

2. How can you apply spiritual warfare against unrighteous anger?

_____

3. True or false: You must forgive your racist offenders. Explain your answer.

_____

4. True or false: The battle against the evil spirit of racism and racism is yours and not the Lord's. Explain your answer.

_____

5. True or false: The battle against the odious spirit of racism and racism is the Lord's and not yours. Explain your answer.

_____

6. True or false: If your soul is laden with negativity, you are unable to receive God's awesome power to deal the loathsome spirit of racism the spiritual blow that it deserves with the Holy Word of God. Explain your answer.

_____

∞∞∞∞∞∞∞∞ ♦ ♦ ♦ ♦ ♦ ∞∞∞∞∞∞∞∞

Reflections:

∞∞∞∞∞∞∞∞ ♦ ♦ ♦ ♦ ♦ ∞∞∞∞∞∞∞∞

Chapter 36 – The Power Over Racism: Philippians 4:8-9

God's beams of radiance and shining rays of victory within you, if you allowed them to do so, would redirect your anger stemming from your racist experiences to positive thoughts, words and actions that would lead to success despite the physical reality of racism around you. If you allowed God to perform His divine work in you, He would make you the head over racism (Deuteronomy 28:13) and take your fully energized spirit and soul to the mountaintop of victory that would leave your prejudiced and racist attackers in a carnal valley of defeat (Psalms 37). So don't

Meditate on Philippians 4:8-9

spend days, weeks or years complaining about your experiences with racism in the workplace or elsewhere; rather, work on discovering your hidden talents that may well take you out of that specific workplace to God's directed higher steps of achievement for you.

Being targeted by racist attitudes is aggravating because they attack your humanity. Nevertheless, be assured that when someone attacks your humanity, they attack God your Maker, and as such they also commit a sin against God, the Creator of all humanity (Isaiah 41:11). God promises you in Isaiah 54:15 that whoever attacks you does so without His permission and will fail. If you stayed focused on God and abided by His Word, He would give you sure victory over your racist attackers (Deuteronomy 1:21, 20:4; Psalms 44:6-8, 60:11-12; John16:33; Romans 8:28; Hebrews 12:3; James 4:7-8; Revelation 12:11). Therefore, if your thoughts and actions remained right and just, that is, in alignment with God's Word, He would fight your daily battles for you (Exodus 14:14; Deuteronomy 1:30, 20:4). Knowing this, then, you must focus your mind on all things that are true, proper and honorable, admirable, worthy, praiseworthy, moral, principled, good, respectable, and upright; think about things that are pure

Focus your faith on God's supernatural power over racism.

and lovely (Philippians 4:8-9)—racism is none of these things, so don't dwell on your experiences with racism.

Focus your faith on God's supernatural ability to take you to higher grounds of triumph over racism and its evils. The Christ-rooted response to racism is to focus on fortifying your heart and mind with the conquering power of God's Word revealed to you by His Holy Spirit through Jesus Christ. Your focus should be on

Trust and obey God's Holy Word for your victory over racism.

tapping into God's brilliant rays of victory within you and rising above the carnal designs of racism, to God's directed mountaintop of victory for you (Psalms 37, 91). You can achieve this through daily close communication with God through prayer, praise, and worship, and frequent spiritual fasting. Ask God for His divine knowledge, understanding and wisdom from His Holy Word, and to direct every step and action that you take daily (Psalms 37:23). The worst revenge that you can have over your prejudiced and racist attacker is to have first spiritual victory and then material (health and wealth) success in your life. Remember that it is God (and not racists) Who gives you the power to get wealth (Deuteronomy 8:18).

By beginning to trust in and obey God's Holy Word and follow the guidance of the Holy Spirit of God Who dwells within you, new horizons will begin to unfold in your life as God begins to show you great and mighty things that you do not know (Jeremiah 33:3). You will become a modern day Jabez (1 Chronicles 4:10), if you learn to trust completely in the belief that our Lord God, the Creator of Heaven and Earth—all things above, below and around you, and the entire universe, has the power to protect you from racism and demolish the evils of racism around you. In prayer, cry out to God like Jabez did: "And Jabez called on the God of Israel, saying, Oh that thou wouldest bless me indeed, and enlarge my coast, and that thine hand might be with me, and that thou wouldest keep me from evil, that it may not grieve me! And God granted him that which he requested." (1 Chronicles 4:10 JKV) Ask God to bless and enlarge your territory beyond the constraints created by the vile spirit of racism and its nasty outgrowth racism. Ask God to give you fresh anointing and keep you from evil so you won't be a racist tool against anyone. Ask God to make you a blessing to many people regardless of race, ethnicity or nationality. Trust that through His grace and

Take your focus off your racist offenders

guidance rooted in Jesus Christ, you, too, can become a conqueror of your daily challenges. Racism is no exception—it is a daily challenge that you must gain spiritual victory over—there is no other alternative, since defeat is not God's option for you.

With undoubting faith, God will give you His rays of hope and courage. Then He will take you from hate to Love, from sorrow and despair to Joy, from ashes to beauty, from a spirit of heaviness to a garment of praise, from feelings of defeat to conquests, from bondage by fear and anxiety to freedom of your mind, from yesterday to the present (now) and the future (by faith), from failure to success, from being a victim of racism to being a solid conqueror of it and victor over it, from disgrace to grace, from indignity to dignity, from valleys to triumphs, and finally, He will permanently illuminate you with His rays of victory and put your racist attackers to shame. You need to draw from God's Holy Word His spiritual power on a daily basis—then you would know and experience His mighty works with quiet splendor—your life is one of His mighty works!

You are one of God's mighty works in Jesus Christ!

If you believed and knew that your life were truly one of God's mighty works in Jesus Christ, then you should also know that the evil spirit of racism has no legal authority in and over your life. You must know and believe this and never take yourself or any other human for granted regardless of race, ethnicity or nationality. Recognizing that every human is one of God's mighty works means that within you, feelings of hatred, disdain, superiority or inferiority must never reside. Know and recognize that because you too are one of God's mighty works, His purpose for you is mighty, and your potential, talents and abilities from Him are also mighty. To know all of this is to have true spiritual knowledge and revelation from God's Holy Word and through His Holy Spirit, Who dwells within you.

Now, take a step of faith in Jesus Christ and move beyond racism to reach for wonderful things that God has in store specifically for you (Jeremiah 29:11). Do not focus your energy on your past or present experiences with racism. Through the combination of your faith, Word knowledge and anointing of God's Holy Spirit through Jesus Christ, you will become empowered by His Word to move the evil spiritual mountains of racist attacks directed against you. Such mountains will be demolished and removed from your path in the mighty Name of Jesus Christ (Mark

Allow God's Holy Spirit to help you to discover your hidden talents.

11:23-25).

Focus your faith on God's Holy Word that will empower you to run and complete the journey of your life by His holy grace—Jesus Christ Himself. You need to stay focused on the Prize, the high calling of God through Jesus Christ. Take your focus off your racist offenders and press on towards the mark for this Prize

You need to stay focused on the Prize, the high calling of God through Jesus Christ.

to which God has called you through Christ (Philippians 3:14). Focus on the truth and holy power of Philippians 4:8-9 which enriches and empowers your mind with power thoughts against racism, and suffocates the negativity of racists and racism. The illuminating power of God's holy Light, His Holy Word, which beams His brilliant rays of victory in you and for you (Psalms 119:105), will through His Holy Spirit, bring a rebirth of your spirit and start the process of renewing and refreshing your soul (Romans 12:2; Ephesians 4:23-24; Acts 3:19).

Chapter Quiz

1. How can you apply Philippians 4:8-9 to rise above racism and the spirit of racism on a daily basis?

   _____

2. How can you apply Philippians 4:8-9 as a power-thought against racism?

   _____

3. Why must you resist complaining about racism and take positive, constructive steps both in prayer and in the natural realm as directed by God's Holy Spirit?

   _____

4. Is there positive spiritual power in complaining about any problem or challenge that you face, including racism?

   _____

5. Why does the devil encourage you to complain about racism rather than to tackle it spiritually with prayer and in the natural realm with positive, constructive actions? Explain your answer.

   _____

6. What does Jeremiah 29:11 say about God's plan for your life? Can the spirit of racism change this;

yes or no? Explain your answer.

7. Why must you not focus your energy on your past or present experiences with racism? What should you focus your energy on, and how should you go about it? Explain your answer.

∞∞∞∞∞∞∞ ♦ ♦ ♦ ♦ ♦ ∞∞∞∞∞∞∞

Reflections:

∞∞∞∞∞∞∞ ♦ ♦ ♦ ♦ ♦ ∞∞∞∞∞∞∞

Chapter 37 – God Sees and Understands Your Pain and Anger

Someone ("Evan") once wrote me an angry email telling me that I was "stupid and naïve" to think that praying and believing God and His Holy Word is sufficient for me or anyone to gain victory over racism. This young man, "Evan", was very angry and frustrated. He said that he lived in a racist environment and this place had a celebrated tradition of racism for centuries. He explained that generations of his family (his parents, grandparents and great grandparents) lived through the cruelty and injustice

> *Jesus Christ set you free from the kingdom of darkness of racism.*

of slavery and racism, and God had remained silent. He said that he often wondered why God had not acted against racists and racism. "Evan" was cynical and asked me why God had not stopped racism in his hometown where he lives. I immediately recognized that "Evan" had a wounded spirit

God sees all wicked, evil, unfair and unjust activities and we must give account of all our actions (Hebrews 4:12-13).

and no longer believed in God's supernatural power and dominion over all things, including racism. "Evan" in his pain had forgotten or never knew that it was God's response to the prayer, worship and cries of his slave ancestors that triggered the chain of events which led to the emancipation of slaves and the end of the Transatlantic Slave Trade in the Western world. Though God waited patiently for centuries for the wicked slave masters to end their evil ways, when His set time of expiration of their wicked ways came, He declared "destroy them" and it happened: "The eternal God is thy refuge, and underneath are the everlasting arms: and he shall thrust out the enemy from before thee; and shall say, Destroy them" (Deuteronomy 33:27).

"Evan" no longer believed that God was, is and will remain the God of justice and righteousness. He did not trust that God's unlimited loving kindness was too boundless to be indifferent to his hurt and pain from his experiences with racism. It may appear to some that if God does not condone unrighteous or sustained anger towards prejudiced and racist individuals, then He must not appreciate the mental or physical pain of those targeted by racism. The fact is that not only does God understand such pain, He feels it with all those who are targeted by racism or any other form of oppression or injustice (Exodus 3:7-10; Isaiah 53:3-11, 61:1-3;), and He will deliver them at His appointed time just as He freed the people of Israel from slavery in Egypt (Exodus 14:13-14; Luke 4:18-19). Jesus Christ has liberated us from the power of all forms of spiritual evil domination.

Racism has no real power over your life.

"Evan," you and I need to know, understand and believe that God is truly on our side; therefore, no one can be against us (Romans 8:31). God offered His Son Jesus Christ as a sacrificial Lamb for our sins. He, Christ, endured scorn, vile injustice, extreme physical torture and pain in order to offer all humanity God's free gift of salvation, and for us to be free of the stranglehold of the devil (John 3:16; Isaiah 53:3-11, 61:1-3): "But he was wounded for our transgressions, he was bruised for our iniquities: the chastisement of our peace was upon him; and with his stripes we are healed" (Isaiah 53:5).

Any racist assault on you is really an assault on God Himself (1 Corinthians 8:12). God understands and feels the pain of any kind of unfairness and injustice, including the wickedness of racism. He allowed His Son and the Savior of the World, Jesus Christ, to go through the worst kind of cruelty, hatred, false accusation, humiliation, victimization, human indignity, persecution, and physical torture, and finally, crucifixion at the hands of humans whom Jesus Christ had blessed and cured of illnesses, fed when they were hungry, and set free from demonic possession. Nonetheless, through the pain and suffering that Jesus Christ endured, came his death and glorious resurrection, and He brought eternal salvation to all humanity, that is, to anyone who will believe in Him and accept Him as their Lord and Savior (John 3:16). So, you see that God Who is the only true God—the triune God, is the true God of purpose, and whatsoever He allows is for a reason that at the moment may be beyond comprehension by our natural or carnal minds. However, either later in life, or when we transition from mortal to immortal and meet face-to-face with God, we will come to comprehend his glorious

> *God wants to help you resolve the hurt and anger within you.*

reason for allowing what might seem now like a tragic event to occur.

Still, at God's set time, at His appointed time, He will declare "destroy" to the vile spirit of racism and its nasty outgrowth racism. Why? He, Jehovah God, has set a date of expiration for the odious spirit of racism that orchestrates and operates racism in willing human hosts (racists) (Deuteronomy 33:27).

If you listen to God's Holy Word, He will become an Enemy and Adversary to your racist attackers and enemies.

In the meantime, God has given us the power through Jesus Christ to trample scorpions and serpents, such as the odious spirit of racism, and over all the power of the enemy, the devil (Luke 10:17-19).

God is not blind, deaf or insensitive to anyone or any situation. He, our Father, Lord God, monitors all activities taking place on Earth, both good and bad (2 Chronicles 16:9a; Zechariah 4:10b). He sees all the actions of wicked, evil, unfair and unjust individuals (2 Chronicles 16:9; Hebrews 4:12-13), and your experience with racism is one of many such deeds. The truth is that if you stood and acted based on God's Holy Word, He would become an Enemy to those who are your enemies and oppose those who oppose you (Exodus 23:22-23; Psalms 35). But if you fight the injustice of racism with your own unjust actions and vile words, doubt God's omnipotent power over the spirit of racism and racism, He will not back you and you will lose the daily spiritual battles and warfare. This means that

God wants to break the cycle of anger and hatred.

you will also be defeated by your racist offenders. The true foundation of your fight against any form of injustice should be built on scriptural principles, on the solid Rock Jesus Christ, Who is the eternal Rock of God of all Ages (Luke 6:47-48; Isaiah 26:3-4; 1 Corinthians 10:1, 4).

Therefore, when dealing with racism and its unseen spiritual forces behind it, we must be still (Psalms 46:10) and wait upon God even as we pray spiritual warfare against them (Ephesians 6:10-18). Let us pray as King David prayed in Psalms 37:1-15: "Fret not thyself because of evildoers, neither be thou envious against the workers of iniquity. For they shall soon be cut down like the grass, and wither as the green herb. Trust in the LORD, and do good; so shalt thou dwell in the land, and verily thou shalt be fed. Delight thyself also in the LORD: and he shall give thee the desires of thine heart. Commit thy way unto the LORD; trust also in him; and he shall bring it to pass. And he shall bring forth thy righteousness as the light, and thy judgment as the noonday. Rest in the LORD, and wait patiently for him: fret not thyself because of him who prospereth in his way, because of the man who bringeth wicked devices to pass. Cease from anger, and forsake wrath: fret not thyself in any wise to do evil. For evildoers shall be cut off: but those that wait upon the LORD, they shall inherit the earth. For yet a little while, and the wicked shall not be: yea, thou shalt diligently consider his place, and it shall not be. But the meek shall inherit the earth; and shall delight themselves in the abundance of peace. The wicked plotteth against the just, and gnasheth upon him with his teeth. The LORD shall laugh at him: for he seeth that his day is coming. The wicked have drawn out the sword, and have bent their bow, to cast down the poor and needy, and to slay such as be of upright conversation. Their sword shall enter into their own heart, and their bows shall be broken."

Offload your anger daily.

Despite racism that you may be dealing with, sustained anger fueled by your emotional pain, which leads to hatred for those who are prejudiced against you, is wrong and will come under judgment by God. One wrongdoing does not justify another. Racist and prejudiced individuals use their human, earthly power to do evil and not good; they hate rather than love others who are of a different race, ethnicity or nationality. Therefore, they (not you) shall bring destruction upon themselves. God promises us that whatever a man sows, he shall also reap (Galatians 6:7). Racists will reap the vile spirit of racial hostility and hatred that they sow and act upon, and without genuine repentance, they shall surely reap God's holy justice against them. Allow God to avenge your racist offenders and give you His holy justice in place of racial injustice (Romans 12:19). Allow God to direct your steps through His Holy Word and Holy Spirit (Psalms 32:8, 37:23; 119:105).

Yes, God understands "Evan's" pain, and yours and mine. He, Almighty Father, understands all of our daily pain, including those inflicted by the oppression, inequity and injustice of racial prejudice and discrimination. Every day He feels and shares your pain with you; He sees and understands how your hurt and pain from your experiences with racism can aggravate you. However, He also sees how destructive the aggravation can be (Psalms 37:8) and that is why He asks you to offload that hurt and anger on a daily basis. God wants to help you resolve the hurt and anger within you by asking you to let go of your burdens and hand them over to Him daily. (Matthew 11:28-30)

Anger and hatred can destroy your soul.

God wants to turn your wounded and defeated spirit into His victorious battle axe (Jeremiah 51:20-23), if you allow Him to do so.

God knows that angry people can hurt other people even when the cause of their anger is justified. God knows that other angry people perpetrate and perpetuate daily acts of racial prejudice and discrimination against you. Fear, anger and hatred fuel racist actions, which in turn fuel more fear, anger and hatred from those who are the targets of those actions. God wants you to break the cycle of fear, anger and hatred towards everyone who has hurt you (Psalms 37:27-28). Fear, anger and hatred can destroy your soul and can cause you to hurt other people either by your words or your actions. This is why God does not do business with fearful, angry or hateful people. However, He is willing to Work with you to rid you of your fear, anger, bitterness, resentment, hatred and vengeance. He will fortify you with His Holy Spirit to help you overcome adversities such as racism. He will redirect your fear, anger, bitterness, resentment, hatred and vengeance to righteous emotions, words and actions, and move your skills, talents and potentials in the right,

> *You are a child of the Most High God and racism has no real power over your life.*

positive direction for victory over the same obstacles that racism set before you. So, when you encounter racism, tune into God's "Spiritual Station," His Holy Word, and let His Holy Spirit empower you with God's Living Word through Jesus Christ Who has given you victory and dominion over the adversities you face such as racism (John 16:33; 1 John 5:4).

Let God's Word remind you that as a child of the Most High God, racism has no real power over your life; only your mind can believe that it does. Let His Holy Spirit caution you not to believe the illusion of carnal power that racists boast about and operate on.

Racism has no real power over your life.

Let the anointing power of God's Word fill you with renewed, conquering power through Jesus Christ. The Holy Spirit also refreshes you with the truth that God has freed you completely from any power of darkness (Colossians 1:13), and racism is no exception. Learn this practice to tune out any racist situation in your mind and tune into the "Power Station" of God's Holy Spirit within you. Above all, let God's Holy Word and Holy Spirit remind you that life is but for a fleeting moment—today we are here and tomorrow we are gone forever (Ecclesiastes 1:1-11)—so that you don't waste your precious time and talents dwelling on the negative, untruthful spirit of racism.

Arise and shine for your light has come and the glory of God is upon you through Jesus Christ (Isaiah 60:1). Rise up today and call the evil spirit of racism what it is—a bogus lie of the devil (John 8:44)—and declare yourself victorious over this foul spirit and its unfruitful product of racism (1 John 5:4; Revelation 12:11).

Arise and shine for your light has come and the glory of God is upon you through Jesus Christ (Isaiah 60:1).

Chapter Quiz

1. What is Luke 4:18-19 and Isaiah 60:1 saying about Jesus Christ liberating you from oppression? How can you apply this Scripture to receive deliverance from the foul spirit of racism? Explain your answer.

_____

2. What does Isaiah 53:3-11 say about what Jesus Christ has done for you?

_____

3. True or false: Because racism is evil, God is against racism. Explain your answer.

___

4. True or false: Because racism attacks your humanity, it attacks God, Who is your Creator. Explain your answer.

___

5. True or false: The Holy Spirit has the power to refresh you with the truth that God has freed you completely from any power of darkness (Colossians 1:13), and racism is not an exception. Explain your answer.

___

6. True or false: God wants you to break the cycle of fear, anger and hatred towards everyone who has hurt you, including your racist offenders. Explain your answer.

___

∞∞∞∞∞∞∞∞ ♦ ♦ ♦ ♦ ∞∞∞∞∞∞∞∞

Reflections:

___
___
___

___

Chapter 38 – Racism Causes Self-Hatred Through Mind Distortion

Self-hatred is a self-denigrating, highly destructive consequence of a distorted mind—one that lacks true knowledge of God's Holy Word (Hosea 4:6)—one who is ignorant about his or her true image in God (Genesis 1:27). As an example, there goes a story (as told by my sister whom we fondly call "Chichi", a sociologist and non-profit philanthropist) about a very wealthy grandmother who had a mixed-race daughter who in turn married a man of another race and had a child. The

When you deny who you are in Jesus Christ, you deny God.

grandmother loved the granddaughter and developed a great bond with her. Everyone assumed that if ever anything were to happen to the grandmother, the granddaughter would inherit all the grandmother's worldly goods because of their very close relationship. One day, the grandmother overheard a conversation between her granddaughter and some of her friends and she was shaken to her bones. The granddaughter was asked if it was true that she was of a certain race, and she denied it vehemently. This conversation greatly depressed the grandmother, but she never let her granddaughter know that she had overhead her conversation with her friends. The grandmother later died, and when her will was read, everyone was shocked because she left everything she owned to charity with a little note for her granddaughter, which read: "You cannot inherit from me if I do not exist."

"You cannot inherit from me if I don't exist."

When you deny who you are, then you deny God, in Whose Image you were created; to deny who you are in Jesus Christ is to deny God's Holy Spirit within you and God the Father Himself. If you are ashamed to accept, receive and acknowledge Jesus Christ, then you cannot inherit His Father's eternal Kingdom (Matthew 10:32-33; Mark 8:38; Luke 9:26; John 5:24-27). Only those who by faith accept, receive and acknowledge Jesus Christ in their heart and confess with their mouth that He is their personal Lord and Savior Who rose from the dead by the power of God's Holy Spirit, will overcome the world (John 3:16; 1 John 5:4). So, you,

God's grace to us through Christ is sufficient for you!

1, and all other believers in Jesus Christ shall inherent God's eternal Kingdom. Through Christ, you have been empowered for victory over all demonic influences in the world (John 16:33; Luke 10:17-19). So, you can defeat racism in your neighborhood, school, workplace, borough, district, county, state, country and in the world by your faith in God through Jesus Christ (1 John 5:4). However, you cannot achieve this with self-hatred or hatred for others.

A lack of Christ-rooted knowledge, understanding and wisdom blinds your mind and leads you down self-destructive paths and ways. Self-hatred stems from a lack of authentic spiritual knowledge, which originates from not having true knowledge of God, in whose perfect Image we exist. Basically, not having authentic knowledge of God, in Whose Image we are all created, is the primary contributing factor to self-hatred. Many other factors can feed or contribute to self-hatred, and oftentimes at the conscious level, an individual may be unaware that they are developing a negative sense of self in their subconscious mind. Self-hatred or self-dislike can appear as a lack of self-acceptance; partial or complete self-rejection; a yearning to be validated by others and lack of fulfillment of this yearning; comparison of yourself to others; qualification of yourself by the definition imposed by others; acceptance of the low "value" placed on yourself by others; and belief in the hierarchy of inferiority or superiority based on race, ethnicity, nationality or any other factor or reasoning. These are by no means the only factors that can feed or contribute to dislike or rejection of who you are. In the absence of true spiritual knowledge, your own spirit can become dormant and asleep, allowing negative fortresses, strongholds and spin-off and lingering effects to evolve and grow within your soul, and all of these contribute to self-hatred.

To reject yourself is to reject the One who created you.

The negative feeling of self-distaste, self-dislike or self-hatred injected into your soul by racism, may be hidden deep in your subconscious mind, and at the same time, it could appear in your conscious mind and impact your thoughts, emotions, actions, attitude, behavior, character and personality. Know that accepting lies of the evil spirit of racism can also lead to acceptance of the spirit of self-distaste, self-dislike or self-hatred that it offers; the latter functions as a remote control by which the obnoxious spirit of racism could destroy you. Also, the vile spirit of racism could also implant racial hostility in your heart against other individuals or groups of people. Now, you see yet another reason why you must continue to resist letting the wicked spirit of racism enter into your heart, and mind to control your emotions and thoughts.

To allow self-hatred to reside within you is to reject God's love in and for you. To reject who you are is to reject the Triune God: God the Father, the One Who created you, and God the Son Jesus Christ and the Holy Spirit Who dwell within you. To reject yourself is to reject God's Kingdom power within you through His Son Jesus Christ Who is your Lord and Savior. To reject yourself is to acknowledge that you lack authentic spiritual knowledge which gives rise to a lack of true self-knowledge, and this indicates a deep spiritual crisis within you and an urgent need for knowledge, understanding and wisdom of God's Holy Word with the guidance of His Holy Spirit Who lives in you. If you

> *To reject who you are is to reject God the Father, the One Who created you, His Son Jesus Christ and Holy Spirit Who dwell within you.*

chose to remain in the cycle of self-hatred, you would leave room within your soul for not just self-hatred but also hatred for others. However, if you allowed God to break the cycle of unhealthy, ungodly deposits of racism, such as, fear, bitterness, resentment, anger, hostility, and hatred within you, He would give you renewed inner spiritual power to transcend any form of racism that is directed against you.

Jesus Christ is "the way, the truth, and the life; no one goes to the Father except by me" (John 14:6). He, Christ, is the only Mediator (1 Timothy 2:5) and the only authentic Way and Truth to God the Father. It is through Christ that we receive eternal life. By your mustard seed faith, start by opening the door to your heart to Christ and accept Him to be your Lord and Savior. Through daily prayer and meditation on God's Holy Word, receive revelation and anointing power from His Holy Spirit, and begin to dwell in the "secret place" with God where you will enter into His awesome, holy presence (Psalms 91:1-3; John 4:24) that keeps you soaring above racism and other adversities through Christ. He, Christ, is God's perpetual grace to you, me and all who have received Him in their hearts.

> *Jesus Christ is "the way, the truth and the life; no one gets to the Father except through me" (John 14:6).*

God's grace through Christ is more than sufficient for you to gain daily victory over racism: "And he said unto me, My grace is sufficient for thee: for my strength is made perfect in weakness. Most gladly therefore will I rather glory in my infirmities, that the power of Christ may rest upon me." (2 Corinthians 12:9)

Chapter Quiz

1. True or false: When you deny who you are, then you deny God, in Whose Image you were created. Explain your answer.

   _____

2. What does self-hatred mean to you? Explain your answer.

   _____

3. True or false: Accepting the lies of the evil spirit of racism about who you are not, could also lead to the acceptance of the spirit of self-disdain, self-dislike, self-loathing or self-hatred. Explain your answer.

   _____

4. What is true spiritual knowledge? Explain your answer.

   _____

5. What is true self-knowledge? Explain your answer.

6. True or false: To allow residence of self-hatred within you is to reject yourself and the Triune God Who created you in His own Image. Explain your answer.

∞∞∞∞∞∞∞∞ ♦ ♦ ♦ ♦ ♦ ∞∞∞∞∞∞∞∞

Reflections:

∞∞∞∞∞∞∞∞ ♦ ♦ ♦ ♦ ♦ ∞∞∞∞∞∞∞∞

Chapter 39 – Self-Hatred Fosters Self-Incarceration

Self-incarceration is a form of self-confining or self-imprisoning and is a byproduct of self-hatred, self-loathing, self-distaste or self-dislike. In a practical sense, self-incarceration is locking up your mind and shutting off any or all possibilities of advancement and achievement. When you are under self-incarceration, you forget that you were made in the Image of an awesome God; you are unable to see your potentials and abilities; rather, you see yourself through the negative views of others or yourself and of defeat, and your knowledge and perception of your true self in Jesus

Self-incarceration is a byproduct of self-hatred.

Christ becomes warped and unreal in your mind. Your soul becomes buried under hopelessness and helplessness, and in your mind, you declare yourself a powerless victim of your circumstances. By sheer ignorance of God's Holy Word and the power you have received through Jesus Christ and the Holy Spirit Who dwell within you (Ephesians 1:18-23), you fall prey to spiritual ignorance and a lack of true self-knowledge (Hosea 4:6). The consequences of a lack of true spiritual knowledge in Jesus Christ are quite grave. You can go down a spiral staircase of self-dislike, self-rejection, self-hatred, low self-esteem and low self-confidence.

Authentic spiritual empowerment will give you true self-knowledge.

You become constantly surrounded by the aura of negativity that will never translate into spiritual or material success. You become like a toy in the filthy hands of the foul spirit of racism and its willing human recruits.

Self-incarceration is an unfruitful negative product of self-hatred. Self-hatred is a rejection of who you are in Jesus Christ that ultimately translates into rejection of yourself. To reject yourself by internalizing the lies of any prejudiced and racist individual is to validate the lies of the vile spirit of racism through that individual by surrendering the power of your own spirit to them. Ironically, prejudiced and racist individuals flaunt a false air of superiority, but in reality these individuals often feel a deep sense of fear, self-doubt, low self-esteem and low self-confidence.

True spiritual knowledge in Jesus Christ births true self-knowledge.

Their feelings of unworthiness propel them to treat others badly as their own misguided way of projecting outward their inferiority complexes, fears and insecurity as false power, control or superiority. Authentic spiritual empowerment will give you true self-knowledge that will reveal to you the insecure state of prejudiced and racist individuals. Know that it is the will of God for you to rise far above your racist offenders first in your spirit, and then in your soul; that is, your heart, mind, thoughts, emotions, will and resolve. Then you can clearly see the foolishness of their racist actions.

Sometimes, the thick white cloud of deceit that manifests as self-hatred, self-loathing, self-distaste or self-dislike, and appears as self-incarceration and self-limitation, is such a strong force over you that you are no longer in a spiritually empowered state to remove the cloud by yourself. When you are in this spiritual canyon, you are actually in a carnal valley of spiritual defeat, and it is time for you to open your spirit and soul to the power of the Holy Spirit of God Who dwells within you. You need to call out your desire to God's anointing Holy Spirit and express your willingness to have the thick midst of self-hatred, self-loathing, self-distaste or self-dislike, removed from your heart. Ask God for true spiritual knowledge and divine wisdom. God gives wisdom to those who ask Him for it (James 1:5; Proverbs 2:6, 9-11).

The ability to apply Christ-rooted knowledge comes from true spiritual wisdom. If you lack true spiritual knowledge and understanding ask God for it (Jeremiah 33:3). He will hear your cry, and in His divine Way He will illuminate your heart and mind with His supernatural enlightenment and wisdom. This knowledge and understanding will help you burst through the thick white cloud of limitation over and around you and you will gain both spiritual and material victory over your situation.

To reject yourself is to validate the lies of the vile spirit of racism.

With true spiritual knowledge of God, you will realize that internalizing the negative attitudes and lies of racists, means accepting spiritual defeat from those who are already spiritually defeated. The individuals to whom you are relinquishing the power of your spirit and soul are completely powerless spiritually and are themselves victims of self-hatred. This is why outwardly they project their self-hatred through prejudiced and racist actions toward others. Having true knowledge of God's Holy Word means that there is no room within you for self-hatred, self-loathing, self-distaste or self-dislike that appears as self-incarceration and self-limitation, or as hatred for anyone, including your racist offenders.

> *There is no room within you for self-hatred, self-loathing, self-distaste or self-dislike that appears as self-incarceration and self-limitation.*

∞∞∞∞∞∞∞∞ ♦ ♦ ♦ ♦ ∞∞∞∞∞∞∞∞

Chapter Quiz

1. What is self-incarceration? Explain your answer.

2. True or false: To reject yourself by internalizing the lies of any prejudiced or racist individual(s) is to validate the lies of that individual(s) by surrendering the power of your own spirit to them. Explain your answer.

3. True or false: The feelings of unworthiness that prejudiced and racist individuals have propel them to treat others badly as their own misguided way of projecting the false belief of superiority. Explain your answer.

___

4. What is true spiritual wisdom? Explain your answer.

___

5. True or false: With true knowledge of God, you will realize that internalizing the negative attitudes and lies of racists means accepting spiritual defeat from those who are already spiritually defeated. Explain your answer.

___

∞∞∞∞∞∞∞∞ ♦ ♦ ♦ ♦ ♦ ∞∞∞∞∞∞∞∞

Reflections:

___
___
___
___

∞∞∞∞∞∞∞∞ ♦ ♦ ♦ ♦ ♦ ∞∞∞∞∞∞∞∞

CHAPTER 40 –
Solidifying God's Word Within You

The kingdom of darkness, the enemy of God's Kingdom of light and truth, perpetrates and perpetuates racism. Reacting carnally to your experiences with racism is one of the devil's strategies to make you disobey God's Holy Word. Knowing that Jesus Christ is in God and God in Him, and Jesus Christ is in you (John 14:19-20), means that there is no room for either the evil spirit of racism within you or for its nasty outgrowth racism to defile your inner or outer person with its evils and lies. Through Jesus Christ, your spirit is housing the greatest power there is and ever will be—God's Holy Spirit whom you received

Jesus Christ has defeated every evil for you.

through His Son Jesus Christ. The same power of God the Father, His Holy Spirit, Who raised Christ from the dead, also dwells in you (Romans 8:11; Ephesians 1:18-23; 1 Corinthians 6:19). So within you lies the holy power of God, the Great I Am. Through Jesus Christ, you are packed with God's supernatural power to overcome racism (John 16:33; 1 John 5:4; 1 John 4:4).

The greatest strategy that you can apply against any form of evil including racism is to solidify the truth of God's Word within you and apply it effectively to overcome the racist situations you encounter. Revelation knowledge of God's Holy Word through His Holy Spirit in you, is thus a prerequisite for applying it in your life. In John 8:32, 36, God promises us: "And ye shall know the truth, and the truth shall *make* you free." So, the first step is to know the truth of God's Holy Word. Then the second step is that the truth of God's Word will *make* us free. Note it says *"make"* us free, and not just *"set"* us free. Free from what? From all of the devil's lies and evil machinations; free from evil domination of our hearts, minds, thoughts, emotions, will and resolve; free from all satanic influences that deviate us from God's destined course for our lives; and yes, free from being ruled by the

> *God has made you more than a conqueror of racism through Jesus Christ.*

devil and devilish thoughts and actions. How can this be possible? In Luke 10:19, Christ tells us that He has given us the power to trample demonic scorpions and serpents and over the power of the enemy who is the devil and we shall be unharmed by him and his evil forces: "Behold, I give unto you power to tread on serpents and scorpions, and over all the power of the enemy: and nothing shall by any means hurt you." Consider the vile spirit of racism a scorpion and serpent spirit that you must trample with the power of God's Holy Word.

You must sustain your spiritual fight against racism with the Holy Word of God firmly solidified within you. God has placed all things under the Feet of Jesus Christ (Hebrews 2:8), Who is our Lord and Savior, and the Redeemer of all humanity. Christ has defeated every form of evil for you, including racism, and He has overcome the world on your behalf (1 John 4:4; John 16:33). He has made you more than a conqueror (Romans 8:37) of your experiences with racism. Now, child of the Most High God, let us begin to apply true revelation knowledge of God's Holy Word and His holy armor against the evil spirit of racism (Ephesians 6:10-18). Knowing that we do not walk in flesh but in spirit and

Reject all lies that racism presents to you.

we do not war after the flesh but against demonic spirits and powers so we do not use carnal weapons of warfare, but we fight evil forces using the awesome power of God to pull down every stronghold or stranglehold against our lives including the despicable spirit of racism. (2 Corinthians 10:3-4; Ephesians 6:10-18) Therefore, through spiritual warfare, let us begin: "Casting down imaginations, and every high thing that exalteth itself against the knowledge of God, and bringing into captivity every thought to the obedience of Christ; and having in a readiness to revenge all disobedience, when your obedience is fulfilled." (2 Corinthians 10:5-6)

> *You have spiritual power over racism because God is in you through Jesus Christ.*

As a child of God who has professed Jesus Christ as their Lord and Savior, you have become spiritually born again (Galatians 2:20; Colossians 3:4; John 3:6-7; 1 Peter 1:23); old things have passed away and you have become a new creation (2 Corinthians 5:17) with a renewed mind in Jesus Christ (Philippians 2:5; 1 Corinthians 2:16). Daily, God's Holy Word will renew your mind (Romans 12:2), grow your faith (Romans 10:17), and make you free from the stranglehold of racism (John 8:32,26); if you read it, meditate on it in your heart, receive and accept it in your heart as *the* truth, and apply it in your mind, thoughts, actions and daily living.

If racism were ever spiritually or mentally defeating to you, it should cease to be so, for your body is a temple of God in which His Holy Spirit dwells (1 Corinthians 3:16-17; 6:19-20). Now, racism has no authority or legal access to your spirit, and Jesus Christ has given you the authority to trample upon any form of evil,

The Power of your mind in Jesus Christ is greater than racism.

including racism (Psalms 91:13). Nothing is too tough for God to accomplish in your life and on your behalf (Jeremiah 32:17). If you trust God and put your faith in Him, He will make you His battleaxe against racism and the vile spirit behind it (Jeremiah 51:20-25). Then, racism will no longer rule your soul; rather, you will rule over racism. God has equipped your spirit (2 Timothy 1:7) to empower your soul to rule over racism.

Reject all lies that racism presents to you (John 8:44; 10:10), including those that deem you to be unworthy, inferior and unable to achieve success in your life. Reject any words of condemnation, whether it comes from a racist or anyone else, for there is "…no condemnation to those who are in Christ Jesus, who do not walk according to the flesh, but according to the

Spirit." (Romans 8:1). Through Jesus Christ, you are a holy and acceptable vessel of God (Romans 11:16). With Christ in you and you in Him you will bear much fruit (John 15:4), and through Him, you have been made holy and blameless before God (Ephesians 1:4) and racism cannot reverse God's absolute truth about who you are in Jesus Christ (Proverbs 30:5; Matthew 24:35). Christ has risen above all evil, whether spiritual or carnal. He is seated in heavenly realms and so are you with Him in spirit (Ephesians 2:6; Philippians 3:20). With Christ, you have been raised far above (Colossians 2:7, 10-11, 3:1, 3-4) the carnal minds of racists, and racism has ceased to have any spiritual or mental stronghold over you (Romans 6:7). God has led you in triumph in Christ, and through you in Christ, God diffuses the fragrance of His knowledge in every place to the glory of His awesome Name (2 Corinthians 2:14). What a beautiful, holy aroma this is! With the power of authentic spiritual knowledge that you receive from God's Holy Word and His Holy Spirit, you will gain triumph over racism, in the mighty Name of Jesus Christ!

Through Jesus Christ, you are a holy and acceptable vessel of God (Romans 11:16).

Racism is designed to cause you to reject yourself and others who may share a racial or ethnic identity with you. How can you reject yourself or others? To do this is to reject Jesus Christ in you, through Whom God's Holy Spirit resides in you. Carnal rejection of anyone is an illusion, because no one can reject the one whom God accepts and loves (John 16:27)—and no one can curse the one whom God has blessed (Numbers 22:12, 23:8; Nehemiah 13:2; Acts 10:15).

The "Stone" (Jesus Christ) the builders rejected has become the Cornerstone (Psalms 118:22; Acts 4:11)—and because Christ dwells within you—you, too, have become the cornerstone that can never be destroyed by racism. Our Lord and Savior, Jesus Christ, was born in an animal barn, what we call a "manger," but He was and still is the Son of the

The "Stone" (Jesus Christ) the builders rejected has become the Cornerstone and you too have become a cornerstone that can never be destroyed by racism.

Most High God; the barn did not change who He was and still is. You may have been rejected because you were born in a place where people refer to as a "Ghetto," but this does not change God's truth about you—that you are His child of great destiny. Remember, God did not create any "Ghetto," human beings did. You are a part of God's chosen race (1 Peter 2:9-10)—those who have been spiritually born again through Jesus Christ. You are free from the condemnation (Romans 8:1) of racism, and because Christ has accepted you, no one is qualified to reject you (Romans 15:7). This is the truth of God's Holy Word about you! Selah! (Pause and think about this!)

Jesus Christ is the true Vine and God the Father is the Gardner, the Vine Dresser, and you, child of God are a branch of His Son Jesus Christ and God expects you to bear good fruit through Jesus Christ (John 15:1-8; Romans 8:16-17; John 1:12). You cannot produce good fruit unless you are attached to the true Vine—Jesus Christ. Racism is not an acceptable reason or excuse for you and me to not bear good fruit.

Regardless of racism that you may face daily, you can and will produce good fruit, if you are attached to Christ Who is the true Vine. Through Jesus Christ, you are a vessel of God to be used for His glory; thus, no one can reject you in reality. You are well-established in Jesus Christ

You are well established in Jesus Christ.

(1 Corinthians 1:30; 2 Corinthians 1:21) to defeat any form of racism that is directed against you. You have been selected, appointed and anointed to be fruitful in Jesus Christ (John 15:16; 2 Corinthians 1:21) and racism lacks the power to render you unfruitful. Jesus Christ has justified and redeemed you (Romans 3:24), and you have

been set apart to do great works in His holy Name. Therefore, racism is not authorized and lacks the power to reverse God's Word in you or through you.

You are to be a "bond servant" only to God (Romans 6:22) and His righteousness (Romans 6:18). The term "bond servant" as used in this scripture is not to be defined or interpreted carnally as one forced to work or to be enslaved with little or no wages. Instead, the term means that you are completely dedicated to God and in obedience to His Word. You are not to be a "bond servant" to any other thing, so you are not to be a "bond servant" to racism either. Racism is a sin against God and offense against humanity. Racism originates from the pit of hell and is against the holy truth of God's Word. You have received God's Holy Spirit, Who guides you into God's truth of all things that have been freely given to you (1 Corinthians 2:12). Let the truth of God's Holy Word sanctify you from the cruel lies of racism (John 17:19).

Racism is not an acceptable reason or excuse for you and me not bearing good fruit.

Through Jesus Christ, you have access to God's power to gain spiritual and mental victory over racism. You have the mind of Christ (1 Corinthians 2:16), and so the power of your mind in Jesus Christ is greater than the carnal mind of any racist plots, schemes or intrigues. Christ has freed you from the oppression of racism (Romans 6:7, 8:1; Isaiah 61:1-3) and now you have liberty in Him (Galatians 2:4). Racism is under our righteous feet in Jesus Christ, and belongs to the kingdom of darkness, and you have been delivered from all darkness (including racism) and brought into God's light (Colossians 1:13).

God's peace which surpasses all understanding, will guard your heart and mind through Jesus Christ (Philippians 4:7), and in Christ you are delivered and protected from the darkness of the abhorrent spirit of racism and its evils (Colossians 1:13). Racism cannot taint your heart and mind because in Christ you are blessed with every spiritual blessing in heavenly places (Ephesians 1:3). Believe this now and always that you are a new creation in Christ; old things have passed away and all things have become new (2 Corinthians 5:17).

Let the truth of God's Holy Word sanctify you (John 17:19).

Racism can no longer assault your renewed spirit and mind in Jesus Christ (Galatians 2:20; Colossians 2:6-7; 3:1-2). You have the armor of God through the power of Christ in you that will destroy any form of racism and the serpent-scorpion spirit behind it (Ephesians 6:13-15;

Luke 10:19). Through Jesus Christ, you have spiritual defensive and offensive warfare to resist the devil's tactics and strategies against you in any form, including racism (Ephesians 6:10-18). Through Christ, you have spiritual power to resist the devil's temptation that is fashioned against you in the form of racist plans, schemes, intrigues and actions. God will never allow any temptation of racism to overrun you (1 Corinthians 10:13).

You are not to be discouraged or dismayed by anything (including racism), for God is with you (Joshua 1:9). You are not to be discouraged by your daily encounters with racism, because the battle is not yours but God's (1 Samuel 17:47). You are not to be discouraged by your misguided feelings of unrighteous anger because of your experiences with racism. God's abundant grace is available to you through Jesus Christ Who is God's grace and mercy to us. Though the unrighteousness of your flesh may battle the righteousness of your spirit as you experience racism (Romans 7:19-25; 8:1-4), the power of God's anointing oil of grace—the power of the Holy Spirit through Jesus Christ, will break the yoke of the burden of racism in

Let Jesus Christ empower you through God's Holy Spirit to rebuke and calm the rough tides created by racism (Mark 4:39; Luke 8:24).

your life by lifting any unrighteous anger from your soul; if you lay down your burden at the feet of Christ in thanksgiving, prayer and worship (Matthew 11:28-30; Isaiah 10:27; 9:4).

The power of God's holy anointing will break the cycle of the fueling and refueling of unrighteous anger within you, and you will react to racism and its evils only in a Christ-rooted manner. Your experiences with racism will not make you bitter or vengeful (Ephesians 4:31) and your experiences with racism will not become a source of sin in your life, because you are dead to sin but alive to God in Jesus Christ (Romans 6:11, 18, 22-23). Thus, the sin of unrighteous anger, bitterness and revenge in response to racism will not reign in your mortal body (Romans 6:12). You have true spiritual power over racism because God is with you through Jesus Christ and no one can be against you (Romans 8:31). Racism lacks the authority and power to be against you for you have declared the victory of Jesus Christ over it (1 John 5:4-5; John 16:33).

You have the Sword of the Spirit against racism—Use it! Apply it against racism!

You have in you the discernment of the Holy Spirit to silence the wicked plots of racists that come against your life and the works that you are doing in

God's holy Name; just like Nehemiah silenced the wicked counsel of the chief instigators (Sanballat and Tobiah) and others against him and his men (Nehemiah 6). Yes, you have the leading of God's Holy Spirit to follow and execute God's assignment to you with accuracy, conviction and courage, and avert the wicked plan of the racist spirit of Haman like Queen Esther did, with her faith and courage, the support of her cousin Mordecai, the cooperation of their fellow Jews (Book of Esther), and their collective prayers and fasting.

Jesus Christ has set you free from the rod of the oppressor (the racist) (Jeremiah 30:8-9), because He, Christ, has broken the yoke of the burden of racism in your life (Isaiah 9:4, 10:27). Yes, you have the power of Christ in you, the power of God's Holy Spirit in you, to reject racism and embrace the absolute truth of God's Word, which states that every creature of God is created of good quality (1Timothy 4:4-5) and has the power to resist and gain victory over evil through Jesus Christ (1 John 5:4; Luke 10:17-19; 1 Corinthians 15:23-28,57). You have the Sword of the Spirit against racism, that is, the Word of God (Ephesians 6:17). Use it! Apply it against racism! Let God's Word target the actions,

You have in you the discernment of the Holy Spirit to silence the wicked plots of racists.

plans, intrigues, schemes and strategies of your racist attackers with the Lord God's precision, guided by His Holy Spirit. Jesus Christ is your "Holy Bridge" over the troubled waters that racism creates (Psalms 23; Psalms 107:29; Isaiah 4:6; Mark 4:39)—Let Him also be your "Overpass" over your troubled encounters with racism— Let Him empower you through God's Holy Spirit to rebuke and calm the wind and rough tides created by racism (Mark 4:39; Luke 8:24). Through Jesus Christ,

Jesus Christ has set you free from the rod of the oppressor (the racist) (Jeremiah 30:8-9).

let God sanctify you with His holy truth, His Holy Word against the lies, injustice, and wickedness of racism (John 17:19). Now, you can sound the trumpet of victory and bring down the walls of racism (Joshua 6:1-27).

∞∞∞∞∞∞∞∞ ♦ ♦ ♦ ♦ ♦ ∞∞∞∞∞∞∞∞

Chapter Quiz

1. How can you solidify God's Holy Word within you? Explain your answer.

_____

2. True or false: The greatest strategy that you can apply against any form of evil, including racism, is

to solidify the truth of God's Word within you. Explain your answer.

3. According to Romans 6:18-22, "…you have been made free from sin and become servants of righteousness." True or false: Therefore, you are to be a "bond servant" to racists. Explain your answer.

4. What do John 8:44 and John 10:10 tell you about the origin of the evil and lying spirit of racism? How can you apply this Scripture to deal victoriously with racism? Explain your answer.

5. According to Ephesians 6:17, how can you apply God's Word as the Sword of the Spirit against racism? Explain your answer.

6. How does 1 John 5:4 empower you to position yourself for victory over the vile spirit of racism? Explain your answer.

Reflections:

_____
_____
_____
_____

∞∞∞∞∞∞∞∞∞ ♦ ♦ ♦ ♦ ♦ ∞∞∞∞∞∞∞∞∞

"Child of the Most High God, it is a marvelous thing to dwell in the secret place of the Most High God, in the Name of our Lord and Savior Jesus Christ."
- Jacyee Aniagolu-Johnson

"He that dwelleth in the secret place of the most High shall abide under the shadow of the Almighty."
Psalms 91:1

∞∞∞∞∞∞∞∞∞ ♦ ♦ ♦ ♦ ♦ ∞∞∞∞∞∞∞∞∞

Now Available:

RAYS OF VICTORY SERIES

∞∞∞∞∞∞∞∞∞ ♦ ♦ ♦ ♦ ♦ ∞∞∞∞∞∞∞∞∞

This Book is:

WORKBOOK SERIES
FOOTPRINTS OF VICTORY OVER RACISM

In the Secret Place With God
(Volume 1)

Illuminating Daily Guideposts for God's Rays of Victory Over Racism

By
Dr. Jacyee Aniagolu-Johnson

∞∞∞∞∞∞∞∞∞ ♦ ♦ ♦ ♦ ♦ ∞∞∞∞∞∞∞∞∞

First Paperback Edition:
ISBN 978-0-9789669-5-9

Also Available:

RAYS OF VICTORY SERIES

∞∞∞∞∞∞∞∞ ♦ ♦ ♦ ♦ ♦ ∞∞∞∞∞∞∞∞

WORKBOOK SERIES
FOOTPRINTS OF VICTORY OVER RACISM
In the Secret Place With God
(Volume 2)

Illuminating Daily Guideposts for God's Rays of Victory Over Racism

By
Dr. Jacyee Aniagolu-Johnson

∞∞∞∞∞∞∞∞ ♦ ♦ ♦ ♦ ♦ ∞∞∞∞∞∞∞∞

First Paperback Edition:
ISBN 978-0-9789669-6-6

FOOTPRINTS OF VICTORY OVER RACISM – VOLUME 1

RAYS OF VICTORY SERIES

∞∞∞∞∞∞∞∞ ♦ ♦ ♦ ♦ ♦ ∞∞∞∞∞∞∞∞

ON THE HAMMOCK:

WITH THE SWORD OF THE SPIRIT

FOR INDIVIDUAL VICTORY OVER RACISM

A Meditation Journal
[40 Days of Daily Meditation]
(Volume 1)

By
Dr. Jacyee Aniagolu-Johnson

∞∞∞∞∞∞∞∞ ♦ ♦ ♦ ♦ ♦ ∞∞∞∞∞∞∞∞

First Paperback Edition:
ISBN 978-0-9789669-8-0

FOOTPRINTS OF VICTORY OVER RACISM – VOLUME 1

RAYS OF VICTORY SERIES

∞∞∞∞∞∞∞∞ ♦ ♦ ♦ ♦ ♦ ∞∞∞∞∞∞∞∞

ON THE HAMMOCK:

WITH THE OIL OF GRACE

FOR INDIVIDUAL VICTORY OVER RACISM

A Meditation Journal
[40 Days of Daily Meditation]
(Volume 2)

By
Dr. Jacyee Aniagolu-Johnson

∞∞∞∞∞∞∞∞ ♦ ♦ ♦ ♦ ♦ ∞∞∞∞∞∞∞∞

First Paperback Edition:
ISBN 978-0-9789669-9-7

FOOTPRINTS OF VICTORY OVER RACISM – VOLUME 1

RAYS OF VICTORY SERIES

∞∞∞∞∞∞∞∞ ♦ ♦ ♦ ♦ ♦ ∞∞∞∞∞∞∞∞

ONE ON ONE WITH GOD

FOR VICTORY OVER RACISM

Daily Prayer Conversations With God for Individual Victory Over Racism

By
Dr. Jacyee Aniagolu-Johnson

∞∞∞∞∞∞∞∞ ♦ ♦ ♦ ♦ ♦ ∞∞∞∞∞∞∞∞

First Paperback Edition:
ISBN 978-0-9789669-7-3

FOOTPRINTS OF VICTORY OVER RACISM – VOLUME 1

RAYS OF VICTORY SERIES

∞∞∞∞∞∞∞ ♦ ♦ ♦ ♦ ∞∞∞∞∞∞∞

My Rays of Victory

BIBLE STUDY DIARY

A Unique Diary for your Signature Penmanship as you Triumph Over Racism

By
Dr. Jacyee Aniagolu-Johnson

∞∞∞∞∞∞∞ ♦ ♦ ♦ ♦ ∞∞∞∞∞∞∞

First Paperback Edition:
ISBN: 978-0-9789669-4-2

FOOTPRINTS OF VICTORY OVER RACISM – VOLUME 1

RAYS OF VICTORY SERIES

150 POWER THOUGHTS FOR VICTORY OVER RACISM

The Power of a Christ-rooted Mindset Over Racism

Excerpts from "Nailing Racism to the Cross"

Dr. Jacyee Aniagolu-Johnson

First Paperback Edition:
ISBN 978-1-937-230-00-5

FOOTPRINTS OF VICTORY OVER RACISM – VOLUME 1

RAYS OF VICTORY SERIES

∞∞∞∞∞∞∞∞ ♦ ♦ ♦ ♦ ♦ ∞∞∞∞∞∞∞∞

150 POWER THOUGHTS
<u>Diary</u>
FOR VICTORY OVER RACISM

∞∞∞∞∞∞∞∞ ♦ ♦ ♦ ♦ ♦ ∞∞∞∞∞∞∞∞

A Journal for Power Thoughts Against Racism

∞∞∞∞∞∞∞∞ ♦ ♦ ♦ ♦ ♦ ∞∞∞∞∞∞∞∞

Excerpts from "Nailing Racism to the Cross"

∞∞∞∞∞∞∞∞ ♦ ♦ ♦ ♦ ♦ ∞∞∞∞∞∞∞∞

Dr. Jacyee Aniagolu-Johnson

First Paperback Edition:
ISBN 978-1-937-230-04-3

FOOTPRINTS OF VICTORY OVER RACISM – VOLUME 1

RAYS OF VICTORY SERIES

∞∞∞∞∞∞∞∞∞ ♦ ♦ ♦ ♦ ♦ ∞∞∞∞∞∞∞∞∞

150 SIGN POSTS TO VICTORY OVER RACISM
(Volume 1)

Empowering Sign Posts for Victory Over Racism

∞∞∞∞∞∞∞∞∞ ♦ ♦ ♦ ♦ ♦ ∞∞∞∞∞∞∞∞∞

Excerpts from "Nailing Racism to the Cross"

∞∞∞∞∞∞∞∞∞ ♦ ♦ ♦ ♦ ♦ ∞∞∞∞∞∞∞∞∞

Dr. Jacyee Aniagolu-Johnson

First Paperback Edition:
ISBN 978-1-937230-01-2

FOOTPRINTS OF VICTORY OVER RACISM – VOLUME 1

RAYS OF VICTORY SERIES

∞∞∞∞∞∞∞∞∞ ♦ ♦ ♦ ♦ ♦ ∞∞∞∞∞∞∞∞∞

150 SIGN POSTS TO VICTORY OVER RACISM
(Volume 2)

Empowering Sign Posts for Victory Over Racism

∞∞∞∞∞∞∞∞∞ ♦ ♦ ♦ ♦ ♦ ∞∞∞∞∞∞∞∞∞

Excerpts from "Nailing Racism to the Cross"

∞∞∞∞∞∞∞∞∞ ♦ ♦ ♦ ♦ ♦ ∞∞∞∞∞∞∞∞∞

Dr. Jacyee Aniagolu-Johnson

First Paperback Edition:
ISBN 978-1-937230-02-9

FOOTPRINTS OF VICTORY OVER RACISM – VOLUME 1

RAYS OF VICTORY SERIES

150 SIGN POSTS TO VICTORY OVER RACISM
(Volume 3)

Empowering Sign Posts for Victory Over Racism

Excerpts from "Nailing Racism to the Cross"

Dr. Jacyee Aniagolu-Johnson

First Paperback Edition
ISBN 978-1-937230-03-6

Rays of Victory Series
Correspondence:

Please send Correspondence to:

Marble Tower Publishing

P.O. Box 1654, Laurel, Maryland 20725

OR

Submit a Contact Request Form at:

www.marbletowerpublishing.com

www.ravbookseries.com

www.ingramcontent.com/pod-product-compliance
Lightning Source LLC
Chambersburg PA
CBHW050417170426
43201CB00008B/442